DEFENSE OF THE MIDDLE EAST
Problems of American Policy

SOME PUBLICATIONS OF THE
COUNCIL ON FOREIGN RELATIONS

FOREIGN AFFAIRS (quarterly), edited by Hamilton Fish Armstrong.

THE UNITED STATES IN WORLD AFFAIRS (annual). Volumes for 1931, 1932, and 1933, by Walter Lippmann and William O. Scroggs; for 1934–1935, 1936, 1937, 1938, 1939 and 1940, by Whitney H. Shepardson and William O. Scroggs; for 1945–1947, 1947–1948 and 1948–1949, by John C. Campbell; for 1949, 1950, 1951, 1952, 1953 and 1954, by Richard P. Stebbins; for 1955, by Hollis W. Barber; for 1956, by Richard P. Stebbins.

DOCUMENTS ON AMERICAN FOREIGN RELATIONS (annual). Volume for 1952 edited by Clarence W. Baier and Richard P. Stebbins; for 1953 and 1954, edited by Peter V. Curl; for 1955 and 1956, edited by Paul E. Zinner.

POLITICAL HANDBOOK OF THE WORLD (annual), edited by Walter H. Mallory.

NUCLEAR WEAPONS AND FOREIGN POLICY, by Henry A. Kissinger.

INDIA AND AMERICA: A Study of Their Relations, by Phillips Talbot and S. L. Poplai.

JAPAN BETWEEN EAST AND WEST, by Hugh Borton, Jerome B. Cohen, William J. Jorden, Donald Keene, Paul F. Langer and C. Martin Wilbur.

MOSCOW-PEKING AXIS: Strengths and Strains, by Howard L. Boorman, Alexander Eckstein, Philip E. Mosely and Benjamin Schwartz.

CLIMATE AND ECONOMIC DEVELOPMENT IN THE TROPICS, by Douglas H. K. Lee.

WHAT THE TARIFF MEANS TO AMERICAN INDUSTRIES, by Percy W. Bidwell.

UNITED STATES SHIPPING POLICY, by Wytze Gorter.

RUSSIA AND AMERICA: Dangers and Prospects, by Henry L. Roberts.

STERLING: Its Meaning in World Finance, by Judd Polk.

KOREA: A Study of U.S. Policy in the United States, by Leland M. Goodrich.

FOREIGN AFFAIRS BIBLIOGRAPHY, 1942–1952, by Henry L. Roberts.

AMERICAN AGENCIES INTERESTED IN INTERNATIONAL AFFAIRS, compiled by Ruth Savord and Donald Wasson.

JAPANESE AND AMERICANS: A Century of Cultural Relations, by Robert S. Schwantes.

THE FUTURE OF UNDERDEVELOPED COUNTRIES: Political Implications of Economic Development, by Eugene Staley.

THE UNDECLARED WAR, 1940–1941, by William L. Langer and S. Everett Gleason.

THE CHALLENGE TO ISOLATION, 1937–1940, by William L. Langer and S. Everett Gleason.

MIDDLE EAST DILEMMAS: The Background of United States Policy, by J. C. Hurewitz.

BRITAIN AND THE UNITED STATES: Problems in Cooperation, a joint report prepared by Henry L. Roberts and Paul A. Wilson.

TRADE AND PAYMENTS IN WESTERN EUROPE: A Study in Economic Cooperation, 1947–1951, by William Diebold, Jr.

WAR AND THE MINDS OF MEN, by Frederick S. Dunn.

PUBLIC OPINION AND FOREIGN POLICY, by Lester Markel and Others.

OUR FARM PROGRAM AND FOREIGN TRADE, by C. Addison Hickman.

THE FOREIGN AFFAIRS READER, edited by Hamilton Fish Armstrong.

THE STUDY OF INTERNATIONAL RELATIONS IN AMERICAN COLLEGES AND UNIVERSITIES, by Grayson Kirk.

FOREIGN AFFAIRS BIBLIOGRAPHY, 1932–1942, by Robert Gale Woolbert.

SURVEY OF AMERICAN FOREIGN RELATIONS (in four volumes, 1928–1931), prepared under the direction of Charles P. Howland.

DEFENSE OF THE MIDDLE EAST

Problems of American Policy

JOHN C. CAMPBELL

Published for the
COUNCIL ON FOREIGN RELATIONS
by
HARPER & BROTHERS
New York
1958

DEFENSE OF THE MIDDLE EAST

Copyright, © 1958, by Council on Foreign Relations, Inc.
Printed in the United States of America

All rights reserved, including the right to reproduce
this book or any portion thereof in any form.

For information, address Council on Foreign Relations,
58 East 68th Street, New York 21

SECOND PRINTING

American Book–Stratford Press, Inc., New York

Library of Congress catalog card number: LC 57-11111

Published in Great Britain and the British
Commonwealth, excluding Canada, by
London: Oxford University Press

TO MY PARENTS
Allan R. Campbell
1879–1957
Gertrude H. Campbell

PREFACE

SINCE the Second World War the Middle East has steadily moved into the forefront of public as well as official attention in this country. The spectacular and in many ways alarming events of the autumn of 1956 and those which have followed have served to bring home certain trends already evident: the unsolved problems of the area, far from approaching settlement, carry the threat of open hostilities and perhaps even of a major war; the Soviet Union has been making substantial gains; the Western alliance, as far as the Middle East is concerned, has virtually broken down, and no clear and comprehensive policy has been found to protect essential American and Western interests. The American public has become acutely conscious of the urgency of these problems and of the need for well-conceived and practical policies to cope with them. This book is an attempt to contribute to a better understanding of the problems and to stimulate thought on policies for the future.

In 1954 the Council on Foreign Relations organized a discussion group on the subject of the defense of the Middle East. Its purpose was to examine, primarily from the standpoint of military policy, the basic factors in the situation and to reach some conclusions on the possibilities of an effective defense of the area against the Soviet threat. Professor Dankwart Rustow of Princeton, who served as Research Secretary of this group, wrote for its consideration a series of informative papers which I have found most useful. In the following year the discussion group was succeeded by a smaller study group, which set itself the task of going more deeply into the problem and placing it in the general setting of the global policies and strategy of the United States. Professor Schuyler C. Wallace, Director of the School of International Affairs of Columbia University, served as chairman of both groups.

As our study group pursued its labors, it came increasingly to look upon the defense of the Middle East as part of a grand strategy in which military, political, economic and other policies must be drawn together into a coordinated whole. This, as the diplomats and military planners have long since discovered, is easier said than done. The maze of problems is such that whatever is done in trying to make some progress on one—whether it be regional organization for defense, economic aid, protection of access to oil, or the Arab-Israel dispute—affects all the others and often adversely. What we attempted to do in the study group was to see what the major elements in the puzzle were and how they might be fitted together in terms of policies that were both promising and feasible. All the members joined fully and freely in the discussions. In addition, at several meetings we had the benefit of the views of special guests, including Ambassador Raymond A. Hare, Major-General Earle G. Wheeler, U.S.A., Mr. John J. McCloy and Mr. Eric Johnston.

The group did not reach many unanimous conclusions. Even had we tried harder to do so, we would not have succeeded. The Middle East is simply too full of questions on which reasonable men can differ.

Such conclusions and statements of fact and opinion as appear in the book are my own. The members of the study group have no responsibility for what is said in it. I have profited greatly, however, by the opportunity to discuss my ideas with them, both individually and collectively. The broad sweep of knowledge and experience represented in the group was invaluable both in clarifying the facts and in providing insights into their meaning. I should like to express my deep appreciation to Professor Wallace and to the entire membership of the group. I should like also to mention our great sorrow at the passing of Samuel K. C. Kopper, who as a valued colleague and friend contributed so much to our deliberations. The group was composed as follows:

Schuyler C. Wallace, *Chairman*
William Staley, *Rapporteur*

Alan N. Alpern	J. C. Hurewitz
Frank Altschul	Samuel K. C. Kopper
John S. Badeau	Hal Lehrman
Lt. Col. Donald Bussey	Walter J. Levy
Gordon R. Clapp	Philip E. Mosely
Admiral Richard L.	Walter R. Sharp
Conolly (ret.)	Theodore Tannenwald, Jr.
James Terry Duce	T. Cuyler Young
Fowler Hamilton	

The first part of the book presents a brief account of the background and development of United States policy in the Middle East as it centered on the defense of that region against Soviet encroachment. It is not a history of the Middle East or of the policies of all interested states. The United States was not the only or even the major outside power in the picture; more often than not the United Kingdom acted as the leading Western power in a great part of the Middle East. But the deliberately chosen theme here is the role of the United States. What I have tried to do is to point up those events which bear on the development by the United States of a broad policy for the area. The treatment is selective, not detailed or exhaustive, because it is intended primarily as a means of introducing the analysis of the problems that confront policy-makers and public opinion today.

It is often said that the United States has had no policy for the Middle East. The charge seems to me unwarranted. The history of our involvement in that part of the world since World War II may show inadequacies and inconsistencies. It is not studded with brilliant diplomatic triumphs. Nevertheless, it represents a policy and deserves analysis as such. What I have tried to do is to present the record and to make whatever judgments seem to be justified by it.

Part Two represents an attempt to define and analyze the political, economic and military problems that now face the United States in the Middle East, and from that analysis to draw conclusions on possible policies for the future. In general, I have tried to avoid the specifics of the questions of the moment and to take the long view. The conclusions are directed principally to the possibility of averting tomorrow's crises, although I hope they are also relevant to those of today. They are, in any case, a call to action today, if we are to have any real power of decision in the future.

I have used the term "Middle East" in the full knowledge that, like the "Near East," it is an elastic definition of an undetermined area. I have taken it to include the following countries: Turkey, Iran, Iraq, Jordan, Syria, Lebanon, Israel, Egypt, Saudi Arabia, Yemen, and the sheikhdoms and protectorates of the Arabian Peninsula. Libya and Sudan, members of the Arab League, are included for most purposes although geographically remote from the central problems. On the eastern edge of the area, Pakistan and Afghanistan, the former a member of the Baghdad Pact, are considered a part of the Middle East in connection with matters of defense. On the western edge, the affairs of Tunisia, Algeria and Morocco form a related story but still a separate one, which I mention only in passing. Allusions to the "Near East" refer to the more limited group of countries at the eastern end of the Mediterranean Sea. Perhaps the purists will not be satisfied, but I think the meaning will be clear enough, and the important thing is what we do about the Middle East, not how we define it. Similarly, on the matter of rendering Arabic names into English, I have tried to use terms familiar to the general reader without departing too often and too drastically from the practice of scholars in the field.

In addition to thanking the members of the study group, I should like to express my appreciation for the information and advice offered by many others. Some I cannot name individually: officers of the Department of State and of the American Foreign Service, officials of other countries, and the many persons in the Middle East who received me with courtesy and hospitality. I am much indebted to my colleagues at the Council on Foreign Relations: to Walter H. Mallory and George S. Franklin, Jr., Executive Directors; to Hamilton Fish Armstrong, Editor, and Philip Quigg, Assistant Editor, of *Foreign Affairs,* in which some of my conclusions appeared in an article published in the issue of April 1957; and to Philip E. Mosely, William Diebold, Jr., and Richard Stebbins, all of whom gave valuable advice and editorial suggestions. My secretary, Miss Claire Couri, provided invaluable assistance at all stages of the project. To Miss Ruth Savord, Donald Wasson, Miss Janet Rigney and the entire staff of the Council Library I owe thanks for their unfailing help in providing the right materials at the right time. Mrs. Elizabeth Valkenier kindly prepared the index, and Miss Lorna Brennan has been most helpful in preparing the manuscript for the press. Finally, I am deeply indebted to my wife for her patience and forbearance throughout the whole affair.

JOHN C. CAMPBELL

The Harold Pratt House
New York
December 1957

CONTENTS

TABLES

MAPS

DEFENSE OF THE MIDDLE EAST

Problems of American Policy

INTRODUCTION

Chapter 1

THE PROBLEM

FOR THE past few years the United States has viewed developments in the turbulent Middle East with "grave concern"—to use a term made familiar by official usage. Each new spectacular event—a raid across the armistice lines in the Holy Land, a riot that overthrows a government in Jordan, a deal for Soviet arms—has provoked a tremor in Washington. Finally, the outbreak of armed violence in October and November of 1956 precipitated this country into a role of leadership which it could no longer avoid without jeopardizing its own interests and those of other free nations.

There should be no doubt of the seriousness of our commitment, as a nation, to take up that role. It has become commonplace to point to this or that area of the world as crucial to the cause of freedom and to the survival of a free society in our own country. The struggle in which we are engaged in these times is world-wide, and its outcome over the coming years will depend on many things, on developments of the mind and of the spirit perhaps as much as on decisions of public policy. Yet an area lost may mean a world lost. After the experience of the last decade, few can deny the special significance of the challenge in the Middle East.

Confronting a situation of recurring crisis, our government has sought by a variety of means to safeguard peace and to advance the national interest. Yet the complexities of the problems seem to defy all efforts to devise consistent and successful policies. We set out to build a military alliance system against the Soviet threat—and provoke a counter-system among some of the very nations we hoped to include. We help support hundreds of thousands of

3

destitute Arabs in refugee camps—where they grow more and more bitter against the West. We seek peaceful settlement and compromise between the Arabs and Israel—only to see passions and tensions rise day by day. We take a stand against aggression—and thereby strengthen those very elements which have done the most to bring Soviet influence into the Middle East.

The Middle East, convulsed by national and social conflicts of its own, is also the scene of a critical phase of the cold war. There is no doubt about our "concern:" for peace, for stability, for human welfare, as also for bases, for oil interests, and for resistance to communism. How is that concern translated into policy? As the kaleidoscope turns, these varied stakes and interests may shift in scope and in value relative both to each other and to a central concept of American national interest. It is worth while trying to define such a central concept both as a means of explaining our policies of the past, successful and unsuccessful, and as a guide to policy in the future. To some the concept of purely national interest may seem too narrow or too selfish, unworthy of our traditions and of our present responsibilities of leadership. But in a world where the principles of the United Nations Charter represent the hopes rather than the practices of nations we have no other choice. And we need assume no inconsistency between what serves our own national interests, broadly conceived, and what serves those of other nations.

The overriding national interest is the security of the United States—put more starkly, its survival. So long as we have no assurance of a workable system of global arms limitation or of a fundamental change in the aims and character of the Soviet regime, we must keep in the forefront of all our calculations and decisions the deadly threat of Soviet power at the service of Soviet policies fundamentally hostile to this country. From this general approach flow a number of concrete propositions with respect to the Middle East. The entrenchment of Soviet power in that strategic region would bring a decisive shift in the world balance, outflanking NATO. Soviet control of Middle Eastern oil could disrupt the economy of the free world. And the triumph of communism in the heart of the Islamic world could be the prelude to its triumph throughout Asia, Africa and Europe. It is fundamental to the United States, then, that the Middle East remain part of the free world. To phrase it in that way, however, shows how far beyond the purely American interest the proposition goes. "Defense of the Middle East"—from Soviet domination as also from that of any other power—is surely the aspiration of the Middle Eastern nations themselves, as it is of all others interested in a just and secure world order.

Containment of Soviet imperialism in the Middle East is thus more than a narrow American interest. But inevitably it carries an implication that the United States, like other great powers, is concerned with the Middle Eastern states and peoples only for the purpose of having them serve its own interests; and this is precisely what it is so often accused of doing. We can and should, therefore, consider United States-Middle East relations in a broader context, as significant in themselves, not just as a function of the world balance between two power blocs. If no Soviet threat existed at all, it would still be in the American interest to find a basis for adjustment between Western and Eastern civilizations, for absorbing the shocks of a revolutionary time, and for creating world conditions in which our own free society can develop and prosper. This more positive, and much more difficult, approach goes far beyond the problem of military defense and physical security. It involves a search for common denominators among peoples of differing cultures, faiths, and historical experience; for a renewal of mutual respect, much of which has been lost; and for a practical partnership in the development of resources. Progress toward those goals would itself be the best possible insurance against the expansion of communism into the strategic Middle East.

From these generalizations a few essential guidelines to policy emerge. The independence of the Middle Eastern nations from Soviet control is vital to the United States. But independence in itself does not mean strength. We must prevent the advance of Soviet power, check and reduce the growth of Soviet influence, to help safeguard that independence. Naturally we have to look at the military problem and to contemplate military action if we have no other choice. But the aim of our policy and conduct should be that this choice never has to be made. "Defense of the Middle East," in American policy, is a concept going well beyond the requirements of military strategy. We have a stake in the strength, stability, and self-confidence of these nations. We have a stake in the attenuation of the bitter conflicts that divide them from one another and of the phobias and violence that mark their internal politics and their attitudes toward the West. If this now "soft" area can find itself, and can find a stable relationship with the West, then it will lose its vulnerability to Soviet penetration or attack, and may even become a source of attraction for the adjacent Moslem peoples of the Soviet Union itself.

No power, of course, no matter how strong, can mold the future of another region according to its own prescription. Neither the United States, Great Britain or the Soviet Union, nor the interplay of their conflicting policies, alone determines the course of the history in the Middle East. We cannot decide upon objectives and policies in the abstract and then expect to apply them in some mechanical way. It is largely a question of direction, of day-to-day decisions made in accordance with a consistent general approach, in the light of the hard facts of life in the region itself. Certain forces and trends should be apparent. It is our task to estimate them correctly, to guide and control them as we can; to march with them when they are favorable, and deflect them when they are not; to ride the tides of history and not be submerged by them.

This the United States has not always done in the past. The record shows much of consistent purpose, clear analysis, and courageous decision. It shows also some inconsistencies and miscalculations. In the first part of this book we shall look briefly at the record of recent years: the major trends of great-power policy, the forces at work within the area, and the specific attempts to organize its defense. In the second part we shall go on to analyze the baffling and even perilous situation which presently confronts the United States and the Western world in the Middle East.

The recent spectacular demonstrations of Soviet prowess in science and military technology add emphasis to the peril and urgency of the task before the free world. The peoples of the Middle East, where Soviet influence and prestige were already rising fast, have been deeply impressed. Added to the many advantages over the West which the Soviet Union has enjoyed in its appeal to those peoples is the growing conviction among many of them that even America cannot save the West, that the future lies with the dynamic leaders of the "camp of socialism." Whether that trend can be reversed will depend in part on what the United States can do to prevent a decisive shift in the balance of military power. It will depend also on what we can do to meet the specific manifestations of the challenge in the Middle East itself.

PART ONE

THE RECORD OF RECENT YEARS

Chapter 2

THE SETTING

THE CLASSIC "Eastern Question" has existed for centuries in one form or another ever since England, France and Russia first began to reach out to seek advantage or to protect national and imperial interests in the strategic areas of the Near and Middle East. Marked by occasional wars, large and small, and by the almost continuous exercise of diplomacy, the struggle has continued as empires have disappeared in war and revolution, societies have been transformed by technological and social change, and backward desert lands have been found to be resting on the world's greatest stores of oil. Three factors have largely determined the changing character of the Eastern Question: the efforts of Britain to preserve a world empire, the southward pressure of the great land mass of Russia, and the forces at work among the peoples of the Middle East itself. It was the impact of the second World War on these three elements and on the interrelationship among them that set the scene for the new phase of the drama, which opened as the war came to an end and as America, for the first time, found itself directly involved.

Retreat of British Power

No element in the Middle Eastern picture after World War II was so fraught with revolutionary implications as the decline of British power. For this power had given the area what stability it had. The historic system of leadership and control through diplomacy, political manipulation, economic influence, prestige and military arrangements had rested in the last analysis on Britain's ability to bring substantial power to bear in the Middle East. Unable, after 1945, to exert such power, the British Government found that its traditional policies and methods could not meet the threats to British interests from both inside and outside the region.

The "British system" in the Middle East, going back over a century and a half, had been aimed at securing the routes to India and the Far East and keeping the area out of the hands of any hostile great power. Throughout the 19th century Britain barred the way to Russian expansion toward the eastern Mediterranean and the Persian Gulf. Its rivalry with France in the area was almost uninterrupted. Twice in this century Britain thwarted the armed efforts of Germany to seize the strategic Middle East as the key to world power. The means of policy changed with the passage of time but the objective of a stable Middle East, willing to cooperate or subject to control, remained constant.

So long as the Sultans reigned at Constantinople, Britain could base its policy on maintaining the independence and integrity of the Ottoman Empire. Though admittedly weak and unable to protect itself, Turkey did have sovereignty over the whole area from the Balkans to the Persian Gulf and had a common interest with Britain in opposing Russian expansion. Despite progressive losses in Europe, it continued to hold its Asian and African territories except Egypt, which came under British occupation in 1882. But when the Ottoman rulers found England on the side of Russia and gambled on a German victory in World War I, the breakup of their empire became an object of British military strategy and, at the end of the war, an accomplished fact which necessitated a new "system" to safeguard British interests. The nationalist Turkey of Mustafa Kemal turned to Soviet Russia in order to avoid partition and domination by the victorious Western powers, but the British were able to keep an influential position in Iran and to establish their power throughout most of the Arab lands. They controlled the new mandated territories of Palestine, Transjordan and Iraq and maintained their protectorate over Egypt. France received the mandate for Syria and Lebanon.

This security system remained substantially intact during the interwar period. Soviet Russia was unable to extend its control into the Middle East, and although Mussolini succeeded in conquering Ethiopia, the permanence of his conquest depended on British sufferance. Even Turkey had by October 1939 become an ally.[1] Nevertheless, the system had shown certain signs of weakness such as the rise of a strong and troublesome nationalism in Egypt and a growing Arab-Jewish conflict in Palestine to which Britain could find no solution. Egypt was given its independence and the mandate for Iraq was ended, but in each case Britain substituted a new relationship for the old, a treaty arrangement safeguarding the necessary military positions and rights to their use.

Great Britain came out of World War II with its hold on the Middle East outwardly stronger than ever. Since the victory at El Alamein it had dominated virtually the whole Arab area with British armed forces and controlled economic life through the Middle East Supply Centre. The Italian colonies were in its hands. Though the mandate system was outdated, London had shown its adaptability in shifting to cooperation with independent Arab states; to this end it gave its blessing to the new League of Arab States and helped to ease the French out of Syria and Lebanon. With this loss France ceased, for all practical purposes, to be a Middle Eastern power, although it continued to make much of its historic and cultural connections and deeply resented being excluded from Western councils when Middle Eastern affairs were considered.

[1] The treaty was directed against any European power committing aggression, but a protocol exempted Turkey from taking any action involving entry into armed conflict with the Soviet Union. Nevertheless, the Soviet Government, then aligned with Germany and seeking a special position for itself in Turkey, was not pleased with this formal alignment of Turkey with the West. See Great Britain, *Treaty Series*, no. 4, Treaty of Mutual Assistance, Cmd. 6165 (London: H.M.S.O., 1940); George Kirk, *The Middle East in the War* (London: Oxford University Press, for the Royal Institute of International Affairs, 1952), pp. 443-446.

The new Labour Government in London gave every indication of its intention to hold on to Britain's traditional positions. This was evident in the sharpness of its reaction to Soviet attempts to get a foothold in the area and to American public statements and private actions with respect to Palestine, which threatened to alienate the Arabs from the West. Appearances were deceptive, however, for Britain's world position had undergone fundamental changes. The war had gravely weakened its financial power. The Middle East Supply Centre was given up. The British could no longer pay the costs of maintaining troops all along the routes of empire. Indeed, great pieces of the empire itself were breaking away. Even in the small area of Palestine, the task of merely keeping order while caught between the fierce nationalism of Jew and Arab was proving too great a drain on British resources and on the patience of the British people. The Arab League, moreover, proved to be no docile instrument or willing partner of British policy. When it became apparent that Britain was not prepared to go all the way toward appeasement of Arab demands, issues such as Palestine and Suez inevitably ranged the strongest forces of Arab nationalism against British interests. The policy of giving up political controls in exchange for keeping bases did not work, for the "unequal treaties" and the bases themselves came under nationalist attack.

Britain simply could not carry alone the burden of maintaining a position of strength in the Middle East. The crucial decisions came in 1947, on Greece and Turkey and on Palestine. In the first case, the British were able to hand over the responsibility to the United States. In the second, they deposited it in the lap of the United Nations and in the following year they simply withdrew their forces and their administration, leaving the fate of Palestine to be settled by an Arab-Jewish war. This precipitous withdrawal of British power from positions long deemed vital was a measure of the unexpected weakness of Britain's postwar economy and also of the willingness of the Labour Government to see the facts and accept their consequences.

Yet the Middle East still had a large place in British calculations. Some positions could be given up if that made it easier to hold on to others, especially if American power could fill the critical vacuums with no loss of over-all Western strength in the area. The British Government still planned on keeping the leadership of a Western effort toward stabilization and, especially after the Communist aggression in Korea, toward an organized defense. Western strength was to rest partly on the new commitments of American power to Greece and Turkey; partly on the as-sumed cooperation or at least tolerance of Egypt and other Arab states; and partly on what remained of the old Brit-ish imperial position: a combination of directly held strong points, special treaty arrangements, and long-estab-lished political influence. Britain held Cyprus and Aden as crown colonies. It exercised ultimate authority in a series of protectorates on the southern and eastern rim of the Arabian peninsula. It still held its major base at Suez and its control over the Sudan, though both had been for-mally challenged by Egypt. It had a special treaty relation-ship with Iraq, including provision for use of two impor-tant military bases, although the failure of the attempt to revise this treaty in 1948 raised doubts whether it could be extended beyond its termination date of 1956. With Transjordan (later Jordan) Britain had a treaty of alliance, base rights, and a position of primary influence through its special role in the establishment, maintenance and com-mand of Jordan's army, the Arab Legion.

The totality of these strong points and treaty arrange-ments made Britain still a formidable power in the area. But the British were not, by 1950, trying to play a lone hand. They were aware of the uncertainty hanging over their bases at Suez, in Iraq and even in Jordan. They felt that other Western powers must be associated with them in their efforts to defend the Middle East. Accordingly, the two major Western initiatives taken at this stage were

multilateral rather than purely British: the Tripartite
Declaration on Palestine, to which the United States and
France were also parties, and the four-power proposal for
an Allied Middle East Command, in which Turkey joined
the three Western powers. The fate of those initiatives
would show how far the whole future of Western influence
in the area would depend not on the West itself but on
the trend of new and vigorous forces arising within the
Middle East.

New Forces within the Middle East

The Middle East itself, after the second World War,
presented a very different picture from before. The most
significant changes flowed neither from the experience of
the military campaigns nor from the influence of the
great political and moral issues of the world struggle.
They were not discernible on the map or in the political
institutions of states so much as in the spirit and temper
of the people. It was the coming to fruition of a longer historical process marked above all by the rise of nationalism.
The war had speeded up this process. During the fighting
the belligerent powers naturally gave precedence to their
own urgent military requirements over the sensitivities of
the peoples who happened to live in this strategically located region. A harvest of protest and violent self-expression against formerly dominant nations was only to be
expected, and the postwar adjustments required in those
nations themselves, exhausted as they were by war and
absorbed in their own more immediate problems, invited
such a reaction.

In some parts of the Near and Middle East, the trend
had begun more than a century before with the disruptive
impact of the West on a weaker and more static Eastern
society. The pattern of reaction was not always the same.
Some "Westernizers" sought full-scale adoption of Western ideas and methods. Others sought to preserve the essential values of their Islamic society while borrowing

from the West the most modern means to resist its domination. Still other political and religious leaders preached simple rejection of Western influence as alien and unwanted. All had in common the desire for national self-assertion. Nationalism was the key to the historic victory of the Kemalist movement and the reconquest of Turkish national territory after the first World War. It lay behind the steady and stubborn resistance of Iran to the encroachments of Russia and Britain on Iranian national independence and integrity. It sparked the periodic Arab outbursts against the British occupation of Egypt or French rule in Syria.

The mood of the Middle East after World War II, however, showed marked variations. Nationalism was not at the same stage in all countries. In some areas where tribal loyalties were paramount or the peasantry remained inert the idea of self-conscious nationhood had little reality. In the Arab world the line was often far from clear between loyalty to individual "nation" such as Egypt or Iraq and the wider loyalty to the pan-Arab idea. Meanwhile the now more powerful challenge of a vigorous Jewish nationalism in Palestine added new explosive elements. Nationalism thus presented for Western policy no single clear issue but a number of complex problems.

Turkey, having gone through the fires of a war for independence a generation earlier, was already a strong and well-established national state. Vigilant throughout the war in guarding its independence and neutrality, it was determined to hold firm against the renewed pressures of the victorious Soviet Union, swollen with wartime gains and probing for more. Sure of themselves, the Turks were not afraid to seek and accept Western support.

Iran's position was quite different. At the end of the war Iran found itself with military forces of the three major Allied powers on its soil and, true to its historic role, dependent on Anglo-Russian rivalry as a means of preventing domination by one or the other. When the Western forces were withdrawn and the Soviet forces were not, Iranian nationalism and Western policy had a common aim in forcing the withdrawal of the Russians and in frustrating Soviet attempts either to hold on to Iranian Azerbaijan or to subvert the national government in Tehran. This aim was achieved in the crisis of 1946. But all was not smooth sailing for the West thereafter, for the British, their position symbolized by the powerful Anglo-Iranian Oil Company, remained an inviting target for Iranian nationalism. It was soon evident that this nationalism was more deeply felt and firmly based than before the war as a result of increased contacts with the outside world and social change within. And Iran, though well aware of the Soviet danger and willing to accept Western aid, clung to its traditional policy of nonalignment as the best guarantee of its independence.

Nationalism in the Arab world took still different forms. Here the Soviet threat was not a matter of real concern to the nationalists. The full force of their agitation was directed rather at the remnants of British and French rule and at the "Zionist invasion" of the Arab world. Although the Arab states in many ways were not yet modern nations, containing many disparate elements and ways of life, there was no question of their ability to apply continuing pressure to Western positions within their territories. The rising middle and professional classes constituted a force with which the European powers could not deal so easily as with the sheikhs, pashas and beys on whom their control had so largely rested in the past. The new leadership was in many ways an unknown quantity.

The Western governments were plagued by the uncertainties of a situation they could not easily diagnose. They could not count on the gradual and orderly development of nationalism in the Middle East under the guidance of responsible national leaders. Rulers could be assassinated; governments could be overthrown; power could fall into the hands of irrational fanatics; a treaty laboriously negotiated with a Middle Eastern government could disappear overnight as the result of street riots and mob scenes organized by that government's political enemies. The tremendous power that could be wielded by those who controlled "the street" put a premium on fanaticism, on demagogy, and on conspiratorial organization. As this fanaticism was almost always directed at "imperialism," "colonialism" and "foreign exploitation," the Communists and the extreme nationalists had little difficulty in using it for their own purposes. The Western powers, as the easily identifiable villains of the piece, became the scapegoats for almost all the ills and troubles afflicting Middle Eastern society, the objects of resentment for all they had done and much they had not done.

The strength and intransigence of Arab nationalism was evident in its inexorable pressure on British positions and in the ceaseless agitation of the Arab League on the questions of Palestine, Suez, Sudan and North Africa. Arab political leaders who wanted to stay in office could not slight or ignore that pressure. Egypt remained unreconciled to the existing treaties covering the British position at Suez and in the Sudan; an Egyptian Prime Minister who tried to negotiate a new agreement with the British in 1946 found himself out of a job. Iraq remained bound to Britain by a treaty of 1930, but the shakiness of the relationship was dramatically revealed by the riots of January 1948 which overthrew a government that had negotiated a new treaty to replace it. Even Jordan, still a ward of the British though given its nominal independence in 1946, was no longer a dependable *pied-à-terre* for Britain in the Middle East after the assassination of King Abdullah in 1951.

If the decline of Britain's position in the face of this nationalist upsurge had not affected the world balance of power, it might have been accepted with equanimity. But the bastions that were falling had had the purpose of holding off the power of Russia. What were the aims of Soviet policy, for which new opportunities seemed to be in the offing? If a "vacuum" was being created, would the Soviet Union attempt to fill it?

The Threat from Russia

Soviet policy in the Middle East has gone through a number of phases since the revolution of 1917, in a changing combination of doctrinaire international communism and coldly calculated requirements of the Soviet state, with swings of the pendulum between aggressive expansion and cooperation with others for collective security. The record includes dramatic shifts and many inconsistencies, but through it all the continuing Soviet objectives in this region are apparent.

The first period after the Bolshevik revolution was marked by the public repudiation of the old Russian imperialism and strident calls for a vast revolt of "Mohammedan toilers of the East" against the Western imperialist oppressors and the local pashas and profiteers. At the very time that Comintern leader Zinoviev was summoning the "peoples of the East" to a holy proletarian war at the Baku Congress of 1920, however, Lenin and Foreign Commissar Chicherin were already coming to terms with non-Communist governments and national movements on Soviet Russia's southern frontiers. In 1921 they concluded a treaty with Mustafa Kemal and helped him in his national struggle. Even the fact that the Turkish Communists returning from the Baku Congress were arrested and thrown into the sea by Kemal's police did not mar the new friendship which was so convenient to both sides. Similarly with Iran the Soviets recognized the existing regime, concluded a treaty, and then withdrew their forces from northern areas of that country, leaving the "Soviet Republic of Gilan" and separatist movements in Azerbaijan to be suppressed by the Iranian Government. Keeping the border states out of the British camp and securing the Soviet frontiers was more important than minor territorial gains or the uncertain prospects of Communist revolution.

Throughout the interwar period the duality of Soviet policy continued. Comintern and GPU agents did their best to build up an apparatus of subversion within the countries of the Middle East. Party congresses debated such questions as the degree of cooperation permissible with bourgeois national movements and proclaimed principles to guide the revolutionary effort in "colonial and semi-colonial" countries. A famous set of "theses" adopted by the Comintern in 1928 permitted only temporary collaboration with nationalist elements, insisting on the independent role of the revolutionary proletarian movement and its drive for the seizure of state power.[2] Soviet and Communist propaganda continued to denounce the anti-Communist governments of Ataturk and Reza Shah along with the "Western imperialists." But this revolutionary strategy bore little resemblance to what the Soviet Government was actually doing in its relations with its immediate neighbors in the Middle East.

The official theme was peaceful coexistence, buttressed by a series of treaties in 1925–1927 which established a pattern of noninterference in internal matters and neutrality in case of war. The more complex and extensive security system devised by Litvinov in the 1930's to protect the Soviet Union against Hitler included new treaties with Turkey, Iran and Afghanistan as well as ties with various European powers and support of the League of Nations. To the network of bilateral pacts, however, were added some multilateral regional arrangements concluded on the initiative of the local governments themselves and not including the U.S.S.R. These were the Balkan Pact of 1934 (Yugoslavia, Rumania, Greece and Turkey) and the Middle Eastern or Saadabad Pact of 1937 (Turkey, Iraq, Iran, Afghanistan). At a time when the Soviet Union was preaching collective security against Nazi Germany and Fascist Italy, it raised no objection to these pacts.[3] But it

[2] Text in George Lenczowski, *Russia and the West in Iran, 1918–1948* (Ithaca: Cornell University Press, 1949), pp. 328-376.

[3] The only Soviet intervention in the Balkan Pact negotiations concerned the possibility that Turkey would be drawn into hostilities against the U.S.S.R. in case of trouble between the latter and Rumania. As a result, Rumania specifically agreed that in that circumstance Turkey would have no obligations under the Pact. See *Survey of International Affairs, 1934* (London: Royal Institute of International Affairs, 1935), pp. 527-528.

was notably cautious and could hardly have viewed with
equanimity the formation of two blocs which, linked by
Turkey's membership in both, stretched along its southern frontiers from the Balkans to the Himalayas. While
these groupings were relatively weak and were not dominated by outside powers then hostile to the U.S.S.R., the
fact that Moscow accepted them at all is out of line with
Soviet policy both before and since.

With the general breakdown of the Versailles system in
Europe, Stalin became convinced of the bankruptcy of
collective security and turned to a policy of collusion with
Hitler. Then the war itself presented him with a series of
new situations holding great opportunities as well as great
dangers. What the Soviet Government said and did with
respect to the Middle East during this period of flux is
particularly revealing of continuing Soviet aims and objectives; at the same time it should be taken with some
reservations because of the very uncertainties of the time.
In the 1939–1941 period the Soviet leadership tried to use
its bargaining position as a nonbelligerent to set limits to
the advance of German power through the Balkans to the
Middle East, to establish Soviet predominance in Turkey,
and also to prevent the Western powers from using their
position in the Middle East for an attack on the Soviet
Union. The Nazi victories of 1940 in the West largely removed the latter danger, but they posed in even more
pressing fashion the question of the balance of German
and Soviet power. Stalin and Molotov showed a lively interest in Hitler's proposal that the area "south of the
national territory of the Soviet Union in the direction of
the Indian Ocean" should be a Soviet sphere of influence.
The trouble with the proposal, from Moscow's viewpoint,
was that if Germany controlled the Balkans and Turkey,
then the Soviet position in the Middle East and even the
security of the U.S.S.R. itself would be at Germany's
mercy. The Soviet counterproposal accordingly specified
conclusion of an alliance between the U.S.S.R. and Bulgaria and a Soviet land and naval base at the Turkish

Straits, in addition to recognition of "the area south of Batum and Baku in the general direction of the Persian Gulf . . . as the center of aspirations of the Soviet Union." [4] The clash of interest was clear to both sides, and the German decision for war was not long delayed.

The German attack in 1941 forced Stalin to concentrate on the fight for survival and on getting Western help in that fight, rather than on dividing up the British Empire. Yet the consistency of his views on the Middle East is apparent from the demands he put forward with respect to Turkey and the Straits in negotiations with his Western allies and the preparations he made for the extension of Soviet control into Southeastern Europe. The Soviet Government also established diplomatic relations with Egypt, Iraq and the Levant states, an indication of its intention to assert its influence in the Arab world. Closer to home, Soviet conduct in Iran during the war provided a remarkable preview of postwar policy. The northern zone under Soviet occupation was cut off from the rest of the country; meanwhile the Soviet Union vastly increased its propaganda and other activities throughout Iran under the protection of its privileged wartime position as an ally and an occupying power. Much of that propaganda was aimed not at Germany but at the Western Allies. Long before the war was over the cold war had begun in Iran.

With the Allied victory over the Axis powers in Europe, Stalin embarked on a gigantic gamble to seize, in the confusion and war-weariness of the immediate postwar period, a strategic position enabling the Soviet Union to dominate the whole Eastern Hemisphere. The main thrusts into Europe and into Eastern Asia were accompanied by a calculated offensive toward the Mediterranean and the Middle East. Military victories in the Balkans and the advent of Communists to power in Yugoslavia, Bulgaria and Albania brought Soviet power to the Adriatic and the bor-

[4] Department of State, *Nazi-Soviet Relations, 1939–1941,* Documents from the Archives of the German Foreign Office, edited by R. J. Sontag and J. S. Beddie (New York: Didier, 1948), pp. 234-259.

ders of Greece. The very existence of an independent Greece was then menaced by Communist rebellion supported from the Soviet bloc. The Soviet Government sought a base in the Dodecanese, put forward a formal claim to a trusteeship over Tripolitania, and expressed interest in areas as remote as Eritrea and Ethiopia. It denounced its long-standing treaty with Turkey and demanded a new regime for the Straits, "joint Soviet-Turkish" bases for their defense, and territorial cessions in eastern Turkey. A revolution was engineered in Iranian Azerbaijan, where Soviet forces prevented the Tehran government from suppressing it. The Soviets then applied pressure to secure an oil concession covering the five northern provinces of Iran, while building up the Tudeh (Communist) Party as an instrument for the seizure of power in the whole country.

This was a serious and many-sided offensive for which the Western powers and the nations immediately threatened were not entirely prepared, but they were able ultimately to check it. Greece was saved by British and later by American support. The West summarily turned down Soviet claims in the Mediterranean. The Turks would listen to no demands for territory or for bases on the Straits. Western opposition and Iranian resiliency combined to induce the withdrawal of Soviet forces and ultimately to bring about the collapse of the Communist regime in Iranian Azerbaijan. Thus the Soviets failed after World War II in their attempts to push forward into the Middle East by force and pressure, just as they had failed after World War I to advance under the banner of world revolution. Their choice of means, moreover, had deliberately ruled out re-creation of the system of pacts and alliances which once had "neutralized" the border area in some degree and kept it free of potentially hostile bases. Now, though their own position in the Balkans was stronger, they had provoked the extension of Western military power and commitments right up to the frontiers of the Soviet Union itself through the American programs of military aid to Greece, Turkey and Iran and the adherence of Greece and Turkey to NATO.

The record of Soviet policy in the Middle East from 1917 to 1950 follows no rigid scheme or pattern. Many Soviet actions were reactions to the policies and moves of others. Yet the record does justify a number of generalizations.

Except at the very outset Communist doctrine has never been the decisive factor in determining specific policies in the Middle East. This is not to say that the Soviet leaders have not consistently believed in the eventual triumph of communism, in the Middle East as elsewhere. Or that they have not been guided by the Lenin-Stalin theory of the natural alliance between the Soviet Union, the exploited colonial peoples of the East and the industrial workers of the West in the struggle to overthrow world capitalism. These considerations are fundamental to their outlook. But their policies have been determined more by the actual course of the contest with other great powers for positions and influence in this strategically located region. In this contest geography has been more important than ideology.

Despite the renunciation of "imperialist" aims and privileges, Soviet policy continued many of the traditional conceptions of Russian strategic interest held by the Tsarist regime, such as control of the Black Sea, egress for Russian naval power through the Straits, and spheres of influence in the Balkans and toward the Persian Gulf. Soviet policy has been dynamic and actively expansionist, however, in the sense of moving in with armed forces or taking an active hand in revolutions, *only* in extraordinary times—times of flux and general collapse, of war or the aftermath of war. Even then, Moscow's hand has often been stayed, and forces have been withdrawn from territory already taken over, when sufficient pressure was applied by other powers or when the immediate strategic or other gains were outweighed by larger objectives. The Soviet strategy of expansion in the Middle East was not to challenge directly the position of rival powers but rather to take advantage of their temporary weakness, lack of concern or disunity, and to avoid the risk of major armed conflict. Even in 1940–1941 when the clash of interest was clear, it was Hitler, not Stalin, who cast the die for war.

Soviet motivation has been both offensive and defensive in character. The two are not separable. "Defensive" thinking is evident in the intense concern over the danger of attack on the U.S.S.R. from the south and with "hostile blocs" and foreign bases in the Middle East; but elimination of rival power is but the preliminary to its replacement by Soviet power. For these purposes the Soviet leadership has utilized a variety of means: political and propaganda campaigns to turn these countries against other powers; special treaties intended to neutralize them or to draw them into a Soviet-sponsored bloc; demands for strategic bases or special rights, or actual attempts to absorb adjacent border areas and create satellite states. Except during a brief interval in the 1930's, the Soviets have consistently tried to prevent any alliances or blocs in this area not under their own sponsorship or control. They have used both threats and promises to keep the Middle Eastern countries out of such blocs. But the Kremlin leaders, much as they have disliked the threats to Soviet security apparent in such alliances or in foreign bases, have not regarded them as intolerable in the sense of automatically requiring military action. Still less have they shown any intention of undertaking a campaign of military conquest to bring the Middle East under their own domination.

They have always made a distinction between their immediate neighbors, the "northern tier" of Middle Eastern states, and the rest of the area. In Turkey, Iran and Afghanistan, where their security has been more immediately involved, they have shown greater sensitivity and have resorted to more direct methods whether in the construction of treaty systems or in pressure, intimidation and the use of force. They have paid particular attention to Iran, which because of its geographical location and political weakness has been the state most susceptible to Soviet pressure and most dangerously open to outside influence. Only with Iran did they insist on a treaty right (1921) to send in Soviet military forces if a third power should intervene militarily in that country.[5]

In the Arab states further to the south, the Soviet leaders relied more on tactics of propaganda, penetration and diplomatic maneuver, doing everything they could at small cost in this traditionally British sphere of influence to make life more difficult for the British and their Western partners. The Soviet role in the Palestine crisis of 1947-1948 is an example. Despite its anti-Zionist attitude the Soviet Government voted in the United Nations for partition in 1947 and quickly recognized Israel in 1948. In so doing it made sure of the departure of British troops and authority from Palestine and of the perpetuation of a Jewish-Arab conflict which for the indefinite future would keep the Middle East in ferment. As Western policy hardened in Turkey and Iran, the Arab world

[5] The relevant treaty clause reads as follows: "If a third party should attempt to carry out a policy of usurpation by means of armed intervention in Persia, or if such Power should desire to use Persian territory as a base of operations against Russia, or if a Foreign Power should threaten the frontiers of Federal Russia or those of its Allies, and if the Persian Government should not be able to put a stop to such menace after having been once called upon to do so by Russia, Russia shall have the right to advance her troops into the Persian interior for the purpose of carrying out the military operations necessary for its defence. Russia undertakes, however, to withdraw her troops from Persian territory as soon as the danger has been removed." A letter of Rothstein, Soviet Representative in Tehran, to the Iranian Government on December 12, 1921, adds that this article is "intended to apply only to cases in which preparations have been made for a considerable armed attack upon Russia or the Soviet Republics allied to her, by the partisans of the regime which has been overthrown or by its supporters among those foreign Powers which are in a position to assist the enemies of the Workers' and Peasants' Republics and at the same time to possess themselves, by force or by underhand methods, of part of the Persian territory, thereby establishing a base of operations for any attacks—made either directly or through the counter-revolutionary forces—which they might meditate against Russia or the Soviet Republics allied to her. . . ." Text in J. C. Hurewitz, Diplomacy in the Near and Middle East, A Documentary Record (Princeton: Van Nostrand, 1956), v. 2, pp. 90-94.

offered the best opportunities for Moscow to break into
the Middle East.

The guiding thread of Soviet policy has been to exploit
the political and social forces prevalent in the Middle
East, primarily militant nationalism, against the West. In
so doing the Kremlin has not felt itself bound by the dic-
tates of doctrine or consistency. It has shown readiness to
support all elements, including "bourgeois nationalists"
and the most reactionary xenophobes as well as its conspiratorial Communist parties. While it did not show at
any time before 1950 that it was able to win popular support for communism or to take over and control the main
currents of nationalism in any Middle Eastern country,
the mere fact of its ability to ally with such forces constituted a formidable threat to the maintenance of Western
power and influence.

How would the West protect its interests? This question
seemed especially urgent after the Kremlin showed its
willingness, through the Communist aggression in Korea
in 1950, to move from the cold war into the realm of military force. The answer depended partly on attitudes and
decisions in London. But no British policy could be effective without the support of the United States, already the
major Western partner in Greece, Turkey and in Saudi
Arabia, and increasingly aware of its own interests in the
area.

Chapter 3

THE GROWTH OF AMERICAN
INTEREST

UNTIL THE first World War the American interest in the Middle East was largely cultural. American diplomacy concerned itself with the protection of American citizens and of their rights to preach, to teach and to trade. American missionaries, though they made few conversions to Christianity, had a significant and beneficial influence in bringing Western thought, ideals and educational methods into the Middle East. They made no small contribution to the growth of nationalism. American opinion, periodically, expressed itself in favor of freedom and against those governments which ignored and suppressed it. The picture of America in the public mind, where it existed at all, was of a benevolent but distant friend. As a government and as a nation, however, the United States took no stand and had no policy.

At the peace table after World War I the United States delegation participated actively in the negotiations and looked forward to a settlement based on the principle of national self-determination in the Middle East as in Europe. President Wilson sent a commission to investigate the situation in Syria, and a proposal for an American mandate over Armenia, fantastic as that idea was, was even presented to the Congress, which declined to approve it.[1] Wilson's defeats in the Senate, however, and at the polls in 1920 killed not only American participation in the League but also any chance of the assumption of responsibilities in the Middle East. In the turbulent develop-

[1] Charles E. Hughes, "Recent Questions and Negotiations," *Foreign Affairs*, v. 2 (December 1923, Special Supplement), pp. xii-xiii.

ments that marked the tearing up of the treaty of Sèvres and the birth of nationalist Turkey, the United States took no part other than to speak up for maintenance of the open door, freedom of navigation in the Straits, and the protection of American property and institutions. It signed neither the Lausanne Convention on the Straits in 1923 nor that of Montreux which replaced it in 1936. As for Palestine, Wilson had given his blessing to the Balfour Declaration and a later joint resolution put Congress on record in favor of the Jewish national home in Palestine, but the specific reservation of the House Committee on Foreign Affairs that the resolution "commits us to no foreign obligations or entanglements" was indicative of the temper of the times. The United States formally approved the British mandate in 1924; for the next two decades Palestine, in American eyes, was a British problem.[2]

During the interwar period, American activity in the Middle East was largely that of oil companies in search of concessions. American companies were able to get a share of the oil industry in Iraq and Kuwait, and to gain exclusive concessions in Bahrein and Saudi Arabia. The official position of the United States in the welter of public and private diplomacy surrounding the scramble for oil was based on the principle of the "open door." Aside from this natural concern to see American firms get their fair share of a promising business, Washington already had in mind the depletion of domestic oil reserves and the desirability of having alternative sources of supply which would not be in foreign hands. No comprehensive national policy emerged, as the United States played no role in the relations between the Western European powers and the increasingly restive peoples under their rule, or in the developing three-way contest among the Axis powers, the Western democracies and the Soviet Union for the control of strategic areas and the support of Middle Eastern gov-

[2] J. C. Hurewitz, *The Struggle for Palestine* (New York: Norton, 1950), pp. 20-21.

ernments and peoples. The growing American involvement in Middle Eastern oil, however, and knowledge of the crucial importance of oil in the war that was approaching pointed the way to the greatly increased American interest in the Middle East that appeared once the war began.

Effects of the Second World War

It was the war itself that actually brought the United States into the Middle East. American engineers and troops were sent to Iran to maintain the lend-lease supply line to Russia. Economic and other experts were there to advise and assist the Iranian Government. American arms and goods flowed into Egypt to build up the strength of the Allied Middle East Command. The United States was a partner of Britain in the work of the Middle East Supply Centre, a sort of economic directorate which planned and controlled the economic life of the whole region in the interest of the Allied military effort. In all the wartime diplomacy concerning such matters as Turkey's possible entry into the war, the position of Egypt and the assurance of Iran's independence, the United States found itself playing a major part by reason of its role as a leading Allied power intent on winning the war and laying the foundations for a stable peace. President Roosevelt generally went along with Mr. Churchill's idea that Britain should "play the hand" in the Middle East, just as the United States played it in the Pacific, but this did not mean disinterest in the future of the region. The President indeed had a very lively interest in the future of the Arab world, which he demonstrated by his visit with King Ibn Saud in Egyptian waters in February 1945 on his way back from Yalta.

Anglo-American relations in the Middle East, as the war came to an end, were not marked by complete harmony. Joint policies had not been worked out beyond the immediate war problems, with the consequence that the occasional American forays in this field often led to friction with well-established British policies and interests: as in the matter of oil concessions, in competition for influence in Saudi Arabia, and above all in the question of Jewish immigration into Palestine. On many counts the major problems for the United States in the immediate postwar period seemed to revolve round rivalry with Great Britain. But these issues, serious as they were, were soon dwarfed by the Soviet challenge to the vital interests of both powers.

Resistance to Russia

Early in 1945 the Soviet Government terminated its long-standing treaty of 1925 with Turkey and made outright demands for bases on the Straits and for a sizeable part of Turkey's territory. Compliance could only mean the eventual reduction of Turkey to satellite status, an aim already apparent in Soviet public demands for a "friendly" government in Ankara. Coming in the period when the Western powers were doing their utmost to lay the basis for long-term cooperation in spite of Soviet duplicity and strong-arm methods, these demands provided a clear test of the will and ability of the West to call a halt to further Soviet expansion, and also of the importance which they attached to the Middle East. At Potsdam both conceded that the Montreux Convention on the Straits (1936) should be revised by its signatories but gave no concurrence to the demands for bases and territory. The United States then took the lead in outlining acceptable changes in the regime of the Straits. Soviet pressure on Turkey continued, however, and was matched by parallel pressure on Iran. The experiment of the "democratic national autonomous government" in Iranian Azerbaijan in 1945 and 1946, sustained by the presence of Soviet troops kept in Iran beyond the evacuation date fixed by treaty, threatened the integrity and the very existence of Iran as an independent state.

President Truman and his principal advisers, particularly Secretary Forrestal, saw the Soviet moves as a direct threat to American security. In the year 1946 they took several crucial decisions that gave proof of a determination not to let Soviet power move into the Middle East: the sending of the battleship "Missouri" to Istanbul; the rejection of Soviet demands on Greece and the Italian colonies in the peace treaty negotiations; the strong stand on Iran, which led to the withdrawal of Soviet forces and the eventual collapse of the Soviet-sponsored regime in Azerbaijan; [3] and the rejection of Moscow's formal demands for a new regime of the Turkish Straits including their "joint defense" by the U.S.S.R. and Turkey.

These American reactions were generally in line with those of Britain, naturally concerned at what Ernest Bevin called a thrust across the throat of the British Empire. But the United States was not just following the British lead. It was taking decisions on its own. These decisions were made in the context of global relations with the Soviet Union; they were the reflection of a hardening of American policy against Soviet encroachment in Europe, the Far East and elsewhere. At a meeting with his advisers called to consider whether the United States, in view of the demands on Turkey, should take a firm attitude or "do as we have in the past—protest, but ultimately give in," the President chose firmness with the full realization that if the Soviet Union did not back down it might mean armed conflict. ". . . We might as well find out," Secretary Forres-

[3] The U.S. attitude on Iran was made manifest through certain public utterances of the President, the strong stand taken by Secretary Byrnes in notes to Moscow and in the United Nations, and the diplomatic and moral support given by the American Ambassador in Tehran to the Iranian Government. The story that Mr. Truman sent an "ultimatum" to Stalin, told by the President himself at a later date (see *New York Times*, April 25, 1952) does not appear to be in accord with any other evidence available. Mr. Truman refers in his memoirs only to having Secretary Byrnes send a "blunt message" to Stalin (see Harry S. Truman, *Memoirs*, New York: Doubleday, 1956, v. 2, *Years of Trial and Hope*, pp. 94-95), but has written later that he "personally saw to it that Stalin was informed that I had given orders to our military chiefs to prepare for the movement of our ground, sea and air forces" (*New York Times*, August 25, 1957).

tal reports Mr. Truman as saying, "whether the Russians [are] bent on world conquest now as in five or ten years." [4]

American firmness also reflected a definite conception of the importance of the Middle East itself to the United States. The Soviet moves in Greece, Turkey and Iran were interpreted as an attempt to penetrate and get control of those countries and then push on to those that lay beyond. That was a threat not just to the lifeline of the British Empire but to the security of the whole non-Soviet world.

The policy of firmness took shape during 1946 as a series of reactions to specific Soviet demands and threats in the Middle East. It was not consciously adopted or presented to the public as a basic and continuing policy until the inability of Britain to keep on supporting Greece and Turkey put the question directly in the spring of 1947. The decision of the United States to take over that responsibility, after full public debate and passage of the necessary legislation by the Congress, marked the definite adoption of a national policy. Henceforward, this country was virtually committed to taking all necessary measures to prevent the intrusion of Soviet power into the Middle East. For though the specific commitment covered only Greece and Turkey and was limited to the provision of military equipment and economic aid, the general statements of the famous "Truman Doctrine" message went much further. Should Greece and Turkey lose their independence, Secretary Acheson pointed out in his testimony to Congressional committees, other states would soon lose theirs; the West had to keep those two countries out of Soviet hands—or be prepared to accept the subsequent loss of the strategic bases, lines of communication and resources of the Middle East. The progressive decline of British strength in the Arab world, moreover, forced the United States to consider the organization of joint defense, and therefore to face the difficult problems involved in reconciling close

[4] Walter Millis, ed., *The Forrestal Diaries* (New York: Viking Press, 1951), pp. 191-192.

association with Britain and a traditionally sympathetic attitude toward Middle Eastern nationalism.

The United States and Palestine

As this general line of policy was developing for the whole area, one particular corner of the Middle East had become the object of an American policy based on quite different considerations. This was Palestine. America, like Britain, was ostensibly seeking a "solution" in Palestine that would safeguard the rights of both Jews and Arabs. But there was a difference in approach between the two Western powers which prevented any effective joint action. Britain was motivated primarily by concern for safeguarding its relations with the Arab world and its strategic position in the Middle East; American policy, while cognizant of those considerations, reflected also a strong humanitarian feeling that a haven in Palestine (but apparently not anywhere else) must be opened to the remnants of persecuted European Jewry, as well as the not inconsiderable pressure which Zionist groups could and did exert in the domestic politics of this country. As a consequence of these factors and of the incompatibility of Arab and Jewish aims, neither London nor Washington, singly or together, was able to develop a consistent or effective policy.

Perhaps there never was any way out of the Palestine problem once the Balfour Declaration had been issued and large-scale Jewish immigration had begun. But whatever possibilities for a settlement there were—both when it was purely a British problem and later when the United States injected itself into the picture and took part in numerous commissions while avoiding all real responsibility—were missed, at a cost which is still being paid. The British, though trying generally in the early postwar period to be conciliatory toward the Arab League, could not meet Arab demands so extreme as to require complete abandonment of the Jews, for they had to consider not only their legal obligations and the actual situation in Palestine but also their relations with the United States. The American contribution to the increasing intractability of the problem took the form largely of periodic presidential statements urging the admission of more Jews to Palestine and private aid to immigration, all of which irked the British and added to the local pressures on them in Palestine itself.

After the problem was shifted to the United Nations in 1947 new factors were added to the equation, such as the expanded opportunities for Soviet influence and the ability of other nations—many with no real interest in Palestine— to get into the act through their voting power in the General Assembly. These factors in any case would have gravely complicated any efforts of Great Britain and the United States to find a way out compatible with their own security interests and on a basis of some reasonable compromise between Arab and Jew. But the very fact that the United Nations was seized of the question bore witness that Britain had given up; henceforth it had no policy other than to terminate the mandate and get out. The United States for its part soon confirmed that it had neither a consistent policy nor a willingness to enforce the solutions which it proposed from time to time.

The United States took a leading part—to put it mildly— in getting the partition resolution through the General Assembly in November 1947. It then declined to contribute any forces to assist in making the resolution stick. A few months later, alarmed by the prospects of what would happen when the British withdrew, it came forward with a proposal for an international trusteeship for Palestine. When this proposal failed of acceptance, American policy reverted with startling rapidity to partition through recognition of Israel's independence a few minutes after it was proclaimed. In the Arab-Jewish war which ensued, American attention naturally was directed toward the overriding aim of keeping the peace. The U.N. efforts to patch up a series of truces, accordingly, had strong American support. But the truce efforts tended to limp behind the fighting, and it was the fighting itself that shaped the situation that was to emerge when the final armistice agreements were signed (see map on page 308). What emerged was an Israel much larger than that of the original U.N. partition resolution, and with it the frustration of Arab hopes to the point where the whole Arab world was bound to be lastingly bitter and unreconciled not only to Israel but also to the powers the Arabs held responsible for their spoliation, humiliation and defeat.

American policy in Palestine was inconsistent and ineffective largely because it was tied to no broad concept of national interest. It was the product of a number of currents which at one time or another produced a variety of political acts and statements. The State Department, in general, stressed the importance of continuing good relations with the Arab world and of cooperation with the British. The Defense Department, especially Secretary Forrestal, was concerned about the future availability of Middle Eastern oil. Both were worried about how the Soviet leadership might profit from what was going on. Both underrated Zionism's political strength in the United States and its military strength in Palestine. The President, on the other hand, was so sympathetic to the Zionist side, by personal conviction and for apparent domestic political reasons, that he did not consistently relate his thinking and actions on Palestine to the broader Middle Eastern policy which on other matters he so courageously followed. In the absence of an agreed estimate of the forces at work in Palestine and of the impact on American interests of the various possibilities—independent Jewish state, trusteeship or whatever—there was no firm standard against which to measure specific policy decisions. Hence the instability, the unpredictability and the dramatic reversals that marked our course of conduct.

Even as the Palestine affair reached its crisis in the war of 1948, the cold war between East and West was brought to new heights of tension with the Communist coup in Czechoslovakia, the defection of Tito, and the Berlin blockade. Faced with what seemed a real possibility of war, the Western powers came together in the North Atlantic alliance and began to build up their military strength. When the Communists struck, however, it was in the Far East, in Korea. That attack, many in American official circles were convinced, was the opening gun of World War III. The Soviet leadership had shown its willingness to resort to open aggression. This might be but the first of a series of aggressions, carried out either directly or with satellite forces against vulnerable countries of the free world. America, therefore, besides throwing back the aggressor in Korea, would have to rearm and to mobilize its own strength as quickly as possible. It would have to look to the free world's defenses, not only in the NATO area but all round the periphery of the Communist bloc. Yugoslavia might be the next to be attacked, or Southeast Asia, or the Middle East. The glaring weakness of the Middle East seemed almost an open invitation to aggression. To Washington and to London the pressing need to do something about organizing a more solid defense there was clear.

Chapter 4

MIDDLE EAST DEFENSE PROPOSALS,
1951–1952

ALTHOUGH THE Soviet Union by this time was an "atomic power," defense of the Middle East was thought of in the West largely in the "conventional" terms of the recent war. The problem was one of planning a strategy by which an invading Soviet land army might be checked and thrown back, while simultaneously building up the military capabilities necessary to carry out that strategy. Traditionally, in two world wars, "allied" defense of the Middle East had been entrusted largely to British and Commonwealth forces. It was natural that they should again form the backbone of any defense, supplemented as might be possible by indigenous forces and by the combined sea and air power which the West could bring to bear in the Middle Eastern theater. The Supreme Commander would be British. Any plan would obviously have to have a necessary minimum of cooperation and good will on the part of the nations which were to be defended. It would have to be a "collective" defense in the sense that they would help or at least not hinder the necessary steps that would have to be taken. Some of them, for political or geographical reasons, obviously would have to be included in strategic planning.

Great Britain, despite the many blows to its old position of predominance in the Middle East, still held the key points and facilities on which defense of the region would logically rest. Above all, it still held at Suez, on the basis of the treaty of 1936, the great base considered indispensable for such defense by both British and American military men. Britain had hoped, as Egypt grew more

39

restive and assertive after World War II, to be able to negotiate a revised treaty that would leave the base in British hands, but Egyptian opinion and policies were moving toward more extreme positions, not toward compromise. Neither direct negotiations nor an appeal by Egypt to the U.N. Security Council produced a settlement. The British thus found themselves faced with a deadlock on the diplomatic front and with increasing Egyptian violence in the Suez area itself. In the summer of 1951 the moment seemed opportune, to both London and Washington, for a new approach whereby the Suez base could be "internationalized" within the framework of a regional defense organization.

The Middle East Command Proposal

Out of these considerations came the concept of an Allied Middle East Command. A formal alliance like the North Atlantic Treaty was hardly possible in the present state of relations among the Middle Eastern nations and between them and the West. The idea of a purely military "command" seemed more practical. Generally speaking, the idea was to re-create something like the British Middle East Command of World War II, with the local governments voluntarily providing the necessary minimum of cooperation and facilities as partners. An "allied" organization, presumably, would be open to less objection from Middle Eastern opinion than would the network of purely British bases and bilateral arrangements that had come under such strong attack.

That was the general approach. When it came to specifics, some difficult questions arose: What form would the new organization take, what nations would be in it, how would it be proposed, and how would it be affected by the disputes and hatreds that were keeping the Middle East in ferment? The United States and Britain asked France and Turkey to join them as sponsors of the proposal: France as one of the "Big Three" with interests in the Middle East even though no longer in possession of territory there; Turkey as a nation whose strength and geographical location were essential to any defense of the region, and a Middle Eastern and Moslem nation whose participation would take the purely Western label off the proposal. Turkey's prime objective had been membership in NATO, and the Turks had resisted the idea that they should belong only to a Middle East defense grouping linked to NATO's command arrangements. But once the decision was taken in the autumn of 1951 to accept Turkey, along with Greece, in NATO, the Turkish Government was quite willing to join also in arrangements for the Middle East.

What was expected of other nations? Iran, the gateway to the Middle East from the north, already had taken the step of signing a military aid agreement with the United States and had begun to receive some equipment. The army of Israel, with some of the best trained forces in the area, might be useful in case of a Soviet attack. The Arab states could hardly provide any significant effective forces, save perhaps Jordan's Arab Legion, but it was essential to have access to their oil and to the important pieces of real estate under their sovereignty. The military planners, however, could not even count on the use of all these resources, meager as they were, because military planning, unfortunately, could not be divorced from the political environment. The year 1951 was one of spectacular manifestations of the nationalist revolt against the West. The crisis in Iran over nationalization of the Anglo-Iranian Oil Company in May 1951, wherever it might lead ultimately, meant for the immediate future a gravely damaged relationship with the West and the prospect of chaos at home. The Wafd government in Egypt was becoming ever more intransigent and committed to policies which left little or no possibility of finding any peaceful outcome of the conflict with Britain over Suez and the Sudan. The Arab states and Israel continued to be at swords' points, with no sign of accommodation on either side. Of all the Middle Eastern states, only Turkey looked at the military problem primarily from the standpoint of defense against Russia.

Into this confused situation the Western powers tossed their proposal for a Middle East Command. Feeling that they had to start somewhere, they decided first to approach Egypt, and only Egypt. The idea was that Egypt held the key position because of the Suez base and its leadership of the Arab League. If Cairo agreed, the other Arab states could be expected to follow. They would be kept informed, but invitations to them were deferred pending Egypt's reaction. Israel was also to be informed and reassured that the scheme would in no way injure Israeli interests. The whole fate of the proposal depended on Egypt.

The avowed purpose of the plan as presented was to defend Egypt and other Middle Eastern countries against aggression from outside. If Egypt were prepared to participate "as a founder member . . . on a basis of equality and partnership," its security would be enhanced, its officers would hold posts of high responsibility in the Command, and its forces would receive necessary training and equipment from other members. As part of the bargain, however, Egypt would agree to furnish to the Command "such strategic defence and other facilities on her soil as are indispensable for the organisation in peacetime of the defence of the Middle East," and would grant "all necessary facilities and assistance in the event of war, imminent menace of war, or apprehended international emergency. . . ." The British base at Suez would be formally handed over to Egypt "on the understanding that it would simultaneously become an Allied Base within the Allied Middle East Command with full Egyptian participation in the running of this base in peace and war." Britain, in return, would give up the Anglo-Egyptian treaty of 1936 and withdraw such British forces as were not allocated to the Command by agreement of its founder members. At the same time Britain made a new proposal on the Sudan under which an international commission, including Egypt, should be established there to watch over constitutional development and tender advice to the British and Egyptian Governments which shared the "condominium." [1]

Egypt's Refusal

The proposal was made on October 13, 1951. It was made at a time when the Egyptian Government had already proposed to its legislature the unilateral denunciation of the treaties with Britain on Suez and the Sudan. The sponsoring powers made their proposal in the hope that, by presenting the alternative of an "international" base at Suez, they could head off the storm and lay a sounder political groundwork for maintaining the Suez base as the focal point for the defense of the entire Middle East. For Western military opinion saw no good alternative to the Suez base. Its geographical location, communications, and facilities for training, storage and repair made it unique.

If there was any real confidence in the West that Egypt would accept the new proposal, it was gravely misplaced. Apparently no attempt was made in advance to sound out the Egyptian Government, already deeply committed to a strongly nationalistic stand on Suez and the Sudan, a stand which for domestic reasons it could not modify. Thus the timing of the proposal could hardly have been more unfortunate. The Egyptian Government did not even give it the courtesy of careful study. Two days after its receipt it was rejected, and the Egyptian parliament adopted decrees denouncing the treaty of 1936 and the Sudan treaty of 1899. [2]

[1] Text of Four-Power Proposal in *Department of State Bulletin*, v. 25 (October 22, 1951), pp. 647-648. Great Britain, *Anglo-Egyptian Conversations on the Defence of the Suez Canal and on the Sudan*, Egypt No. 2 (1951), Cmd. 8419 (London: H.M.S.O., 1951), pp. 43-46.

[2] Egypt, Ministry of Foreign Affairs, *Records of Conversations, Notes and Papers Exchanged between the Royal Egyptian Government and the United Kingdom Government (March 1950–November 1951)* (Cairo, 1951), pp. 167-179.

These moves killed the whole Anglo-American plan for organizing the defense of the Middle East. Anglo-Egyptian relations deteriorated as the British denounced Egypt's unilateral repudiation of treaty obligations and prepared to hold firm at Suez against provocation and violence. The United States felt compelled to back the British on the issue of the sanctity of treaties. Thus the Western powers, instead of getting Egyptian cooperation to defend Suez, Egypt and the Middle East, found themselves faced with open Egyptian hostility and increasing violence in the canal zone itself.

In an explanatory statement issued a few weeks later the Western powers toned down their original proposal and tried to answer some of Egypt's arguments. They stressed that no derogation of sovereignty was intended; that Egypt would be an equal partner; that arrangements for bases and facilities were a matter for subsequent specific agreements; that the main task at first would be the provision of military aid to the Middle Eastern states.[3] These points may have had some effect on other Arab states but they made no impression on Egypt. The West persisted in the line that Egypt did not "understand" the Middle East Command proposal. The Egyptian Government simply chose not to understand it as a proposal for cooperation among equals but rather as a device to prolong the British occupation of Egyptian territory with the added backing of the United States.

The Middle East Command, accordingly, was stillborn, though its sponsors maintained they would go ahead with it anyway. For a few months they declared their offer to be still open, then turned their attention to other possible ways of making a start on the organization of Middle East defense. The explanatory statement of November 10 had stressed military planning as opposed to the actual build-up of forces under the Command. Although it brought no change in the negative Arab attitude, the British Chiefs of Staff were anxious to get planning started anyway. If

[3] *Department of State Bulletin,* v. 25 (November 19, 1951), pp. 817-818.

they could not do it at Suez, with the Egyptians, they would do it at Cyprus, without the Egyptians and with as many states as were willing to come along. In that way they might establish the nucleus of a defense organization which the Arab states might join later when they saw it was a going concern. The revolution in Egypt which brought General Nagib and his army associates to power in Egypt in July 1952 later gave the West transient hopes of a more "realistic" attitude in Cairo. Meanwhile Britain, the United States, France, Turkey, Australia, New Zealand and South Africa could proceed on their own. Cyprus would be only the planning headquarters; it was not considered an adequate substitute for Suez as a base.

The United States, however, was never more than lukewarm about a Middle East defense organization that included but one Middle Eastern nation among its participants. It was all right for British, American and Turkish military men to exchange views and do a bit of quiet planning. But an organization with so little support from the nations of the region itself would not represent a position of strength. In case of war, of course, the West would have to act with whatever local support it could muster. A large part of the purpose of a peacetime defense organization, on the other hand, was precisely to demonstrate the will of the local nations themselves to share in the common defense. Without Egypt or any Arab state, without Israel, without Iran, it could hardly be anything but what its opponents said it was, an organization of Western powers to protect Western interests. This was the fundamental reason why the Middle East defense organization never took form.

Reasons for Failure

The whole effort to build some kind of collective defense against the Soviet threat to the Middle East thus ended in failure. What went wrong? Certainly the tactics and timing of the approaches left something to be desired.

More fundamentally, the real difficulty lay in the attempt
to create a military command and base structure without
sufficient underpinning of political understanding and
agreement. Even the promise of arms and of "social and
economic advancement" was not enough to overcome the
effects of the deep political cleavages separating some of
the Middle Eastern nations from each other and from the
West or the general disbelief among the Arab governments in the reality of a Soviet military threat.

The most obvious miscalculation concerned the attitude
of Egypt. The Western powers made the proposal in terms
which they thought reasonable, but if they had correctly
gauged the Egyptian mood they could hardy have thought
it worth while to make it at all. Egyptian nationalism made
it virtually impossible for a government in Cairo, whether
of the King's favorites or of the Wafd or of General Nagib,
to accept anything but the evacuation of British troops
from Suez, certainly not a proposal which looked like a
plan to keep them there under an "Allied" label. The miscalculation in Egypt, moreover, practically eliminated the
chance of winning over any other Arab states to military
cooperation with the West. Iraq was favorably inclined
toward just such an arrangement, to substitute a multilateral undertaking for the existing bilateral treaty under
which Britain held two bases in Iraq. Lebanon was generally sympathetic to the Western powers, as was Ibn Saud.
Syria, though divided on the issue, and Jordan, closely
tied to Britain by treaty and subsidy, might well have gone
along. But none of them could be expected to defy Egypt
on a decision taken against the "imperialists" in the name
of nationalism and the sacred sovereignty of an Arab state.

The principal object of Arab concern was Israel. While
the American and British Governments were well aware of
that fact, they saw that they could not do much about it
at the moment, whereas the need for an organized defense against the Soviet Union was urgent. They therefore
did their best to keep the Arab-Israel conflict to one side
while they proceeded with the business at hand. Merely to

avoid trying to get Israel and the Arab states under the same roof to plan military strategy with the West, however, did not solve the problem. The difficulty lay in the very attempt to organize any defense organization covering this area when the Arab states still considered themselves at war with Israel.

Israel, meanwhile, was turning more and more from a neutral to a pro-Western line in the cold war and was convinced of its own value as a possible ally. But could it be expected to take its eyes off the main objective, that of forcing the Arabs to make peace, or to look on the idea of a regional defense organization other than as a means of achieving that objective; or on the actual Western proposals as anything but "appeasement" of the Arabs at Israel's expense? Could the Arab states regard them as anything but an attempt to divert them from their own main objective of exacting revenge for the disaster of 1948 and to force their acceptance of the *status quo* with Israel? Owing to Egypt's quick rejection of the Middle East Command and its consistently negative attitude thereafter, these attitudes were not put to the test. Yet it was clear from the reaction of both sides that, quite aside from Suez and all the tangled problems of Anglo-Egyptian relations, the great unsettled questions of Palestine stood as a mountainous barrier in the way of all Western efforts to win the cooperation and support of the peoples of that part of the Middle East.

Finally, there was the absence of Iran. Geographically, Iran was in the first line of defense. If it were lost, Turkey could be flanked from the east and south; probably even Suez could not be held. From a military standpoint it was obvious that any Middle East defense organization ought to include Iran, but in this case as in others, the years 1951 and 1952 presented political conditions which made its inclusion out of the question. With moderate elements in eclipse, Iranian nationalism was being whipped up to fever pitch and directed entirely against Britain. The United States, while continuing its vain efforts to mediate, was trying to preserve some small measure of influence in Iran and to keep its military mission there. But until a settlement could be reached on the oil dispute, Iran had to be left out of all consideration of Middle East defense. Indeed, as the internal situation went from bad to worse, it was a real question whether the combination of fanatic anti-British nationalism and growing Communist influence might not lead the whole country into the Soviet orbit.

In sum, we may conclude that the conditions for the success of Anglo-American efforts in these years could hardly have been less favorable. Any progress on arrangements for defense had to await progress toward settlement of the major political disputes. Second, clearer understanding was necessary as to the interests and political commitments of the nations concerned, so that the limitations as well as the possibilities of defense would be apparent. In the Middle East the Western powers had tried to reverse the sequence of what had been done in Europe. There a solid alliance based on a community of attitudes and interests had been established, then a joint military organization created; here the military command structure and planning arrangements were to be brought into being first and superimposed on a welter of political conflicts. It simply would not work. If anything could be concluded by American policy-makers from the experience of those years, it was that the old roads led nowhere and that some new approach would have to be tried.

Chapter 5

THE ORIGINS OF THE BAGHDAD PACT

THE NEW Republican Administration came into office ready to take a "new look" at all existing policies for national security, both in the strictly military field and in foreign relations generally. Some policies, such as support for NATO, obviously would be carried on without basic change. In an area such as the Middle East, where no comparable position of strength had been built, the new look was bound to be far more searching. Secretary of State Dulles decided to do the looking himself in a fact-finding expedition that took him to all the principal Middle Eastern countries in the spring of 1953.

The Secretary's trip marked the beginning of some new directions in American policy. While the basic purpose of strengthening the area against Soviet pressures and possible aggression remained unchanged, some of the approaches and methods were altered. The Secretary's conclusions, similar to those reached by others who had been working closely with the problem, may be summarized as follows: (1) that any sound regional defense organization must spring from the desires of the peoples and governments of the area in question; (2) that most of the Middle Eastern peoples and governments, as of that time, were unwilling to be associated with the West in such a defense organization; (3) that the states of the "northern tier" of the Middle East were the most aware of the Soviet menace, the most likely to do something about it, and the best situated to provide protection to the area as a whole.[1]

[1] "Report on the Near East," Address by Secretary Dulles, *Department of State Bulletin*, v. 28 (June 15, 1953), pp. 831-835.

49

The Northern Tier

The "northern tier concept" seemed to offer the opportunity to strengthen those nations that wanted to be strengthened, without permitting troublesome problems like Suez and Palestine to hold up progress where it could be made. The step-by-step approach would mean putting aside for a time any comprehensive joint planning for regional defense, but cooperation could be expanded when and as individual states made their choice for it.

The cornerstone of any northern tier alignment could only be Turkey, the strongest state in the Middle East. Already a member of NATO, Turkey had committed its armed forces wholly to the NATO command. Together with Greece and Yugoslavia, with which it had signed a treaty of friendship in February 1953, it provided indispensable territory and manpower for the defense of the eastern Mediterranean area. Turkey happened to be, also, the only firm base from which the Western alliance system and Western power could be extended into the Middle East. The Turks were willing to take the initiative, for they saw as clearly as American strategic planners that their own country, and with it the entire NATO position, could be outflanked by a Soviet encircling move through the distressingly vulnerable countries farther to the east. But beyond those weaker immediate neighbors, Iran and Iraq, lay Pakistan.

For some months Washington had been eyeing Pakistan as another potential position of strength, an eastern cornerstone for a Middle East defense system. With a population of some 70,000,000, almost half of them in the western part of the country, with its strong military traditions and a reservoir of fighting men, Pakistan might conceivably play the military role that British India had played before partition, providing manpower and supplies for the defense of the Middle East. Its leaders had, moreover, shown an interest in aligning their country with the West and in securing arms from the United States. Their reasons were eminently practical. They wished to strengthen their country's international position, especially against India. Concern over Soviet aggression, either directly against Pakistan or in the Middle East, was hardly a major factor in their decision.[2]

By the end of 1953 the general knowledge that the United States and Pakistan were negotiating some kind of military agreement had provoked protests from Afghanistan and a veritable storm in India where many voices were raised decrying any step that would upset the existing ratio of forces between Pakistan and India, "bring the cold war to India's doorstep," and undermine the policy of neutrality for South Asia. These protests, though largely discounted in advance, gave Washington some cause for concern, but after Vice-President Nixon's visit to Karachi in December 1953 the United States could hardly have backed out without offense to Pakistan. In the following February the decision was announced, and a military assistance agreement was negotiated and signed in May. It was a regular arms aid agreement, with no provision for United States bases in Pakistan and no alliance obligations. But one part of the arrangement was the understanding, which the United States regarded as linked to the aid, that Pakistan would cooperate in regional defense.[3] Pakistan was, indeed, already negotiating with Turkey.

On April 2, 1954, Turkey and Pakistan signed a treaty of friendship and cooperation for security.[4] It was no military alliance, providing only that the parties would study the means and extent of their cooperation for collective defense to meet an attack from outside. It was actually

[2] Mohammed Ahsen Chaudhri, "Pakistan and the United States," *Pakistan Horizon*, v. 9 (December 1956), pp. 200, 206.

[3] See statement of President Eisenhower, February 25, 1954, in *Documents on American Foreign Relations, 1954* (New York: Harper, for the Council on Foreign Relations, 1955), pp. 373-374; for text of agreement, see Department of State, "Mutual Defense Assistance Agreement between the United States of America and Pakistan," *Treaties and Other International Acts Series*, no. 2976 (Washington: G.P.O., 1955).

[4] Text of agreement in *Documents on American Foreign Relations, 1954*, cited, pp. 376-378.

intended, as American diplomacy had envisaged, as a constructive step toward better ensuring the security of the whole Middle East, and was specifically open to accession by other states. Not bearing the stigma of Western participation that had marked the proposed Middle East Command, it might eventually attract Arab support. By itself the pact had an element of incongruity, the two countries being so widely separated geographically with no means of being of much help to each other in case of war. That very fact drew attention to the invitation to others to join and to the states which might do so. The logical land bridge, Iran, now rid of the anti-Western Mosaddeq regime and working its way slowly toward political stability and a settlement of the controversy with the West on oil, was not yet ready to consider adherence. Iraq seemed a more likely candidate.

Iraq's Choice for the West

The United States had taken a decision on military aid to Iraq during the preceding year. Under the premiership of Mohammed Fadhel Jamali negotiations were brought to a speedy conclusion and a military assistance agreement was effected by an exchange of notes on April 21, 1954. While the Iraq Government made no formal commitment with respect to regional defense, it was understood between the two governments that Iraq would play its part in regional defense. As in the case of Pakistan, the Turks were ready to take the lead in negotiations for a bilateral treaty. For Iraq, however, the decision to ally with Turkey and thus indirectly with the West was one of great moment to take, for it raised the whole question of relations with the other Arab states and the possible breaking of the "solidarity" of the Arab League. It was almost sure to provoke opposition from anti-Western forces throughout the Arab world and possibly riotous protest at home, but General Nuri es-Said, who was serving as Prime Minister later in 1954, secured the assent of eight former premiers

in the presence of the King, taking a chance on being able
to control any domestic opposition, legal or illegal. The
main problem then was to make it palatable to Egypt,
where press and radio were already stirring up Arab
opinion, including the "street" in Baghdad and other
cities of Iraq, against the new course.

Iraq's leaders reasoned that they had to strengthen their
country. The Soviet threat had some meaning for them.
Soviet air bases were but a few minutes' flight from Iraqi
territory; the large Kurdish minority made Iraq vulnerable to Soviet subversion; the Communist Party of Iraq,
though outlawed, was a source of potential trouble. Besides its fear of the U.S.S.R., Iraq had various reasons for
seeking arms and other aid: to consolidate Iraq's own
political stability and further its economic progress with
Western help, to aid the Arab cause against Israel and,
even more significant, to play a leading role in the Arab
world.

Within the Arab League as then constituted Egypt had
always had the strongest voice. Iraq had vainly contended,
since the negotiations preceding the League's birth in
1945, for a federal relationship among the Arab states,
particularly those closely linked by geography and economic interest. As a trial balloon Iraq had proposed an
Arab federation at the meeting of the Arab League Council in January 1954. It met no positive response from the
sister Arab states. Premier Jamali then revived the old idea
of unity of the Fertile Crescent, to begin with a federation
of Iraq with Syria and Jordan. Egypt, of course, would have
opposed it, as would Saudi Arabia. The United States
Government, when asked for support, would do nothing
in the absence of an express desire for union on the part
of the peoples concerned and was exercised over the effect
on Israel, whose reaction was bound to be negative and
might be explosive. Despite these negative results, Iraq did
not lose its zeal for Arab federation, nor did it wish to
weaken the bonds of the Arab League; but it felt the time

had come boldly to pursue the idea of alignment with Turkey, Pakistan and the Western powers.

The Reaction of Egypt

In the summer of 1954, shortly after Nuri es-Said took office as Prime Minister, he talked in Baghdad with Salah Salem of Egypt and later with Abdel Nasser in Cairo. The stories of what transpired do not agree, but according to the Iraqi version Nuri clearly announced what he intended to do; Egypt agreed but urged him to hold off until the agreement with Britain on the evacuation of Suez was concluded. When that agreement was signed in October, Iraq began negotiations with Turkey. The matter came up again at the meeting of the Foreign Ministers of the Arab League in December, when further misunderstanding developed. Iraq's intentions, again according to the Iraqi side of the story, were made clear; it could not postpone indefinitely steps required for its own security just to please Egypt. According to Egypt, however, it was agreed that no Arab state would make an alliance with a non-Arab state. At any rate, when Iraq and Turkey announced in January 1955 that they were about to conclude such a pact, the lid blew off in Cairo. Egypt denounced Iraq as a traitor to the Arab cause and did everything possible to rally Arab opinion against Nuri es-Said. Abdel Nasser claimed also that the Western powers had agreed to let Egypt take the lead in building a stronger Arab regional organization not linked to the West; now they had set about wrecking that possibility.[5]

Misunderstanding or deception, Iraq's course brought out into the open a real conflict of interest. Egypt, itself not prepared to line up with Turkey and the West, could not resign itself to seeing any other Arab state defy Egyptian leadership by doing so; there could be but one collective defense pact and that was the Arab League Collective Security Pact. In its own bargaining with the

[5] Interview, *New York Times*, April 4, 1955.

West the Egyptian regime wanted the weight of the whole Arab world behind it. But now Iraq had broken ranks and threatened to carry other Arab states along with it.

The Turkish-Iraqi pact, signed at Baghdad on February 24, 1955, pledged the two nations to cooperation "for their security and their defense." [6] Just how they would cooperate was left to later, more detailed agreements. Appropriate language to mollify Egyptian and Arab nationalist sensibilities was included in references to other international obligations and in a separate exchange of letters supporting U.N. resolutions on Palestine. Abdel Nasser was not impressed. It was the fact of the conclusion of the pact, not its terms, that broke the solidarity of the Arab League and threatened Egypt's leadership. It looked for a time as if Egypt would break up the League by insisting on Iraq's expulsion or by withdrawing itself. In the end the League survived because neither rival wished to take the responsibility for its breakup, but behind its transparent façade each bent its energies to lining up the other Arab states. Iraq, with the heavy-handed cooperation of Turkey, tried to extend the new pact in the Fertile Crescent area; Egypt organized a new grouping in which the common defense was to be organized under common (Egyptian) command. In this contest the Egyptians scored all the successes. Saudi Arabia, following its traditional anti-Hashemite policy, supported the Egyptian campaign politically and financially. No other Arab state decided to take advantage of the clause of the Turkish-Iraqi pact inviting the accession of "any member of the Arab League or any other state effectively interested in the peace and security of this region." Meanwhile Cairo's Voice of the Arabs was filling the air with abuse of Nuri es-Said and calling upon the people of Iraq to throw him out.

Nuri, an old hand at maintaining order at home, may not have been worried by this campaign. But Iraq was now on the defensive. The attempt to combine a pro-Western policy with leadership in the Arab world did not succeed.

[6] Text in *Middle East Journal*, v. 9 (Spring 1955), pp. 177-178.

The United States and the Baghdad Pact

Once again, a Western initiative to organize the defense of the Middle East had run afoul of Arab nationalism and Arab politics. The American decision to grant arms aid to Iraq and to encourage its participation in regional defense had involved the risk that in gaining Iraq the West might have to write off the rest of the Arab world. But there was at least the chance that Iraq's "realism" would find an echo in other Arab capitals. On this point it is possible that more careful preparation and execution might have brought Lebanon, Syria and Jordan into the arrangement along with Iraq. The initiative for collective security, Mr. Dulles had said, must come from the Middle Eastern nations themselves. Premiers Menderes and Nuri es-Said took the initiative on this occasion. It was their decision to go ahead when and as they did. Following the conclusion of the pact, it was Menderes who undertook to sell it to Lebanon and to press it strongly, even threateningly, upon Syria. Lebanon, however, stuck to its traditional middle position. Syria discarded its relatively moderate government for a new one more susceptible to Egyptian influence and more suspicious of the West. An American decision to join the alliance at the start might have made the difference in persuading Lebanon, Syria or Jordan to come in, but Washington chose caution and the initiative was left to other hands.

What opportunity there may have been to strengthen Iraq's relative position and influence over those of Egypt was lost partly because the violence of Egypt's reaction was not entirely anticipated. Although one could find warnings in the output of Cairo's press and radio, Abdel Nasser himself had given numerous private assurances of his desire for cooperation with the West. Even Premier Menderes had had hopes of an understanding with Egypt and was planning a visit to Cairo when Egyptian delays induced him to go off to Baghdad first. After that he heard no further kind words from Egypt. Abdel Nasser moved rapidly to form an informal Egypt-Syria-Saudi Arabia-Yemen alignment that later took the form of a series of bilateral and multilateral pacts under Egypt's leadership and military command.[7]

The Role of Great Britain

Any consideration of the entry of Iraq into the northern tier alignment requires a look at the role of Great Britain. The British Government had not shown any great enthusiasm for the northern tier concept or for the Turkish-Pakistan agreement, with its damaging effect on Western relations with India. British ideas on defense of the Middle East still revolved round Suez and the various bases which Britain held by treaty. It was because of the relationship with Iraq, where two of the most important British bases were located, that the growing set of northern tier agreements suddenly took on more attraction for London. These bases were held under a treaty due to expire in 1956 and not likely to be renewed. Several years before, Baghdad street mobs had already wrecked one attempt to keep the bases under a new treaty, and after agreeing to evacuate Suez it would be tempting fate for Britain merely to sit tight on existing arrangements with Iraq.

The Baghdad Pact between Turkey and Iraq offered the kind of opportunity the British needed. It was open to all states "interested in the peace and security of the region." Nuri es-Said, long a friend of the British, was quite willing to deal them in. On April 4, 1955, Great Britain adhered to the Baghdad Pact and signed at the same time with Iraq a bilateral treaty, under which Iraq assumed responsibility for its own defense and eventually took over the two bases, Habbaniya and Shu'aiba. The

[7] Egyptian-Syrian treaty, October 20, 1955; Egyptian-Saudi Arabian treaty, October 27, 1955; joint Egyptian-Saudi Arabian-Yemen treaty, April 21, 1956. For unofficial translation of texts of first two treaties, see *Middle East Journal*, v. 10 (Winter 1956), pp. 77-79. See also G.E.K., "The Turco-Egyptian Flirtation of Autumn 1954," *The World Today*, v. 12 (November 1956), pp. 447-457.

British promised to help in maintaining the bases and in training and equipping the Iraqi air force, and British aircraft would have landing and overflight rights in Iraq.[8] It seemed a happy solution for all concerned.

Great Britain's accession to the Baghdad Pact, however, put a new face on the picture. Whereas at the start the initiative and sponsorship had been largely American, hereafter the United Kingdom as the only Western member of the pact naturally assumed a role of leadership. As Sir Anthony Eden said in explaining Britain's accession, "our purpose . . . was a very simple one. I think that by so doing we have strengthened our influence and our voice throughout the Middle East." [9] With Suez being evacuated and with only Egypt's promise on which to depend for its use in case of war, Britain looked all the more to its position in Iraq as a means of protecting the security of British interests in the Middle East, especially in the Persian Gulf area. Membership in the Baghdad Pact seemed the best available means of protecting the oil supplies so necessary to Britain's economy. It might also check the erosion of the British positions throughout the Middle East, especially if Jordan were brought in.

The Test in Jordan

Jordan's fate became a test of strength between the British and the anti-pact forces in the Arab world led by Abdel Nasser of Egypt. The British Government was prepared to offer Jordan, as a price for joining the pact, a revision of the treaty of 1946, which still had ten years to run, and an increased subsidy. In January 1956 it sent Sir Gerald Templer, Chief of the Imperial General Staff, to persuade the Jordanian King and Cabinet of the wisdom of the proposal. Success was expected, and the first official reactions were favorable. Then the thunder from the

[8] For text, see Great Britain, *Treaty Series*, no. 50, Cmd. 9544 (London: H.M.S.O., 1955).
[9] House of Commons, *Parliamentary Debates*, Weekly Hansard, no. 320, col. 897 (April 4, 1955).

streets, toppling three governments within a week, showed
how gravely London had miscalculated the strength of
the opposing forces both within Jordan and outside. The
"old reliable" leaders and the young King could no longer
control the situation, now that two-thirds of Jordan's inhabitants were Palestinians, and more than half of those
were refugees. Stimulated by Egyptian agitation and
propaganda, and by Saudi money, local nationalists and
the "mob" sounded the knell of Britain's tutelage in
Amman. The dismissal a month later of Glubb Pasha,
British Commander of Jordan's Arab Legion, was the
logical denouement, to be followed in due course by the
termination of the Anglo-Jordanian treaty and British
rights to bases in Jordan. It was the end of all hope that
the Baghdad Pact might soon be extended to include
other Arab states beside Iraq. Lebanon was confirmed in
its decision to keep its middle position and stay out, while
Jordan seemed destined to follow Syria into Abdel Nasser's
camp.

Accession of Iran

Counterbalancing these setbacks in the Arab world had
been the success in completing the alliance across the
northern tier. Pakistan acceded to the Baghdad Pact in
September 1955, and Iran joined in October. The first
decision was expected, since Pakistan and Turkey had
started the whole thing; the Pakistan Government was
merely waiting for the best possible moment from the
standpoint of its domestic situation and the arrangements
for arms aid from the United States. For Iran, on the other
hand, it was a major new decision. Historically Iran had
sought security in neutrality, in trying to preserve a balance between predatory great powers by nonalignment
and nonprovocation. Since the unhappy Mosaddeq experience and the settlement of the oil dispute, however,
the Shah had definitely turned toward the West. His intention was to join the northern tier grouping at such

time as he felt that the support from the West would be sufficient to counterbalance the risk of antagonizing the Soviet Union. Specifically, he wanted the assurance of American protection and some modern weapons for his army. Actually, when he took his country into the Baghdad Pact in October he did not yet have full satisfaction on either count, but had become convinced that the risk was worth taking. The decision was not made under American pressure, although there was no doubt of Washington's gratification, and the Shah had reason to believe he had opened the door to increased support from the West.

The United States Stays Out

The five pact members met at Baghdad in November 1955 to set up the formal organization, including a Council of Ministers and special committees for military planning, economic cooperation, communications and countersubversion. A permanent headquarters was set up in Baghdad, with a Secretary-General and staff. The United States, represented at the meeting by an observer, gave its blessing to these arrangements. It was not prepared itself to join the alliance, despite the urgings of all members, for a variety of reasons: the State Department wished to keep whatever chance still remained of working with Saudi Arabia and Egypt; it did not want to provoke any new Soviet move into the Middle East; it did not wish further to antagonize Israel, which had declared its hostility to the pact; and it did not relish the prospect of a debate in the Senate on ratification which might throw its whole Middle Eastern policy into the arena of domestic politics. On the occasion of Sir Anthony Eden's visit to Washington in February 1956 he and the President publicly spoke kind words for the Baghdad Pact, and when the next meeting of the Council was held at Tehran in April, the United States announced its decision for full participation in the committees on economics and countersubversion and for permanent liaison with the military committee. It was in the pact but not of it, a participant for practical purposes but without the legal commitments.

To the extent that the formation and growth of the Baghdad Pact could be considered the results of American diplomacy, the State Department looked upon its handiwork and saw that it was good. In 1953 the northern tier was a concept in the mind of Mr. Dulles and his associates. By the summer of 1956 it was a five-nation regional security organization covering the previously open gap between NATO and SEATO. It included the strongest and most populous countries in the Middle East. They had stood firm in rejecting the Soviet threats and protests which had accompanied each step of the way. Iran, the key country from a geographical standpoint, had made a clear decision for alignment with the West. The anti-Western solidarity of the Arab League had been cracked by the inclusion of Iraq. There now existed a barrier to Soviet imperialism, not a formidable one but still a barrier.

The story of how the pact was formed and how it grew is not the chronicle of failure and futility that marked the efforts of 1951 and 1952 for a Middle East defense organization. Nevertheless, the story shows clearly enough how far the West still was from a position of strength in the Middle East. Militarily, the pact offered no prospect of effective defense. Turkey, its forces already committed to NATO, could not be expected to do more in the east than try to hold its own territory. Iraq and Iran were woefully weak; Pakistan was absorbed in its disputes with India. All three had joined primarily in order to get arms from the United States rather than out of faith in the concept of regional security. Britain had joined in order to save its position in Iraq and to bolster a sagging position throughout the Middle East. The refusal of the United States to join had left all members with a feeling they had been deceived and let down. Iraq was now isolated in the Arab world and its government's position was gravely weakened. The gap between the northern tier and the southern tier of Arab states had been fatefully widened, creating opportunities for Soviet penetration of the Arab world which Moscow was not slow to exploit. Western gains in the north were matched by losses in the south. Fathered by American initiative, the pact was left weak and unformed by virtue of the disparate interests of its members and the half-heartedness of American support, uncertain of its future in the growing crisis which its very existence had helped to create.

Chapter 6

THE CHALLENGE OF ABDEL NASSER

ON JULY 19, 1952, a group of young army officers organized and led a revolution which sealed the fate of the monarchy and the old political system in Egypt. This was no ordinary *coup d'état* by military adventurers. Its success was due to profound and widespread public discontent with King Faruq, the parties and the politicians. Reform was the watchword of the new ruling group. Their mandate, as they and their supporters saw it, was to begin the building of a new Egypt, to eliminate corruption, to attack the basic problems of poverty and backwardness. Only with such revolutionary changes could they rescue the army from its futility and weakness and revenge the humiliation suffered in Palestine. Only thus could Egypt properly play its rightful part as leader of the Arab world.[1]

The new regime, headed by the popular General Mohammed Nagib, received a rather cordial welcome from the Western powers, which had no more reason than the Egyptian people to be fond of King Faruq. Perhaps, they thought, Nagib would embark on the same kind of modernizing revolution that Ataturk had carried through in Turkey. Perhaps he would be interested in enlisting Western help and good will. Perhaps the plans for a Middle East defense organization could now be rescued from near oblivion.

It was soon apparent that in matters of foreign policy the new government's position did not greatly differ from that of its predecessor. A group which had been swept into power by the outraged national pride of so many

[1] John S. Badeau, "A Role in Search of a Hero," *Middle East Journal,* v. 9 (Autumn 1955), pp. 373-384; Gamal Abdel Nasser, "The Egyptian Revolution," *Foreign Affairs,* v. 33 (January 1955), pp. 199-211.

Egyptians could hardly have taken anything other than the spirit of nationalism as its guide. The young officers who had made the revolution, the Revolutionary Command Council which henceforth ruled Egypt, had no special feelings of friendship for the West. Indeed, they had been nurtured for years on a hatred of British imperialism as the source of Egypt's troubles. General Nagib, as titular head of the government, was bound to be wary of making concessions which the old regime would not make. The problem of Suez was no nearer to solution, a Middle East defense organization no nearer to reality.

The Suez Negotiations

Nevertheless, it did seem possible that fresh impetus could be given to the negotiations with Britain. There was no better way for the new rulers to consolidate their regime than to get the British out of the Sudan and out of the Suez base. And the British, by this time, were ready to leave both, provided satisfactory terms could be arranged. As for Sudan they wished only to be sure that the Sudanese would have a free choice of their future status. When Egypt accepted this point, compromise became possible and an agreement was reached in February 1953. As for Suez, since Egypt still would not agree to the immediate transformation of the base from British to "international" status, then the next best thing was to turn it over to Egypt with certain guarantees covering its maintenance in peace and its use in time of war. The United States was prepared to help the negotiations along with encouragement and advice to both sides.

General Nagib was displaced by Colonel Gamal Abdel Nasser in September 1953 and disappeared from the political scene early in 1954. This brought about no basic change in the Egyptian position, and by that time the negotiations were already well advanced. By mid-1954 both Britain and Egypt were prepared to initial "heads of agreement," with two sticky problems remaining to be settled: the availability of the base in time of war and the status of the British technicians who would maintain the facilities at the base for a number of years after the evacuation of British armed forces. Even these points finally proved susceptible of compromise, and the formal agreement was signed in October 1954.[2]

British forces were to be out of the Suez base in 20 months from the signature of the treaty. For a period of seven years the British would have the right to reoccupy the base in case of an attack "by a foreign power" on any member of the Arab League or on Turkey, but would withdraw when the emergency was over. During that period British technicians, not in uniform, would help Egypt to maintain the complex facilities of the base. With respect to the canal the treaty said only that the parties recognized it as an integral part of Egypt and as a maritime communication route of economic, commercial and strategic importance, and pledged themelves to respect the Constantinople Convention of 1888 guaranteeing freedom of navigation.

For the Egyptians this was the end of a long struggle to be rid of foreign troops; British forces had been in Egypt since Gladstone ordered a "temporary" occupation in 1882. For the British it was the best bargain they could make in a situation that was becoming increasingly difficult. There was no denying the historic strategic importance of Suez, which the "rebels" in the Conservative Party were loudly pointing out. It could not have been easy for Winston Churchill to preside over the liquidation of what had been the key base on the lifeline of empire, the fulcrum of Britain's whole military strategy in the Middle East. Yet such a great all-purpose base appeared increasingly vulnerable in an age of nuclear weapons and its value would certainly have been greatly diminished if Britain had to maintain it indefinitely in a hostile environment, which was the prospect. A decision to do so,

[2] For text, see Great Britain, *Anglo-Egyptian Suez Canal Base Agreement,* Egypt No. 2 (1954), Cmd. 9298 (London: H.M.S.O., 1954).

moreover, would mean giving up all chance of securing Egypt's voluntary cooperation in Middle East defense. Withdrawal, on the best terms obtainable, was the indicated course. The British Chiefs of Staff were not happy about it. Cyprus as an alternative lacked many of the natural advantages of Suez, but at least it was a base under British sovereignty on which they could fall back.

The American role in these British-Egyptian negotiations has been the subject of criticism to the effect that the United States put pressure on the British to induce them to agree to give up Suez and thus bears responsibility for the weakening of the Western position through the loss of this key base. The American Ambassador in Cairo, Jefferson Caffery, was indeed kept fully informed of the course of the negotiations and used his powers of persuasion on both sides to help move them toward agreement. The American purpose, which was not disguised, was to hasten the day when Egypt would be prepared to cooperate voluntarily in Western defense. As Egypt would not give such cooperation so long as Suez was a British or an 'international" base, the question before the Western powers was this: Would they be in a stronger position, in the long run, if the British simply held on to the base whether Egypt liked it or not, or if they evacuated it and took a chance on Egypt's cooperation in the future? In the American view the second course was the better choice. Perhaps the fact that this view was made known to both British and Egyptian negotiators gave the latter a certain advantage. But it cannot fairly be said that it was American pressure that got the British out of Suez, except that they had to take account of our desire to see an accord reached and to begin aid programs to Egypt. The decision to evacuate was a British decision based on British calculation of what was in the best interests of Britain and the Western world.

How well the bargain would stand up in the future was a real question. The provisions were specific enough. They appeared to meet Britain's strategic needs. But the

British were under no illusions as to the value of Egyptian promises as opposed to having Suez in their own hands. Whether the base would actually be maintained for possible British use, and whether Egypt, once freed of British troops, would in practice agree to their return under any conditions were matters of serious doubt. The fate of the Anglo-Egyptian treaty of 1936 afforded an example of how little the treaty pledges might be worth a few years hence. The withdrawal of British troops, moreover, meant the removal of the only sure safeguard for continued use of the Suez Canal. In the last analysis it would come down to the degree of good faith and cooperation that could be established by the Western powers with Egypt, which meant, for the foreseeable future, with Gamal Abdel Nasser and those elements on which his power rested. It was he who made the final concessions necessary to get the British to agree to evacuate Suez. But it was he also who got the credit and the acclaim, from Egyptians and from Arabs elsewhere, for taking a great forward step toward emancipation from Western domination. In the future he would undoubtedly weigh the advantages of the acclaim certain to follow such diplomatic "victories" against whatever he might hope to gain by collaboration with the West.

Egypt and the West

The British and American Governments were at first quite hopeful, once the Sudan and Suez affairs were settled with Egypt, that Abdel Nasser would prove "reasonable" on the subject of defense cooperation. Specifically, they hoped Egypt would join the alliance system then taking shape along the "northern tier." During the negotiations over Suez, Abdel Nasser had given Western representatives reason for that impression, but neither the British, as a price for evacuation, nor the Americans, as a price for mediation, had tied him down to a specific commitment. Whether they should have done so is a matter for debate.[3] It seems likely that insistence on such a commitment would have made the Suez agreement impossible, for the Egyptian leader maintained later that the "cooperation" he had in mind was a strengthening of the Arab League with Western support and without any alliance with the West or with Turkey.[4]

In any event the Western powers, once the agreement was made, looked forward to a new era of cooperative relations with Egypt. The United States made available $40 million in economic aid which had been held up pending agreement on Suez. It was prepared also to provide military aid under the mutual security program. Henry Byroade, the new American Ambassador in Cairo, set out to win Abdel Nasser's confidence and put relations between the two countries on the soundest possible basis.

The Egyptian Prime Minister, however, was not rushing into any close relationship with the West. He accepted the economic aid. He inquired into the conditions on which military aid would be supplied and found them unacceptable, particularly the requirement for an American "military assistance advisory group" in Egypt to supervise and report on the use of the aid provided. As for an alliance, he pointed out to his Western friends that the Egyptian people were not ready for so drastic a step. They would have to have time to get used to the fact of independence from foreign occupation. To them the idea of an alliance with the West still meant inequality and domination.

Events, instead of waiting for the Egyptian people to get used to the idea of alliance with the West, soon began to push the Egyptian Government into some crucial decisions, and those decisions established a policy which was more and more antagonistic to the Western powers and

[3] J. C. Hurewitz, "Our Mistakes in the Middle East," *Atlantic*, v. 198 (December 1956), pp. 46-52, argues cogently that the U. S. missed a great opportunity by not securing Egypt's commitment at least to a bilateral military aid agreement.

[4] Interview, *New York Times*, April 4, 1955, and Abdel Nasser's speech of July 26, 1956 (text in *L'Orient*, Paris, v. 1, January 1957, pp. 45-63).

more and more favorable to their enemies. In January 1955 Turkey and Iraq, with the blessing of the United States, announced their intention to conclude a defensive alliance. In February Israel carried out a large-scale military raid on Gaza. The first of these events broke the solidarity of the Arab League and threatened Egypt's leadership of the Arab world. The second exposed Egypt's military weakness. Together they brought Abdel Nasser and his colleagues to the conviction that they would have to act swiftly to assert Egypt's position against Israel, against Iraq, and if need be against the West. They now had a freedom of action they did not enjoy before the agreement on Suez, and would find help where they could.

Out of this situation developed the whole series of moves and countermoves that eventually destroyed all confidence between Egypt and the West: the Egyptian diplomatic and propaganda offensive against the Baghdad Pact; the unwillingness of the United States to meet Nasser's request for American arms on his terms; his arms deal with the Soviets; the Western offer on the High Aswan Dam; the riots in Jordan that thwarted the Western attempt to extend the Baghdad Pact; Nasser's delay on the Dam offer and further flirtation with the Soviets; the withdrawal of the offer; and the nationalization of the Suez Canal Company.

There is no point in trying here to assess blame for this series of developments, except insofar as it may help us to judge where the miscalculations of the past may hold a lesson for the decisions of the future. If it be assumed that the American estimate of late 1954 was correct—that Abdel Nasser was basically friendly toward the West and needed only time and considerate treatment to bring Egypt into a relationship of mutually beneficial cooperation—then mistakes surely were made somewhere along the line. If, on the other hand, the Egyptian regime was by its very nature and situation bound to remain at odds with the Western powers, including the United States, the drama could have had no other outcome than it did. To try to penetrate the problem one must try to penetrate the character and motives of Abdel Nasser himself and to estimate the forces he represents and on which he depends.

What Does Abdel Nasser Stand For?

The Egyptian Government has given wide circulation to a small book called *The Philosophy of the Revolution,* said to be written by Gamal Abdel Nasser.[5] Whether or not it provides the inspiration and explanation for the concrete acts and policies of the Egyptian Government, we may assume that it represents the general line of thought by which Abdel Nasser has been guided. Through the whole story—his revolutionary ideas and activity as a student, his experience in the Palestine war, the motives of the present and the dreams of the future—the main enemy is always the same, "Imperialism." It may take the form of British occupation forces, or of Jews in Palestine, or of corrupt Egyptian politicians serving British interests; these are but different heads of the imperialist hydra that must be slain. The whole outlook of Abdel Nasser and his associates was formed in and by this struggle.[6] They knew little of world history and had no grasp of the forces which had produced the second World War and the less violent but no less deadly Communist onslaught on freedom which followed it. The world, as they looked out on it from Cairo, was primarily the world of three "zones" described in *The Philosophy of the Revolution*: the Arab zone, the African continent, and the lands of Islam. In these zones Egypt, and especially those selected by destiny to guide Egypt, had a great role of leadership to play. In each zone the great struggle for liberation would have to be carried on to victory over the enemy who still held many of these lands and nations in subjection, who con-

[5] Gamal Abdel Nasser, *Egypt's Liberation: The Philosophy of the Revolution* (Washington: Public Affairs Press, 1955).
[6] Anwar el Sadat, *Revolt on the Nile* (New York: John Day, 1957). This book by a close associate of Abdel Nasser illustrates the point even more sharply than *The Philosophy of the Revolution*.

trolled their seas and skies and exploited their oil and other resources for his own benefit.

There is at least a strong presumption that these ingrained feelings, these profound emotional drives, explain much of the subsequent conduct of the Cairo regime. For these drives are not limited to Abdel Nasser or to the few army officers who fought their way with him to the top. They represent strong popular currents of Egyptian and Arab nationalism that had been gathering force for decades. Abdel Nasser and his friends were not entirely free agents. To beat the drums against imperialism was for them not merely to satisfy their own desires but to win and to consolidate their political power. This is not to say that every Arab is more concerned about imperialism than he is about the economic conditions in which he lives or the inadequacies of his own rulers. Nationalist leaders, however, have had a great measure of success in turning all discontents into the channel of protest against the West and the West's "creature," Israel.

Abdel Nasser seemed so sincere and reasonable in his conversations with Western diplomats or with visitors from the West that the natural reaction was to trust in what he said when he spoke of cooperation. But what he said in his speeches in the public squares of Cairo and Alexandria, and what his controlled press and radio shouted forth to the people of Egypt and the Arab world, had a different theme and a different tone. The ominous parallel lines followed by the broadcasts of Cairo and Moscow had long been evident. Which was the real Abdel Nasser, the sober statesman or the ranting demagogue? Probably both. It need not be assumed from what has happened that his various assurances to Western diplomats were nothing but a campaign of deliberate deception. But all the dominant elements of his political position and of his developing public personality, interacting with each other, were pushing him in the direction of nationalistic self-assertion against the West. When he thought soberly about reform and development of his own country, he

must have recognized the benefits of good relations with
Western Europe and especially with the United States.
But his attention was turned more and more from domestic to international affairs, to the championship of
Arab nationalism. Only by defying and combating the
West could he play the "role in search of a hero" about
which he wrote in *The Philosophy of the Revolution,* the
role of leading the Arab people to the destiny that was
rightfully theirs.

Viewed against that background, Abdel Nasser's crucial
decisions taken in 1955 and 1956 cannot be attributed
solely to arbitrary whim or to the mistaken approaches
and tactics of the Western governments. He was obviously
attracted, since the Bandung conference and his meeting
with Nehru and Tito on Brioni, by the possibilities of
neutralism. He was intent on arming quickly. He was determined to keep for Egypt the leadership of Arab nationalism from the Atlantic to the Persian Gulf. His natural reaction to the Israeli raid on Gaza in February 1955
was to seek arms wherever he could get them. His natural
reaction to the Western-sponsored Turkish-Iraqi pact of
that same month was to oppose it and to rally the Arab
world against it.

Arms Deal with the Soviets

It may be that if the United States had found some way
to provide Egypt with arms, Abdel Nasser would not have
turned to the Soviet Union. The Department of State had
adequate warning that he might do so. Its failure to see
the magnitude of the danger and to act in time may have
been a costly mistake. As grant aid in arms equipment was
not possible so long as Egypt would not agree to conditions required of all recipients under the mutual security legislation, the question was whether arms could be
purchased by Egypt. The United States after long delay
agreed to make available some of the items on the Egyptian shopping list, but while desultory negotiations were

in progress on whether some other means of payment than dollars, which Egypt could not spare, might be acceptable, Abdel Nasser suddenly concluded his deal in September 1955 for large quantities of arms from the Soviet orbit.[7]

By this one bold stroke he declared his independence of the West and proclaimed his leadership of the Arabs. The effect in the Arab world was prodigious. Everywhere the new leader was acclaimed. The feeble reaction of the United States, consisting of the hurried sending of an Assistant Secretary of State to Cairo to express concern, served only to multiply the fervent applause. The magnitude of his political success probably surprised even Abdel Nasser himself. In any event it proved to be a great turning point in his career. It made him a world figure. And it apparently convinced him that he could continue to play the Soviet card with nothing to fear from the West.

The High Aswan Dam

The interplay over the proposed High Aswan Dam has to be considered in that new context of Egyptian self-confidence and Western distrust. The United States Government, in December 1955, decided to go ahead with an offer of $56 million as an initial grant on which (together with a British offer of $14 million) the World Bank loan of $200 million depended. It saw this decision as a last chance to preserve some Western influence in Egypt; if the Soviet Union, already the main source of arms, should finance the dam as well, it would be in a position of nearly complete control over the Egyptian economy.

The whole story of what happened in the following months is not publicly known, but a few points seem clear enough. Abdel Nasser, either because he wanted better terms from the West or sought to provoke a better offer from the Soviets, delayed his acceptance and raised a num-

[7] The agreement was signed with Czechoslovakia, but the negotiations were begun and the vital decisions were made on the Communist side by the Soviet Union, as Abdel Nasser himself publicly acknowledged in his speech of July 26, 1956.

ber of conditions requiring further negotiation. The
United States negotiated patiently with him but, as
months went by, was increasingly disturbed over the bur-
geoning contacts between Egypt and the Soviet bloc: trade
deals, technical missions, and arms shipments of a magnitude that gave new dimensions to the picture as it had
been seen the previous autumn. These facts raised legitimate doubts as to Egypt's ability to carry its part of the
High Dam scheme and to repay the World Bank loan, for
its main export, cotton, appeared to be mortgaged almost
totally to the Soviet bloc for some time through the accumulation of obligations.

To these doubts were added others on the political side.
Egypt was reveling in its new role of Arab leadership. Its
propaganda against the Baghdad Pact and the Government of Iraq was incessant and violent. Its hand in the
anti-Western riots in Jordan was obvious. Its radio broadcasts were encouraging unrest and revolt in Africa, beyond
the confines of the Arab world. The Egyptian press was
filled with denunciation of the West, but had no word of
blame for the Soviet Union. Finally, in May 1956, Egypt
established diplomatic relations with Communist China.
As matters were developing, the Aswan Dam offer seemed
more and more incongruous to the United States. The
Appropriations Committee of the Senate directed that
none of the mutual security funds could be used for the
dam without its prior approval.[8] It would have been difficult enough for the Administration to defend such a grant
to an Arab state before Congress in an election year. When
that Arab state, after stalling on the offer when it was first
made, became increasingly hostile in all its public acts and
utterances, it was only to be expected that there would be
a new look at policy toward Egypt and, as it turned out, a
withdrawal of the offer. The calculation or knowledge that
the Soviet Union, despite the stories from Egyptian sources,

[8] *Mutual Security Appropriation Bill, 1957*, U.S. Senate Committee on
Appropriations, S. Rept. 2579 to accompany H. R. 12130, 84th Cong., 2nd
sess. (Washington: G.P.O., 1956), p. 4.

was not prepared to undertake the project itself may have rendered the decision easier to make.[9]

The manner in which the offer was withdrawn, to the accompaniment of a statement saying the ability of Egypt to devote adequate resources to assure the project's success, even with the projected outside financing, had become more uncertain, was taken by Abdel Nasser as an attempt to humiliate him and his country. He certainly overplayed the "insulting" character of the statement, but that a clear rebuff was intended can hardly be doubted, for Washington might have continued to delay and to point out obstacles still to be surmounted. That it was the first clear manifestation of a new American attitude toward Egypt was also apparent, one which took more account of the resentment of Turkey and other pro-Western states that Egypt was getting more from the United States for being naughty than they did for being good.[10]

How great a change in American policy had taken place? In all likelihood there would be no more aid to Egypt, though existing programs might be completed. Diplomatic relations would be on a correct but minimum level. Abdel Nasser would be left to go his own way in his association with the Soviets; perhaps only first-hand experience would

[9] Senator Fulbright, on the basis of unpublished documents submitted by the Department of State, has stated that the U.S.S.R. had made an offer more attractive to Egypt than that of the Western powers and the World Bank (*Congressional Record*, v. 103, August 17, 1957, p. 13394). However, the denial by Shepilov that it had done so (*New York Times*, July 22, 1956) and the failure of the Soviet Government to do anything about it after July 19 cast doubt on the firmness of any such offer.

[10] Secretary Dulles, in a press conference on April 2, 1957, while defending the "courteous manner" in which the reply was given, said that "the Egyptians, in a sense, forced upon us an issue to which I think there was only one proper response. That issue was, do nations which play both sides get better treatment than nations which are stalwart and work with us?" (See *Department of State Bulletin*, v. 36, April 22, 1957, p. 642.) But if that was the test it could have been applied at the time the offer was made, for Egypt had shown by the arms deal with the Soviets that it was playing both sides and was no stalwart ally of the United States. The Secretary, at the same press conference, seemed to reject the thesis set forth by his friendly biographer, John R. Beal (*John Foster Dulles*, New York: Harper, 1957, p. 259) that the cancellation of the offer was "a truly major gambit in the cold war."

show him the dangers involved. But American policy did not swing all the way to the position that the Egyptian regime had become so hostile to American interests that the United States should hope and work for its disappearance. It was merely a question of recognizing that the earlier policy, the policy of aiding the regime and expecting a pro-Western or at least benevolently neutral Egypt in return, had to be abandoned; and that the High Dam offer, which seemed ever more anachronistic, had to go with it. The transfer of Ambassador Byroade, who had come to be a symbol of the old policy, marked the change.

Expropriation of the Canal Company

If the United States and Britain, which followed suit by withdrawing its own similar offer, had dealt a mortal blow to what little remained of hopes for Egyptian cooperation with the West, Abdel Nasser's reply, the seizure of the Universal Suez Maritime Canal Company, brought relations near the point of complete rupture and even of armed hostilities. The strength of the Western reaction, particularly from Britain and France whose interests were most directly threatened, was perhaps stronger than the Egyptian leader had expected. But it only confirmed him in his defiance and in his new friendship with the Soviet Union, which stoutly defended the seizure in its diplomacy and its propaganda. As the Western powers called conferences and talked of international control of the Suez Canal, Nasser, despite nominal concessions, stood firm on his original position, sure that he had enough support from the Communist bloc and from the ex-colonial nations of Asia to weather the storm.

The magic formula for striking such telling blows at the "imperialists" and getting away with it was a fairly simple one. As long as anti-Western actions were taken in the sacred name of nationalism and sovereignty, the Western nations could not hope to mobilize world opinion or U.N. action against them. And insofar as they raised the possibility of the use of force in reply, Egypt could count on the West's fear of provoking a world war and on its reluctance to antagonize the whole uncommitted world.

Leader of the Arab World

Most of all perhaps, Abdel Nasser could take heart from the tremendous outpouring of support from the rest of the Arab world. There was no doubt of his success in capturing the imagination of the Arab peoples. While he had some adherents among the old ruling groups, for the most part he drew his support from the emerging middle class, the educated and half-educated intelligentsia, the army officers, and those elements constituting the street mob which so often plays a decisive influence in Arab politics. He won this impressive support because his successes corresponded to the profound emotional desires of so many Arabs: to assert their pride in themselves, their feeling of unity, their right to equality, their sovereignty, their place in the sun; to humiliate those who so often had humiliated them; to gain revenge for the disaster of Palestine. Their support was not entirely self-generated, however. It was stimulated by Cairo's powerful "Voice of the Arabs" broadcasts, by pressures and subtle influences of one kind or another on the press, and by the activities of Egyptian agents. The total effect was to create a powerful wave of Arab opinion behind one leader such as had not existed since the days of Saladin.

Not all elements in the Arab world were overcome by enthusiasm for Abdel Nasser. It was not comfortable to be an Arab ruler and see one's supposedly loyal subjects so devoted to the ruler of another state. King Hussein of Jordan was anything but master in his own country where thousands of Palestinian Arabs looked to Abdel Nasser as the man to redeem their homeland. King Saud could not view with equanimity the potentially disruptive Egyptian influence in his own backward realm. The Christians in Lebanon obviously feared that a wave of intense Arab nationalism, with an admixture of Moslem fanaticism, would engulf their historic position and the special role of Lebanon as a link with the Western world. Old-line political leaders and a few pro-Western nationalists in Syria and Jordan resented the changes which were pushing them aside and bringing pro-Egyptian and some pro-Soviet elements into positions of power. In Iraq these traditional elements still held the reins but in the face of a strong and increasingly bold opposition. Even in Egypt there were some who would have preferred greater political freedom or social reform at home to the regime's smashing diplomatic victories in the international field. Yet all these elements throughout the Arab world had little in common with each other save distaste for the President of Egypt, and had no means of coordinating their opposition to him.

Alternatives for the West

The rising prestige and influence of Gamal Abdel Nasser throughout the Arab world, his obvious hostility to Western interests, and his growing dependence on the Soviet Union faced the Western powers with a critical decision on how to deal with a trend which, if unchecked, seemed likely to push them out of the Middle East. One approach was to accept the new virulent Arab nationalism as a fact of international life, to recognize that Abdel Nasser had largely captured it, and to try to come to terms with him. According to this view he was not yet so deeply committed to the Soviet Union as to have lost his independence of action or to be unwilling to compromise with the West. Mere blind opposition to him or attempts to overthrow him would only consolidate his support and throw him and the whole Arab world irrevocably into the camp of the U.S.S.R. A second approach, while putting no faith in Abdel Nasser, recognized the reality of Arab nationalism and sought to encourage forces in the Arab world that would counterbalance his influence. A third approach frankly looked to strong action, possibly even including the use of force, as the only way of disposing of the menace. According to this view, further appeasement was folly and would lead to the loss of the few remaining Western positions; Abdel Nasser was a "cardboard Pharaoh" who had won a great following because no one had stood up to him; if the West would only call his bluff, his fickle followers would fold their tents and silently steal away.

It may not be justified to label these views as specifically American or British. All three had their adherents among Westerners of various nationalities and also among pro-Western Middle Easterners concerned over the deteriorating situation. It is fair to say, however, that after the seizure of the Suez Canal Company in July 1956 the British and French Governments developed their policies on the basis of the third approach: that Abdel Nasser would have to go even if it meant the use of force. The United States was also disillusioned with the President of Egypt and would have liked to see him "cut down to size." But it saw no alternative regime on the horizon and definitely did not favor the use of force, even if no other way could be found to make him accept international control of the canal. This difference of approach among the Western powers led eventually to the decision of the British and French Governments, in October 1956, to take forceful action on their own initiative, without consulting the Government of the United States.

Chapter 7

BREAKDOWN OF THE ARMISTICE
IN PALESTINE

THE ARMISTICE agreements signed in 1949 by Israel and its Arab neighbors reflected the outcome of the fighting of the previous year and of the truce and mediation efforts of the United Nations. They did not represent satisfactory terms of settlement for either side. The people of Israel were gratified to have made good the independent existence of the Jewish State and secured control over the greater part of Palestine, but they could not feel easy about borders which left their new state only ten miles wide at one point and cut through the heart of the intended capital, Jerusalem. The Arab states, for their part, accepted the armistice terms only because they had been beaten. They were not reconciled to defeat or to the continued existence of Israel.

Nor were the Arabs of Palestine reconciled to the fate which had befallen them. Instead of the "Arab Palestine" which had been the hope of their national leaders, instead of the Arab state in a partitioned Palestine provided for in the United Nations resolution of November 1947, only two isolated pieces of Palestine territory remained outside Israel: the small Gaza strip which Egypt occupied and administered, and the hilly area on the west bank of the River Jordan which was annexed by King Abdullah of Jordan. The shadowy "Arab Palestine Government" that had existed briefly at Gaza during the war was forgotten. And some 726,000 Arabs whose homes had been in the area now held by Israel were refugees in the Gaza area, in Jordan, in Syria and in Lebanon.[1]

[1] The refugees have never been officially counted, and there has been considerable controversy over their number. The original estimate of 726,000

Responsibility for the existence of the refugee problem is a subject of bitter partisan controversy. Israel maintains that these Arabs left because they were urged to do so by Arab leaders, who promised they would soon return with the victorious Arab armies; Arab spokesmen assert that they were driven out by Zionist attacks and fear of annihilation. Suffice it to say that the problem would not have arisen in its present form if the Arab states had not rejected the U.N. partition proposal and marched into Palestine, and that it was a combination of the causes cited by both sides which produced the exodus, but to what precise degree each was responsible seems impossible to determine.

The Mirage of a Peace Settlement

The armistice agreements, as all concerned recognized, were not a final settlement. The United Nations, in helping to get the agreements negotiated and in taking cognizance of them, had looked forward to the negotiation of a peace settlement under U.N. auspices. It had set up for that purpose a Palestine Conciliation Commission,

---

was based on all the information available to the U.N. Economic Survey Mission in 1949; it is obtained by taking the Arab population of the territory that became Israel on the basis of the last census under the British Mandate (with estimates of the increase up to 1948), and subtracting the number that remained. Since 1948 some 30,000 of the refugees returned to Israel, but the total number outside has been steadily swelled by natural increase. In 1957, according to the Director of the U.N. Relief and Works Agency, they numbered 933,556 (517,388 in Jordan, 221,058 in Gaza, 102,586 in Lebanon, 92,524 in Syria). This total may be somewhat higher than is justified owing to two factors: (1) influx into the refugee camps of some Arabs not refugees, and (2) the practice of not reporting deaths in the camps, in order to keep ration cards. See *Final Report of the United Nations Economic Survey Mission for the Middle East* (1949, II B.5, pt. 1) (Lake Success, 1949), pp. 22-23; *Annual Report of the Director of the United Nations Relief and Works Agency for Palestine Refugees in the Near East, . . . 1 July 1956 to 30 June 1957*, U.N. General Assembly, *Official Records*, 12th Session, Supplement no. 14 (New York, 1957), pp. 12-13. For Israel estimates see Israel Office of Information, *The Arab Refugees* (New York: International Press, 1953); for Arab estimates see Sami Hadawi, *Land Ownership in Palestine* (New York: Palestine Arab Refugee Office, 1957).

composed of France, Turkey and the United States. Events were to show that these hopes were woefully misplaced, for the war of 1948 had not solved the basic problem of how Arab and Jew were to live together, or side by side. Neither was ready for a peace of reconciliation.

The Arabs, indeed, were not ready for a peace of any kind. The outcome of the war had been a crushing blow to their hopes and to their pride. The revelation of their weakness and of their disunity had shattering effects on the political life of the Arab states themselves, as feelings of humiliation and frustration boiled over in a series of assassinations, *coups d'état* and revolutions. Through it all ran the thread of continuing hatred of Israel and the idea of revenge.

All the Arab governments refused to recognize Israel. They fought its admission to the United Nations. They refused all economic relations. They blockaded Israel where they could, as at the Suez Canal and the Gulf of Aqaba. Their leaders openly pledged themselves to "restore the rights of the Arabs of Palestine." Some were frank in anticipating a "second round" of fighting in which Israel would be annihilated. Others voiced confidence that the Arabs could outlast Israel, that the "artificial" state would not be indefinitely supported from outside, and that the boycott and blockade would destroy it in the end. Mixed with the bombast and confidence was an element of fear. The Arabs had been made acutely aware of Israel's military superiority. They were not yet prepared to stand up to a new test of strength. With continuing Jewish immigration into Israel they feared the generation of pressure for expansion that would lead Israel to strike out and take more territory.

Because it takes at least two to make a negotiated peace, the Arab attitude ruled out any possibility of it, as the Palestine Conciliation Commission discovered. Israel, for its part, consistently expressed its desire to sit down with the Arabs and talk peace terms. Basically, Israel's attitude was the more reasonable in that it wanted peace while the

Arabs did not, but from the viewpoint of the latter what Israel wanted was recognition and legal confirmation of unjust gains won by the sword. Israel's attitudes, moreover, did nothing to disarm Arab suspicions or mitigate Arab hostility even if that had been possible. The new state was full of self-assurance after its spectacular victories. It had no idea of reopening territorial questions, other than perhaps minor boundary adjustments. Everything on its side of the armistice lines was "sacred" national territory. On that territory new immigrants were being settled, communities were springing up, agriculture and new industries would be developed. While applying itself with single-minded purpose to its own development, Israel paid remarkably little heed to the necessity of coming to some terms with the fact of living in the heart of the Arab world. Other than legalizing the return of a limited number to be reunited with their families, and releasing some refugee funds from Palestine banks, the Government of Israel did nothing toward solution of the problem of the Arab refugees. It merely offered compensation, in principle, for their property while barring their return, meanwhile opening the doors wide to Jewish immigration.

Violence on the Border

Owing to the irreconcilable attitudes on both sides the United Nations had to give up its efforts for a negotiated peace and concentrated on keeping the uneasy "peace" that existed under the armistice agreements. For that purpose it had created a United Nations Truce Supervision Organization (U.N.T.S.O.) with the task of watching over the borders. Unfortunately, despite its untiring efforts, U.N.T.S.O. had neither the numbers nor the authority to do an effective job in the absence of the full cooperation of both sides, which it never had. The Arab governments were unable or unwilling to curb the infiltration of Arab refugees across the borders into Israel, where they stole or damaged property and sometimes killed Israeli citizens. Israel soldiers and police, on the other hand, often crossed into Arab territory to take preventive or retaliatory action.

The United Nations observers did what they could to investigate these incidents. Serving as neutral chairmen of the four mixed armistice commissions on which Israel and its respective Arab neighbors were equally represented, U.N.T.S.O. officers did their best to determine the facts and to vote accordingly on one side or the other. Their reports show their general fairness and good will, but they do not disguise the fact that it was essentially a sterile process. Regardless of the investigations and the findings, the incidents continued, increasing in frequency and in seriousness. Israel, more often than not, was uncooperative with the mixed armistice commissions and began to seek its own remedy against infiltration by conducting large-scale raids.[2] In the first such raid, on the town of Qibiya in 1953, 53 Arabs were killed. Such acts, intended to teach the Arabs a lesson and force the Arab governments to control infiltration, may have had that effect for a time, but inevitably they inflamed feelings and increased the danger of war.

Role of the United Nations

When the incidents were of sufficient size or importance, or when one of the parties found a reason to put its case to the world, they came before the U.N. Security Council. Generally the result was a resolution which might condemn one or both parties, but such resolutions had no real effect on the situation because they were not followed up by any action in the way either of specific enforcement or sanctions or of strengthening the U.N. machinery so that it could prevent future incidents. In 1951 the Security Council supported Israel in its contention that Egypt's interference

[2] Elmo H. Hutchinson, *Violent Truce* (New York: Devin-Adair, 1956). Commander Hutchinson, U.S.N.R., former chairman of the Israel-Jordan M.A.C., is a strong partisan of the Arab cause, but this fact does not vitiate the general validity of his story of Israel's non-cooperation based on his own experience.

with shipping through the Suez Canal destined for Israel, on grounds of belligerent rights, was unwarranted, but nothing was done to make Egypt change its practice. Israel's raid on Qibiya was given "the strongest censure" by the Security Council, but Israel merely shrugged off the reprimand and resorted to the same measures again when it thought the situation required it.

Both sides, accordingly, got the idea that they could flout the United Nations when they desired and that the world organization was of no particular use to them in maintaining their national interests. They used it as a place to make their views and their demands heard, but they were not overawed or even seriously influenced by its authority or its prestige. In the case of Israel, a state with whose birth and continued existence the United Nations was so closely associated, this attitude was all the more remarkable as an indication of the failure of the United Nations, and thus of those members who could have but did not take the lead to act effectively through the United Nations, to face up to the dangerous situation that was developing.[3]

The Tripartite Declaration

The United States and its Western allies, in pursuing the aim of keeping the peace in Palestine, had not, however, put all their faith in the United Nations. By May 1950, a year after conclusion of the armistice agreements, it was evident that no peace settlement was in sight. The United States then took the initiative to put a Western guarantee behind the armistice settlement. After consultation among American, British, and French representatives a Tripartite Declaration was issued. Its first main pledge was that the three Western powers would not permit any armed aggression across the existing armistice lines in Palestine, and if it took place they would take appropriate action against

[3] *Israel and the United Nations, Report of a Study Group set up by the Hebrew University of Jerusalem* (New York: Manhattan Publishing Co., for the Carnegie Endowment for International Peace, 1956), pp. 218-223, 292-294.

the aggressor "both within and outside the United Nations."
The second pledge was that they would strive to maintain
a balance in the supply of arms to Israel and the Arab
states and to prevent the creation of any "imbalance" that
would endanger the peace.[4] The Tripartite Declaration
may have made some contribution to stability, especially
by slowing down the arms race. So long as they could
count on Israel and the Arab states to take it seriously, the
Western powers at least had the opportunity to work toward their other aim, a more permanent settlement.

In retrospect one may point to these years, before Russia
was prominently in the picture, as the period when the
West lost its chance to bring about a settlement which might
have closed the door to Russia's entry. Yet it is a real question whether the chance ever existed. The United States
and British Governments were well aware of the importance
of tackling the interrelated questions that must form the
bedrock of any settlement: boundaries, Arab refugees, the
status of Jerusalem, use of water resources. These were not
just items for some future peace treaty but matters of immediate moment that were poisoning the atmosphere and
threatening to erupt in violence. The Arab refugees were
not only a burden on the international community and a
challenge to the moral sense of mankind, but also a source
of infiltration and killing on the frontiers and a breeding
ground for communism. The dispute over water had to be
settled by international agreement, or both sides were likely
to take action on their own terms. Israel's preparations for
diversion of water in the Banat Ya'qub area near the Syrian
border in 1953 were stopped at the behest of the United Nations, but Israel had warned it would not wait forever and
Syria in turn had warned that a resumption of work on
Israel's project would be met with force. As for Jerusalem,
the inability of the United Nations to do anything about
its resolutions calling for an international status for the city
and surrounding area left the situation right where it was
when the war stopped, with the Holy City itself cut in two

[4] Text in *Department of State Bulletin*, v. 22 (June 5, 1950), p. 886.

by the truce line and enveloped by a continuing tension as one bloody incident followed another.

Efforts to Promote a Settlement

With the obvious failure of the Palestine Conciliation Commission, the United States and Britain turned to old-fashioned diplomacy as the best means of moving toward a settlement. As in the case of the proposed Middle East Command, they chose Egypt as the key country to approach first. Without Egypt, they felt, no other Arab country would dare take a step toward peace with Israel. Once Egypt had shown the way, as the armistice negotiations had demonstrated, the others might be expected to follow. The trouble was that the time never seemed to be propitious. The Nagib-Nasser regime in its early period, immersed in its domestic problems and appealing for popular support, would not even consider serious negotiations on Palestine. Later, when Nasser was firmly in control and appeared to be working his way gradually toward cooperation with the West, it was still not possible to broach the question until the negotiations over the British evacuation of Suez were completed.

When the Suez agreement was finally reached, in October 1954, the U.S. and British Governments were engaged in a thorough study of all the possibilities. This study covered all the thorny questions and sketched out tentative settlements in considerable detail, including frontier adjustments, draft security treaties, transit and free port arrangements, repatriation and resettlement of refugees, and a special status for Jerusalem. It seemed at least possible that these matters could be discussed by the two Western powers separately with Egypt and with Israel, without any direct confrontation between the two parties, a procedure which had just succeeded in settling the long and bitter dispute between Italy and Yugoslavia over Trieste.

No one can be sure what might have come of these endeavors had not Israel's raid on Gaza in February 1955, which resulted in 69 casualties and revealed the utter weakness of Egypt's military defenses, frightened Nasser into turning all his attention to the need for strengthening Egypt and asserting his and Egypt's position in the Arab world. Because of the agreement on the evacuation of Suez, he was in a position to do so. At this same time the Soviet Union, which since the previous year had taken a pro-Arab position in the United Nations, turned to a policy of enthusiastic support of the Arab case against Israel. Soviet diplomacy at Cairo backed up what Moscow's propaganda was telling the Arabs through press and radio. From that point onward the chance that the Western powers could talk Egypt into a settlement with Israel virtually disappeared.

Statements of American and British Policy, 1955

In August of that year, in a speech at the Council on Foreign Relations, Secretary Dulles outlined what the United States would do to support a settlement.[5] It would guarantee the permanent frontiers agreed upon by the parties; it would help financially to carry out an agreed plan to repatriate or resettle the Arab refugees; it would help Israel and its Arab neighbors to put into effect the regional plan for the use of Jordan waters currently being discussed with the interested governments by Eric Johnston, special representative of the President. These were the most far-reaching proposals that the United States had made, but they aroused very little favorable comment on either side. They depended so much on agreements between the two parties on matters so hopelessly in dispute that they seemed to have practically no current significance. Abdel Nasser was already negotiating with the Soviet Government, and by the time Prime Minister Eden made his companion speech at London's Guildhall two months later the notorious arms deal had been consummated. Eden came closer to the substance of the Arab-Israel dispute when he spoke of the need for a territorial compromise somewhere between the armistice lines and the boundaries of the U.N. partition resolution

[5] *Department of State Bulletin*, v. 33 (September 5, 1955), pp. 378-380.

of November 1947.[6] Without satisfying Arab opinion this proposal, as might have been expected, evoked a howl of protest in Israel. So negative was the reaction that the Western powers did not follow up these speeches with further endeavors to promote a settlement. They were not going to try to force a solution on both sides, and any hope of agreement between the two seemed quite vain.

Arms for Israel?

One thing the Soviet-Egyptian arms deal did was to blow off the lid which the Western powers, under the Tripartite Declaration, had been trying to keep on the arms race. Now that Egypt, and presumably other Arab states, could look to the Soviet bloc for all the weapons they wanted, the West could no longer control the situation by regulating the supply of arms to both sides. Its choice was whether to try to keep a rough balance by supplying Israel as the Soviets supplied the Arabs, thus in fact pushing the arms race to higher levels, to refrain from supplying Israel and hope the situation might become somewhat stabilized, or to bring about a limitation of Soviet deliveries to the Arabs by agreement or by force. The United States, with British concurrence, chose the second alternative. Despite urgent appeals from Israel, it decided against providing the arms that country felt it needed for defense against the new Soviet bombers and tanks Egypt was receiving. It was a courageous decision politically, and it may have been soundly based on knowledge that even the heavy Soviet deliveries to Egypt would not, in the present state of Egyptian military competence, upset the balance against Israel. Yet it did contribute greatly to the growing feeling in Israel that it was standing alone against an enemy who was daily growing stronger as he acquired new weapons against which Israel had no defense.

By the end of 1955 the danger of renewed conflict in the Near East was greater than at any time since 1948. The

6 *New York Times,* November 10, 1955.

armistice agreements had been repeatedly violated by both sides. An especially severe raid by Israel against Syria in December claimed many innocent victims and shocked world opinion without putting a stop to the Arab incursions. Indeed, early in the following year these incursions were being undertaken by trained bands of fedayeen or commando groups, as well as by individual marauders. These bands, organized from Palestinian refugees by the Egyptian authorities, penetrated deep into Israel territory to kill and destroy. Israel felt that it must reply with periodic reprisal raids. The situation became so tense that the U.N. Security Council asked the Secretary-General to visit the area personally. His intervention with both sides brought a momentary easing but no basic change.

On the occasion of Sir Anthony Eden's visit to Washington early in 1956, the United States and British Governments had recognized that finding a basis for permanent settlement had to take second place, for the moment, to the urgent need to prevent the outbreak of hostilities. A new Arab-Israel war could do untold damage to Western interests as well as to those immediately involved, and it might spread sooner or later into a world conflict. The two governments took the opportunity to reaffirm the Tripartite Declaration and to announce the establishment of a tripartite working group that would plan precise military measures to be taken in the event of a crisis. What the working group ever worked out has not been officially divulged. At any rate, there was no announcement or evidence of joint plans for action, a fact which was bound to cast doubt on the real value of the Tripartite Declaration.

Arab Aims and Policies

To understand the drift toward war during the course of 1956, it is necessary to recapture the psychological mood on both sides. Arab opinion had been elated by Abdel Nasser's arms deal with the Soviets. Here was the promise of armed strength such as the Arabs had never known before, and with it the support of a great power that was unreservedly on their side. There was a new ring of confidence in the declarations of Arab leaders that they would right the wrongs done to their brethren in Palestine. Abdel Nasser himself came to be looked on by many Arabs as the new Saladin who would restore Palestine to its rightful owners. Yet it would be a mistake to say that the Arab leaders, including Abdel Nasser, had set any time schedule for the destruction of Israel, despite rumors to the effect that in some given number of months, when such-and-such an amount of equipment had been received and so many Egyptian pilots and tankmen had been trained by their Soviet advisers, the Arabs would march on Israel. Nevertheless, Abdel Nasser, having sold himself to the Arab masses as the man who finally could do something about Israel, might find himself under growing and eventually intolerable pressure to go ahead and do it.

The real danger to peace on the Arab side lay not in the danger of a calculated decision to attack Israel so much as in the instability that threatened to precipitate reckless action or a crisis into which Israel also would be drawn. Syria, since the election of 1954, had drifted more and more into the hands of the parties of the left, allied with the Communists and supported by powerful elements in the army. The old parties and leaders had at first been able to keep something of a balance, but the continued successes of Abdel Nasser and Soviet support of Arab nationalism strengthened all those who followed the pro-Egyptian and pro-Soviet line and increased the danger of a leftist *coup d'état* or of a move against Israel.

In neighboring Jordan British influence was rapidly fading after the failure to get that country to join the Baghdad Pact, the ouster of Glubb Pasha, and growing attacks on the Anglo-Jordanian treaty. The young King, insecure on his throne, was trying to get help from his brother Arab rulers to replace Britain's diplomatic and financial support, which he needed desperately but was under pressure to renounce. The main trouble was that two-thirds of his own people were Palestinians who had no loyalty to the dynasty or even to the state. The riots of late 1955 and early 1956 had seemed to show that whoever could control the mobs in the streets of Amman and Jerusalem would control the destiny of the state, if it survived at all. Pulled one way by the dynastic tie to Iraq and another way by the Egypt-Syria-Saudi Arabia bloc, Jordan bid fair to be torn apart if at any time internal order broke down, and there was always Israel, which would surely seize the west bank of the River Jordan before allowing any other Arab state to occupy it. Jordan's weakness in the face of a number of heavy Israeli raids in September and October was only too apparent. Ben-Gurion stated that Israel would react with force if Iraqi forces entered Jordan, and Britain in turn warned Israel against any rash move. The British Government affirmed its intention to stick to its treaty of alliance with Jordan, but Arabs and Israelis both could legitimately wonder what sense to make of that. Would the British, already at swords' points with Egypt on the Suez Canal question, get themselves into a fight with Israel on behalf of an Arab state that did not appear to want British protection?

The approach of elections in October 1956 brought all these problems to the fore. The clear-cut victory of the extreme nationalist, leftist and pro-Egyptian groups largely representing the Palestinian elements of the population opened the way for Egypt to move quickly to exploit the situation. Within a week Jordan had agreed to place its armed forces under Egyptian command. Jordan had not fallen apart, as many expected. It seemed rather to have fallen into the hands of Abdel Nasser.

The State of Mind in Israel

If we now look at all these developments from the viewpoint of Israel, the perspective is of course quite different and makes possible better understanding of why, in October, Israel took its fateful decision for war. Following the Soviet-Egyptian arms deal and the continued refusal of the United

States to meet Israel's request for arms, the sense of desperation grew. That Egypt may not have set any specific time schedule for a campaign to destroy Israel was not a source of any particular comfort to Israel's citizens. They knew only that the Arab leaders had sworn publicly to annihilate them and that now for the first time they were getting the means to do it. They saw Israel's past advantages in superior weapons, skills, training and morale rapidly dwindling in the face of Arab numbers disposing of an unlimited supply of Soviet planes, tanks and heavy guns.

Added to this disturbing calculation was the new element of terror caused by the raids of the fedayeen. Israelis had lived for eight years under siege, behind long and indefensible frontiers, inured to conditions of insecurity. But the new raids were of a different character, suicide squads against whom no part of Israel and no individual citizen was safe. They had penetrated to the city of Tel Aviv itself. Evidence accumulated that these bands were coming over all the frontiers, from Lebanon, Syria, Jordan and Egypt, but were nevertheless organized under central direction from Egypt. Although in May Ben Gurion had accepted Secretary-General Hammarskjold's plea for a renewed pledge against violation of the armistice lines, he felt he could not afford to let Israel's citizens be subjected to this terror. Consequently, Israel undertook a series of heavy raids against Jordan in October. But the fedayeen activities did not cease.

By this time Israel had lost all faith in the armistice system. Where only three years before it had extolled the armistice agreements as the only firm legal basis for relations between Israel and the Arab states, now those agreements were looked on as having lost all validity because the Arab states had violated them and the United Nations had not been able to enforce them.[7] The Israel Government re-

[7] Statement of Abba Eban to the Ad Hoc Political Committee, December 1, 1952. Summary in U.N. General Assembly, *Official Records,* 7th Session (A/AC.61/SR.29) (New York, 1953); full text in Abba Eban, *Voice of Israel* (New York: Horizon Press, 1957), pp. 93-122. See also Ambassador Eban's statement of November 3, 1956, U.N. General Assembly, *Official Records,* 1st Emergency Special Session (A/PV.563) (New York, 1956).

garded U.N.T.S.O. as useless, a mere recording device keeping a tabulation of border violations and incidents but doing nothing whatever to protect Israel. Nor was the Security Council any more helpful. It ignored the many Arab incursions while going out of its way to condemn Israel's attempt to defend itself by retaliatory raids. As for the Tripartite Declaration, Israel derived no feeling of safety from its existence. President Eisenhower, in April, had re-emphasized the determination of the United States to assist any Middle Eastern nation attacked.[8] But would the United States or Great Britain really protect Israel against an Arab attack? After the denial of arms, the leaders of Israel were feeling "ultrarealistic" about the help they might expect from the United States. They appreciated the financial support, but they felt no assurance at all that the United States would be willing or able to act in time to save Israel from Arab assault. Ben-Gurion and his colleagues came firmly to believe, as they had in 1948, that Israel would have to depend for its survival on its own will and its own strength.

The Decision for War

Such were the factors that led Israel to the point of denouncing the armistice and sending its army into Egypt. When the decision was taken we do not know. Perhaps it was inevitable ever since the moderating influence of Moshe Sharrett was removed from the cabinet in June. But as late as October 15 Ben-Gurion made a speech in the Knesset renouncing preventive war and emphasizing Israel's policy of deterrence.[9] If that speech represented his convictions at the time, what happened in the next two weeks to change them? Certain moves on the part of the Arabs indicated increasing danger: intensification of the fedayeen raids and

[8] Statement of April 9, 1956, *Department of State Bulletin*, v. 34 (April 23, 1956), p. 668.
[9] State of Israel, Government Press Office, unnumbered press release (full text in English translation).

Abdel Nasser's rapid move to draw Jordan into his anti-Israel military alliance. Other events in the world at large seemed to make the present a more favorable time for a showdown than any time in the future. The Soviet Union was absorbed in its troubles in Eastern Europe and unlikely to take a strong line in the Near East. The United States was in the midst of an election campaign and likely to avoid decisive action. France had come to Israel's support by providing fighter aircraft and other needed arms. Israel's relative military position was probably better than it ever would be again. These were the circumstances in which Ben-Gurion made his decision for military action. The Israel army jumped off on Monday, October 29, with the double aim of destroying the bases from which the fedayeen attacks had come and of somehow disposing of the menace which Abdel Nasser and his leadership of Arab nationalism posed to the existence of the State of Israel.

Critique of American Policy

Looking back over the record, one may ask where American policy failed. Without attributing to the United States a control of events which it did not and could not have, can we point to mistakes made or opportunities missed which might have made the difference between relative stability in the Near East and the crisis which developed in October 1956? Leaving aside judgments on the wisdom or unwisdom of our role in the creation of Israel, in attempting to deal with the resulting situation we were faced with the discouraging fact that the armistice agreements which closed the Palestine war were basically unstable, for the Arab states did not accept them either as a just resolution of the Palestine question or as a temporary settlement to be followed promptly by a negotiated peace. Any Western attempts to promote solutions of the basic issues or to enforce the armistice regime had to be related to general policies with respect to the Arab world. And since, on the one

hand, the Western states needed the good will of the Arab
world to maintain their military position and their sources
of oil, and on the other were trying to work out acceptable arrangements with Egypt on such matters as the Suez
base and the status of the Sudan, they found they had very
little bargaining power with the Arabs on the question of
Palestine.

The fact that American policy was closely linked with
British during this period did not simplify matters. It
meant that every dispute between Britain and an Arab
state had its deleterious effect on attempts to work toward
Arab-Israel settlements. Moreover, as far as Arab opinion
was concerned, the United States itself did not come into
court with clean hands; in the view of most Arabs, America's pro-Zionist policy and American financial support were
responsible for Israel's victory in 1948 and its continued
existence. The policy of "impartiality" between the Arab
states and Israel, proclaimed by the new Eisenhower Administration in 1953, did not impress Arab nationalists
when it became apparent that no attempt would be made
to coerce Israel on the major issues in dispute or to deprive
it of American economic support.

Since the Western powers in fact were not prepared to
force Israel into concessions on territory and on the return
of the refugees, they never had any chance to get the Arab
states to talk seriously about settlement. Arab leaders often
cited past U.N. resolutions (on partition of Palestine, repatriation of refugees, and the internationalization of Jerusalem) as the basis for a settlement. Israel would not even
consider such terms, pointing to the fact that the Arab
states themselves had not accepted the U.N. partition plan
and had taken up arms to upset it. The clock, said Israel,
could not be turned back; hundreds of thousands of Jewish refugees had since entered Israel.

The United States Government had plenty of warning
that the situation in the Near East was deteriorating and
that the Israel-Arab conflict was increasingly harmful to
Western interests. Perhaps it could have done more to keep

the question of a settlement before the United Nations, invoking whatever procedures were available for its discussion as a world problem. Perhaps it should have made a greater effort to mobilize world opinion in regard to the plight of the Arab refugees, so that both Israel and the Arab states might have been put under real pressure to share with other states the burden of solving it as a human, and not just a political, problem. But we can feel no assurance whatever, in view of the bitterness of the feeling on both sides, that anything concrete could have been accomplished.

The other line of possible action, given the near hopelessness of the chances for a basic settlement, was to stabilize the armistice regime so that violence would be minimized and both sides would gradually become accustomed to the *status quo*. To do so would have required convincing both that violence would not in fact be tolerated. They could not have been so convinced, events showed, without strong statements of intent on the part of the Western powers, especially the United States, backed up by the capacity and will to prevent violence. That meant, for infiltration and border raids, a strong and effective U.N. force on the ground, and for larger-scale aggression, mobile power that could quickly be brought into play. As to statements of intent, the Tripartite Declaration might have been adequate had there been anything behind it. On the enforcement side, however, the U.N.T.S.O. machinery was hopelessly inadequate to keep the peace in Palestine, and the Western powers never showed that they were prepared to stop any aggression in its tracks with superior force.

As a result, resolutions of the Security Council and appeals of the Secretary-General were ineffective. Both Israel and the Arab states felt they could act without regard to the United Nations or the West. Even though when the crisis broke, at the end of October, the United States showed that it could and would act promptly and with decision, the fact remains that in the crucial months before the actual crisis the Arab-Israel conflict, like the Suez dispute, was out of control. America had to face a harrowing decision in November, involving a hard choice of evils, because easier though admittedly difficult decisions had not been made earlier.

Chapter 8

THE CRISIS OF 1956

IN THE period of three months between Abdel Nasser's seizure of the Suez Canal Company and the end of October the two questions of Suez and Palestine, interacting with each other, both moved toward a violent climax. The salient feature of this story was the failure of the Western powers, bound together by their common interests in free and secure transit through the canal and in keeping the peace in Palestine, to find effective policies to protect those interests. They approached the moment of crisis without any common estimate of the situation or plan for united action, indeed, without even having maintained adequate communication with each other. The consequence was serious damage both to the interests of the West in the Middle East and to the fabric of the Western alliance itself.

The Suez Canal Dispute

It is unnecessary here to trace the detailed story of the dispute over the Suez Canal. Egypt's expropriation of a foreign-owned company was not so different from similar acts by other governments in the past, such as the nationalization of the Anglo-Iranian Oil Company in 1951, except that this particular company had been managing an international waterway and by its mere presence there had represented a kind of institutional guarantee of the freedom of navigation enshrined in the Constantinople Convention of 1888. It had also been making substantial profits. Over twenty years ago Sir Arnold Wilson had raised the question whether control of a great international highway by a commercial company, bent on paying as large dividends as possible, was consistent with modern ideas and modern

99

needs.[1] By 1956 it was clearly no longer consistent with Abdel Nasser's idea of modern Egypt's needs.

The Western powers, stung by his dramatic and unexpected move, protested against it as seizure of "an international agency" for national purposes and a threat to the freedom and security of the canal. They did not, however, attempt to test its legality before the International Court of Justice or to insist that the company be restored to its former position; the concession was to expire in twelve years anyway. Great Britain and France, while not forswearing the possibility of a resort to force, adopted at least temporarily the position that they could accept the expropriation (assuming full compensation to the owners, as Egypt had promised), conditional on the establishment of a new system of international control and management of the canal, in which Egypt and the principal canal-using countries would be represented. The United Kingdom, France and the United States agreed upon this approach in London on August 2, and elaborated it in the eighteen-nation plan that emerged from the conference of twenty-two nations also held in London later in the same month.[2]

The approach was logical but abstract. The maritime nations of the world had a vital interest in freedom of transit and had a right to adequate assurance that they would continue to enjoy it in the future as in the past; Egypt, while the canal was within its territory, could profit from it only if it served its purpose as an international waterway. The difficulties arose because in the atmosphere and political conditions of 1956 no such rational approach was possible. Egypt had taken over the canal as a grand political gesture, an assertion of "sovereignty," an act of defiance against the

[1] Sir Arnold T. Wilson, *The Suez Canal* (Oxford: Oxford University Press, 1933), p. vii.
[2] Texts of the tripartite communiqué and of the eighteen-nation plan appear in Department of State, *The Suez Canal Problem* (Washington: G.P.O., 1956), pp. 34-35, 291-292. This documentary collection also contains the texts of the Constantinople Convention and other relevant agreements. See also D. C. Watt, ed., *Documents on the Suez Crisis* (London: Royal Institute of International Affairs, 1957).

West. Abdel Nasser himself had announced it as a "declaration of independence" from imperialism. He had won great acclaim in the Arab world. He had refused to attend the London conference. How could he be expected to jeopardize all he had won by accepting a system of international control, which would have been more restrictive of Egypt's sovereignty than the concession to a foreign-owned but still legally Egyptian company which he had just annulled? He might have been prepared to discuss the Indian proposal for an advisory board representing the users and reporting to the United Nations, but his outright rejection as "collective colonialism" of the eighteen-nation plan, presented to him in September by Australian Prime Minister Menzies on behalf of its sponsors, was a foregone conclusion.

On the side of the Western powers also, particularly Britain and France, the matters in dispute were not considered on their merits alone. Their concern with maintenance of freedom of transit through the canal, especially for vital oil shipments, was real enough, but it explains only in part the nature of their reaction to the seizure and their attitude toward Egypt. If Suez was a word charged with emotion for Egypt, so was it also for Britain. Despite the loss of India and the crumbling of imperial positions in the East over the span of a decade, despite the recently completed withdrawal of British forces from Suez itself, the canal had remained a symbol. Britain's whole position as a world power seemed now to be at the mercy of a nation for which many Britons had no respect at all, and of a posturing demagogue who had bedeviled British interests all over the Middle East and even beyond it. Could Britain's fate be allowed to depend on his whim? In many ways the seizure of the Canal Company was the last straw, both for the Government and for a great part of the public.

Similarly, the French reaction reflected the frustration generated by years of trouble and conflict in North Africa, where Egypt's moral and material support of nationalist forces was blamed for the persistence of the rebellion in Algeria. French opinion seemed virtually unanimous in favoring strong action in reply to Abdel Nasser's coup. Concern for the rights of the many French shareholders in the expropriated company explains this in part, but even more it was the growing feeling that France could not endure further humiliation, a conviction that *il faut en finir*.

To both British and French Governments the Suez issue seemed to present the crucial point at which the two nations had to assert themselves. Their aims, therefore, went beyond freedom of transit through Suez. They had to turn the tide that was running against them. They had to defeat, or somehow get rid of, Abdel Nasser. Sir Anthony Eden, in a speech on August 8, committed himself publicly to a test of strength which could find its logical end only in the fall of one of the two protagonists.[3]

Negotiation or Use of Force

In these circumstances the immediate and unresolved question was not what kind of international regime for the canal could be negotiated, but whether force would be used to impose a solution on Egypt. The British Government came close to deciding to use force at the very start, in a play for quick success before Egypt or anyone else was prepared for it. But Britain's military forces were not ready for action on such short notice, and within a few days both foreign and domestic pressures were such as to persuade the Government to put off the idea of using force and to call a conference instead.

As the scene shifted from the Conference of Twenty-two to the Menzies mission, to the Conference of Eighteen, to the Suez Canal Users' Association and finally to the U.N. Security Council, the question of the use of force remained unresolved. More than that, it began to poison relations between the United States and its major European allies. The British and French were not content with a "solution by negotiation" which consisted in devising progressively weaker schemes for Egypt to reject. They felt that at some

[3] *The Times* (London), August 9, 1956.

point a solution would have to be imposed on Egypt. The
United States, however, while agreeing with the principle
of international regulation of the canal, took a strong stand
against any use of force. It did so in confidential negotiations. It did so publicly. The effect was to deprive Britain
and France of whatever means of pressure they might have
derived from the threat of force. To them the Users' Association, largely an American invention, made sense only as
a means of bringing Abdel Nasser to terms, even by con-
voying ships through the canal in defiance of his new company's regulations and taking over control of operations.
Mr. Dulles, however, renounced "shooting our way through
the canal;" to him, so it seemed in London and Paris, the
Association was just another delaying device, and Nasser
was thriving on delay. The Egyptian Government, while it
remained suspicious of British and French intentions, could
at least take comfort in the knowledge that the West was
in fact not united, and that the attitude of the United States
seemed to rule out coercion.

The Disunity of the West

It serves no purpose to try to apportion blame for this
unfortunate situation. The United States bears a responsibility for its unwillingness to see the seriousness of what its
allies regarded as an issue vital to them and to give them
at least some promise of a common course of action that
would meet their needs. If force was ruled out, all other
means of pressure and persuasion might have been explored.
Instead, it became apparent that the United States did not
even favor severe economic measures beyond the freezing
of Egyptian assets in the United States, which it had done
at the start.

That Britain and France felt deceived and disillusioned
with Secretary Dulles' "preaching" and with American policy was not wholly the result of their own sinister designs
or lack of political wisdom. On the other hand, the record
on their side is hardly distinguished by statesmanship. The

obsession of the need for a "showdown" with Abdel Nasser colored British and French thinking, but there was no corresponding strategy except somehow to force an international system or a Users' Association down his throat. British and French leaders seemed mesmerized by the supposed parallel with the appeasement of Hitler in the 1930's and the imminent disaster of a new "Munich." They tended to underestimate both the sincerity of the American "moral" objection to force and the seriousness of the American conviction that the contest with communism for the Middle East and the whole uncommitted world could not be successfully waged, and might even be irreparably lost, by a reversion to 19th century strong-arm methods.

In any event, communication between Washington on the one hand and Paris and London on the other, so far as the Suez question was concerned, virtually broke down during the latter half of October. No clear and authoritative warning of what was in the wind was conveyed by the British Government to the United States. The U.N. Security Council, on October 13, adopted a six-point resolution which Britain, France and Egypt publicly accepted as the agreed basis for a negotiated solution, although the Soviet representative at the same time vetoed the other part of the resolution, which approved the eighteen-nation plan already rejected by Egypt.[4] The one point of the six on which the Western nations counted to protect their position was that the operation of the Canal should be "insulated from the politics of any country," whatever that might mean in law or practice. While the United States, gratified at this apparent progress, awaited the start of direct negotiations between the parties more immediately concerned, decisions were being made in Tel Aviv, Paris and London to apply more drastic corrective measures to the intractable problems of dealing with Abdel Nasser.

[4] U.N. Security Council (S/3675), October 13, 1956; text also in *Documents on American Foreign Relations, 1956* (New York: Harper, for the Council on Foreign Relations, 1957), pp. 342-343.

The Charge of Collusion

Since the beginning of the Suez crisis the connection between Palestine and Suez must have become apparent to the Western European powers and to Israel, just as it had always existed for the Arabs in theory and in propaganda if not always in fact. Israel had already been shaken by the withdrawal of British military forces from Suez, which gave Egypt a much freer hand for action in Palestine. The crisis over the canal, from which Israeli ships had always been barred, brought out more clearly the obvious parallel between the interests of Israel and those of the West in their common antagonism to Egypt. We cannot be sure to what extent Israel's leaders thought they could gain their own ends by acting as the cutting edge of Western policy, or to what extent British and French statesmen saw the advantages in having Israel do, or begin, the job they wanted done. We can be sure, however, that some thinking along these lines took place, and that it led to ever closer relations between France and Israel and finally to the dovetailed if not concerted action which marked the outbreak of the crisis at the end of October.

It had been a cardinal objective on the American side to prevent the problems arising from the seizure of the Canal Company from becoming enmeshed in the Arab-Israel dispute. The flouting of that policy by France and Britain indicated how deluded, or how indifferent to the importance of solidarity with the United States, they had become.

The question of "collusion" is still not wholly clarified, and for our present purpose of examining the problems of American policy perhaps that does not greatly matter, interesting as it may be as a political issue and as a point for historical investigation. The closeness of the collaboration between France and Israel seems clear enough. France sent considerable military equipment, especially fighter aircraft, to Israel in September and October, and some officers with it. Diplomatic and military contacts were

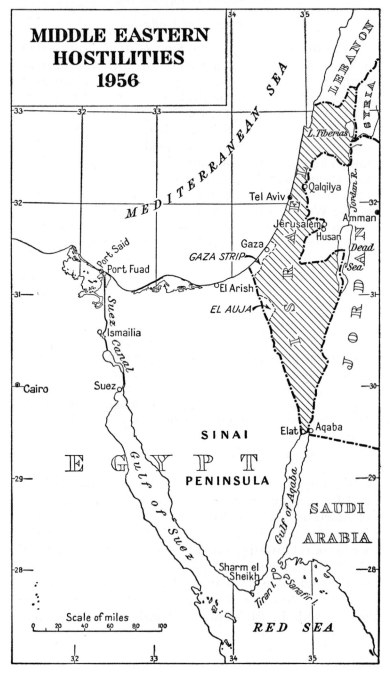

MIDDLE EASTERN
HOSTILITIES
1956

multiplied. And when the crisis came, French naval units and aircraft, under French orders, provided important operational assistance to Israel's forces. Planes of the French air force participated in Israeli operations in Sinai.[5] Whether or not the French actually encouraged Israel to attack Egypt—which is quite possible—they had a very good idea of what was in the wind, though perhaps without knowing the precise date, which was concealed from all but a handful of persons in Israel itself.[6] The Israel Government undoubtedly looked forward to help from France, both diplomatic and material, though it may not have planned for or even desired the kind of military intervention to which France and Britain actually resorted; that intervention, indeed, spoiled rather than aided Israel's chance of making substantial gains from its enterprise.

Great Britain was not in such close relations with Israel, but was in more or less constant touch with France after October 16, the date on which those who charge a plot say that it was hatched in Paris by Eden, Lloyd, Mollet and Pineau. The two powers were coordinating their military planning and preparing their forces on Cyprus for action, while Britain assembled an invasion force at Malta. The British Government may not have known just when and where Israel would strike but, as Sir Anthony himself conceded, it was aware of the possibility. He had discussed with the French "every possible hypothesis" in the Middle East, including presumably the one which materialized.[7]

[5] See especially the report of James Morris in the *Manchester Guardian*, November 20, 1956, and Merry and Serge Bromberger, *Les Secrets de l'Expédition d'Egypte* (Paris: Editions des 4 Fils Aymon, 1957), pp. 21-32, 114-134. This book, undocumented, goes into great detail both on secret official conversations and on military plans and operations. If its "secrets" have any authenticity, and most of them have the ring of truth, they must have come from high French official sources, of which the most likely is the Ministry of Defense.

[6] Bromberger, cited, pp. 55-56, indicates that Ben-Gurion informed Mollet of Israel's plans at a secret meeting at an airport near Paris on October 22.

[7] For Eden's final statement, December 20, 1956, see House of Commons, *Parliamentary Debates*, Weekly Hansard, no. 375, cols. 1460-1464 (December 20, 1956). The full knowledge and collusion of the British Government was

There can be no doubt that the Prime Minister and his Government had long been seeking the right combination of circumstances to do something forceful about Suez, and that the information coming to their notice in the latter half of October, even before the 29th, convinced them that the opportunity had arrived.

The American Response to the Crisis

Israel's attack on Egypt took place on Monday, October 29. For a time it was not clear whether it was a real invasion or another retaliatory raid in greater "depth," but it was plainly no border incident; within a matter of hours Israeli columns were operating fifty miles and more within Egyptian territory. The reaction of the United States was to put the case immediately before the Security Council and seek to end the fighting; this was what seemed to be called for both under the Tripartite Declaration and under the U.N. Charter. Before the Security Council could act it was informed by the British and French representatives of the ultimatums delivered by their own governments to Israel and Egypt on that day, October 30, directing them to keep their forces ten miles from the Suez Canal, the Israel army on the east and the Egyptian army on the west; British and French forces would occupy the canal zone anyway, using force if they were resisted.

This intervention transformed the situation, turning it from a local Middle Eastern conflict into a Western attack on Egypt. The ultimatum could be interpreted in no other way despite the official reasons given: to stop the war and to protect British subjects, British shipping and the canal. Those who made this crucial decision did not inform the

---

charged but not conclusively proved by the Labour Party leadership, and was vigorously denied by the Government. An extreme but well-argued statement of the charge by left-wing Labour spokesmen appears in Michael Foot and Mervyn Jones, *Guilty Men 1957* (New York: Rinehart, 1957). It is interesting that John R. Beal's semi-authorized biography (*John Foster Dulles*, New York: Harper, 1957, p. 277) flatly calls the affair a plot in which Britain, after October 16, was a full-fledged partner.

United States in advance because, as M. Mollet later admitted, they feared Washington would not approve their action and might upset their schedule.[8] But they apparently counted on a measure of understanding and "benevolent neutrality" even without advance consultation and looked to American influence as a counterweight to any Soviet inclination to intervene.

Probably the British and French expected a quick military success, whereby they would seize the canal and oust Abdel Nasser before anybody else could do very much about it. If so, they planned and conducted their military operations badly; they underestimated the capacity of the United Nations for speedy action; they underestimated the reaction of the Soviet Union, which took the form of threats of rocket warfare against Western Europe; and they overestimated the unwillingness of the United States, on the eve of an election, to take any strong action at all. The result was that the General Assembly, with the United States in a leading role, passed quickly and overwhelmingly a series of resolutions calling for a cessation of fighting and the withdrawal of foreign forces from Egypt. The combined pressure of the United States, the Soviet Union, U.N. resolutions, world opinion, lack of the united support of the Commonwealth, and the strong opposition of the Labour Party sufficed to bring Britain by November 6 to the point of calling it off, with only Port Said captured. France had no choice but to follow suit immediately, and Israel, its military victory won, had already stated its readiness to stop fighting.

The position of the United States should hardly have been a matter of doubt. Regardless of what had gone before, including the provocations on the Egyptian side, regardless even of its own failure to prevent this deterioration to the point of open hostilities, the United States was now faced not just with a troublesome situation but with the fact of open aggression on the part of Israel, Britain and France against Egypt. As in the case of Korea in 1950,

[8] Interview, *New York Times*, December 10, 1956.

even though this was not a Communist aggression, the conviction was strong that we had to act as we did unless we were willing to see the end of the United Nations and of all the hopes for an effective world security system which it represented. In addition to these reasons of principle were some eminently practical ones. A failure of the United States to take the stand it took would have risked the permanent alienation of all those nations of Asia and Africa, most of them newly independent or not yet independent, which were being so ardently wooed by the Communist powers.

As a practical matter the U.S. Government did not believe that the Western powers, even if temporarily successful in using force against Egypt and the Arab world, could make such a victory "stick" over the long run. This had been the lesson of the earlier occupation of Egypt and the lesson of Syria, the Palestine mandate, and North Africa. As for the idea of getting rid of Abdel Nasser, the United States had no reason to be fond of him, but it was not convinced that there was any alternative—the British had none—or that the use of force was the way to find one. The Administration was also unwilling to let the Soviet Union reap all the benefits of acting on behalf of the Arab peoples in a case like this in which the aggression was clear. In this way it had the chance to save some credit for the West with the Arabs, now more bitter than ever against Great Britain and France.

The Price of Failure

The results of the abortive campaign, from the viewpoint of those two powers, were indeed disastrous. Because of the slowness of their military operations they were unable even to occupy more than a fraction of the canal zone. Even if they had seized it all, it is not certain they would have gained anything except more territory from which to withdraw "forthwith," as they did from Port Said. They did not succeed in toppling Abdel Nasser; on the contrary they helped him to win a great political victory. They did not restore their dwindling prestige in the Middle East, but sent it plummeting rapidly toward zero. Their failure at Suez was practically an invitation to Arab nationalists to step up the pressure against French rule in Algeria and against the British positions in Jordan, Iraq and the Persian Gulf area. The Suez Canal, which they had gone in to protect, was closed to all shipping for months as a result of the fighting and especially of deliberate Egyptian acts of destruction. The pipelines from the oilfields of Iraq to the Mediterranean were cut by the blowing up of the pumping stations in Syria. All Western Europe faced a serious oil shortage. Later efforts of the British Government to claim real gains from the Suez action—such as foiling a Soviet plot to seize the Middle East, the prevention of a world war, the creation of a United Nations police force, and the bringing of American interests and power more directly into the area—were not very convincing.

Although Sir Anthony Eden stepped down, the British and French Governments did not fall, perhaps because the majority of the British people and almost all the French shared their conviction of the essential rightness of their action even when it failed and refused like them to admit the humiliation that normally accompanies failure. Despite this bold front, the results cannot properly be described as anything but an unmitigated disaster. The adventure into which the two governments leaped, in an effort to prove that they could still play the role of great powers, proved beyond all doubt that this was now beyond their strength. Even in dealing with smaller and weaker nations, their former wards, they could not act except in the context of the policies of the United States and of the Soviet Union. The United States was occupied with an election, the Soviet Union with revolt in its satellites, but neither was so occupied that it could not intervene in the Middle East. Their intervention, for once on the same side, gave London and Paris no choice but withdrawal.

Role of the Soviet Union

It was embarrassing to the United States to find itself in the company of the Soviet Union in condemning its traditional allies and threatening them with chastisement. The American position was based on definite and independent reasons and not subject to change just because the Soviet representatives in the United Nations happened to vote the same way. Paradoxically, both the United States and the Soviet Union came to this point of apparent coincidence of policy through their separate attempts, directed against each other, to fit the narrower issues of Palestine and Suez into the broader question of the fate of the Middle East in the cold war.

Moscow had made its basic strategic decision in 1955, or even before, to play the card of Arab nationalism in every possible way against Israel and against the West. From this decision flowed its votes for the Arab cause in the United Nations, its arms deliveries, its trade deals, and its unceasing stream of pro-Arab propaganda. The crisis of 1956, for Moscow, was a confirmation of the correctness of its strategy and an opportunity for redoubled efforts, which helped also to distract attention from the suppression of freedom in Hungary. The Western powers, two of them anyway, seemed to be intent on digging a grave for themselves in the Middle East. To help them do so and to bury American interests along with them, Moscow made every possible appeal to Arab and Asian nationalism, to anti-colonialism, to the principles of sovereignty and the rights of small nations, victims of aggression. America was pictured not as helping Egypt and the Arabs but as scheming to replace European with American imperialism. Behind the propaganda front the Soviets were pushing ahead to consolidate and enlarge the positions they had already won in the Arab world.

These moves were methodical, not reckless. The Soviet leaders wanted to convince the Arabs that Russia would fight if necessary while the United States would not; but they took no step which would spread the war in the Middle East. True, they intervened diplomatically in a dramatic way by proposing joint Soviet-American action against the "aggressors" and by threatening Britain and France with missile warfare if they did not withdraw from Egypt. They talked a great deal about sending "volunteers" to fight for Egypt. While the notes to Britain and France came as a shock to the recipients and may have had a bearing on the British decision to stop the invasion and withdraw,[9] it would be a good guess that they were in fact a bluff. And it is doubtful that there was a real intention to send "volunteers;" the proposal was a good experiment for testing reactions both in the Middle East and in the United States. Soviet willingness to use force cannot be excluded. If the fighting had continued, with Asian and other opinion inflamed against Britain and France, the Soviet leaders might have taken the chance on a military intervention. In any case, the moves they took illustrated their intention to reap the greatest possible harvest from Western mistakes, fears and divisions.

Both the Soviet Union and the United States, under the surface of their apparent common front in the United Nations as defenders of the victim of aggression and upholders of the Charter, were doing their best to capitalize on that role in the Middle East and to forestall each other's moves there. In this competition the Soviets had certain real advantages: their earlier record of support for Arab nationalism; their insistence on the immediate and unconditional withdrawal of all foreign troops from Egypt and the Gaza strip; and their hard talk to Israel, even calling into question its future existence as a state. On these points the United States could not match the aban-

[9] Government spokesmen were several times pressed in the House of Commons to explain the reasons for their decision, but all they would say was that, on receipt of assurances that Israel and Egypt had accepted a cease-fire and that the international force would be established, Great Britain had attained its objectives and would therefore agree to cease hostilities. See House of Commons, *Parliamentary Debates,* Weekly Hansard, no. 369, cols. 75-80 (November 6, 1956); no. 373, cols. 1261-1263 (December 5, 1956).

don and irresponsibility of Soviet threats, promises and propaganda. In fact, it found itself enmeshed in a series of complex and difficult questions involving the when and the how of Western and Israeli withdrawal, stabilization of relations in the area after hostilities, and progress toward more permanent settlements. On all these matters its decisions had to take account of its future relations with the countries of the area, including Israel, of the badly strained Western alliance, and of the need for meeting the over-all challenge of the advance of Soviet influence, the answer to which had not yet been found.

The Denouement

Two lines of thought appeared in America's early reaction to the crisis. One was that the Sinai and Suez aggressions, like any aggression in open violation of the Charter, must be "liquidated" as soon as possible by a cessation of hostilities and a withdrawal of invading forces. This, the dominant theme of American policy, represented a somewhat rigid legal approach in requiring a return to the *status quo ante* with no change that could be interpreted as a reward for aggression. The other line of thinking, more political than legal in its emphasis, tended to regard the armed action against Egypt not as an isolated crime against the peace but rather as the culmination of a series of actions and reactions in which Abdel Nasser's role was not simply that of innocent victim. Even without passing judgment on that point, some looked to the fact of hostilities, the changed situation and the new prestige of the United Nations as providing the opportunity and the means for a fresh approach to the basic problems out of which the hostilities had grown. What that would mean in practice, however, would be using bargaining power created by the military action to force Egypt to accept solutions that had previously been unacceptable. In concrete terms, the question was whether the invading forces would be kept in Egypt until some settlements were reached with respect to the Suez Canal and the points at issue between Egypt and Israel, and whether, if the withdrawal of those forces was required, the presence of the newly formed United Nations Emergency Force might serve the same purpose.

While attracted by this second line of thought, American officials were never able to find a way to do anything about it, restricted as they were by the legal and political considerations that underlay the original stand. On several occasions Secretary Dulles stressed the importance of immediate progress toward permanent settlements, and the U.S. Government had put before the United Nations the idea of special committees to go to work on the basic problems of the Suez Canal and Palestine.[10] That was as far as the initiative went.

The job which the Assembly had given to Secretary-General Hammarskjold bristled with difficulties: to organize a U.N. force, get it to Egypt immediately, and obtain Egypt's agreement to its location and functions. The Secretary-General was breaking new ground in the role of "executive" of the General Assembly and interpreter of its resolutions. His negotiations with Abdel Nasser were delicate, in view of the vagueness of his mandate and the legal limitations on the Assembly's resolutions, which have the force only of recommendations to member governments. On every point Egypt had to be persuaded and could not be coerced. His function as he saw it was to help in getting foreign troops out of Egypt and in restoring the previously existing Armistice Agreement, the only legal basis for regulating relations between Egypt and Israel. The U.N. force, accordingly, was to be used to these ends, not as a means of forcing Egypt to agree to new settlements on Suez and Palestine.

The United States might have taken a more understanding view of the interests of its European allies and

---

[10] U.N. General Assembly, *Question Considered by the Security Council at Its 749th and 750th Meetings . . . 30 October 1956*, 1st Emergency Special Session (A/3272 and A/3273), November 3, 1956.

of Israel, once they had agreed to the cease-fire, and might have tried to establish a stronger role for the U.N.E.F. It was restrained from doing so by the practical difficulties of getting a two-thirds majority in the General Assembly for such a course, the danger of losing recently gained Arab and Asian good will, and an unwillingness to make the Secretary-General's job any more difficult. Critics of this relative inaction on the part of the Administration felt that it was unnecessarily hard on our friends and showed too much scruple or fear in its reluctance to offend the President of Egypt; also that it tended to leave to Mr. Hammarskjold the pursuit and protection of American interests, which were not strictly his business.

As far as the United Kingdom and France were concerned, their willingness to withdraw in a matter of weeks simplified the problem, although U.S. relations with them remained at a low point for some time. Public opinion in both countries continued to resent our joining the Arab-Asian and Soviet blocs in what seemed to them like vindictive resolutions, and our apparent willingness, by the delay in putting prepared organizational arrangements into effect, to use their oil shortage as a means of political pressure.[11] But their only course was to swallow their pride and resentment, and to extract themselves as soon as possible from untenable positions. In any event, by Christmas British and French troops were out, U.N. forces had moved eastward from the canal zone, and the dispute over the canal was as far from solution as ever, or farther still since Abdel Nasser now considered Egypt released from the six principles of the Security Council resolution of October 13. The possibility of internationalization appeared to be dead beyond recall.

[11] During November the U.S. Government refrained, because "the international situation was extremely delicate," from authorizing operation of the Middle East Emergency Committee of thirteen U.S. oil companies organized to expedite supplies to Europe. However, private companies on their own shipped some 15 million barrels of oil products to Europe in that month. (*Petroleum Survey,* U.S. House Committee on Interstate and Foreign Commerce, Preliminary Report, 85th Cong., 1st sess., Washington: G.P.O., 1950, pp. 14-22).

Aqaba and Gaza

With Israel the difficulties were greater because Israel had won a military campaign and did not want to lose the fruits of victory. The attack in Sinai had grown out of a desperate feeling of insecurity. Israel could hardly be expected meekly to return to the same conditions, even when standing alone against overwhelming majorities in the United Nations. Ben-Gurion had indeed torn up the armistice at the time of the attack, saying that it no longer existed and must be replaced by a negotiated peace. Because Egypt and other Arab states would not talk peace with Israel, and the United Nations would not compel them to do so, it came down to a question of what kind of *de facto* situations would emerge in regard to the withdrawal of Israel forces, the control of the entrance to the Gulf of Aqaba, and the status of the Gaza strip.

Israel retreated step by step. World opinion may have had some influence. The threats and pressure from the Soviet Union could not be ignored. But the big factor was the "friendly persuasion" of the United States. Ben-Gurion could not afford to alienate the country on which Israel depended for its economic existence, nor could he lightly take the responsibility for the world conflict which might result from failure to heed warnings from Washington. On the question of Sinai, Israel was not disposed to hold out and took the decision to withdraw from all but the Sharm el-Sheikh area opposite the Strait of Tiran at the entrance to the Gulf of Aqaba. It would have preferred some scheme for the internationalization or demilitarization of Sinai, but no support developed for limiting Egyptian sovereignty in this territory which had always been a part of Egypt.

On Aqaba and Gaza, however, Israel was less accommodating. Freedom of navigation to and from the port of Elath through the Gulf of Aqaba had become, in Israel's eyes, a matter of life and death. As for the Gaza strip, Israel's position was firm in its insistence on administering

this territory, never a part of Egypt, which had been used
as a base for raids against Israel. On these two questions
the authority and negotiating abilities of the Secretary-
General were not enough to bring a solution. The indicated next step was the voting of sanctions by the United
Nations, which the Arab-Asian bloc was urging. It was at
this point that the United States felt compelled to step
in and take an active role. The question of sanctions was
a dangerous one, both internationally and domestically.
The Administration did not wish to be caught between
the General Assembly and the United States Congress,
where sentiment was against sanctions. It did not wish to
lose the political gains it had made in the Middle East and
Asia by its stand against aggression. On the other hand it
did not wish to see a renewal of the fighting and recognized
that Israel, on these two questions, had some legal and
political justification for its position.

Following a diplomatic note from Secretary Dulles
which offered Israel something beside moral precepts, direct negotiations produced a set of understandings on the
basis of which Israel agreed to withdraw its troops from
Sharm el-Sheikh and its troops and administration from
Gaza.[12] It is not quite certain just what the force of these
commitments, or understandings, or "not unreasonable
expectations" may be. Yet because they did represent a
price for Israel's withdrawal, and were assumed publicly
in the full view of American and world opinion, they
were not mere words to be forgotten or interpreted away.
Israel soon experienced some disillusionment in that the
expectation of a U.N. administration for the Gaza strip
proved illusory when the softness of U.S. policy and of
Mr. Hammarskjold's handling of Egypt opened the door

[12] Aide memoire handed to Israeli Ambassador Eban by Secretary of State
Dulles, February 11, 1957, in Department of State, *United States Policy in
the Middle East, September 1956–June 1957, Documents* (Washington:
G.P.O., 1957), pp. 290-292; statement by Ambassador Lodge to the U.N.
General Assembly, March 1, 1957 (same, pp. 322-327).

for Abdel Nasser to step in and take over.[13] Yet the U.N.E.F. remained in the Gaza strip and at Sharm el-Sheikh, for how long no one could be sure. Even should they be withdrawn, the United States still had assumed a strong moral commitment to see to it that the right of "innocent passage" through the Strait of Tiran was maintained (unless the International Court of Justice should rule differently), and that Egypt did not use the Gaza strip as a base for renewed attacks of the fedayeen on Israel.

With the final withdrawal of Israel troops behind the old armistice line the crisis may be said to have reached its end. Peace in the Middle East, in the sense of the absence of large-scale military operations, had been restored, and a world conflict had been avoided. There was some possibility that the presence of the U.N.E.F. on the border, although not admitted to Israel's side of it, might cut down the volume of raids and sudden death. But the world was no nearer to solutions on Suez and on Palestine than it had been before the crisis broke out. The hostility between Israel and the Arab states was deeper than ever. Aside from the psychological effects of Israel's spectacular *Blitzkrieg* and Abdel Nasser's success in snatching political victory from military defeat, things were more or less back where they were before the fighting started.

Looked at in the larger sense of the world balance, however, the results of the crisis were no mere restoration of the *status quo*. For the debacle of Britain and France and the advance of Soviet influence into the Middle East forced a new and urgent decision on the United States. Even as it was upholding the law of the Charter against its Western European allies it had to find some way to save vital Western interests in the Middle East and to redefine its own role there. The first step along this way was the proposal which came to be called the Eisenhower Doctrine.

[13] Hamilton Fish Armstrong, "The U. N. Experience in Gaza," *Foreign Affairs*, v. 35 (July 1957), pp. 600-619.

Chapter 9

THE EISENHOWER DOCTRINE

THE CRISIS of 1956 patently called for a review of American policy in the Middle East. After the excitement of the immediate reaction to the outbreak of hostilities, the appeal to the United Nations and the acceptance of a cease-fire, official Washington had to take stock of certain very ominous facts. One was that Great Britain had virtually abdicated its role as a great power in the Middle East. Another was that the Soviet Union had intervened in the crisis, not by armed force but still strongly enough to raise justified fears that the Kremlin would take full advantage of the division among the Western allies and push forward just as fast and as far as it could. The Soviet "ultimatums" to Britain, France and Israel and the threat to send "volunteers" had enhanced Soviet prestige throughout the Arab world. Egypt and Syria seemed more and more receptive to Soviet influence and suggestions.

The strong stand of the United States against the aggression of its major European allies, in the absence of any previously formulated and plainly understood American determination to keep Soviet power out of the area, presented Moscow with opportunities to move in ostensibly as a defender of the U.N. Charter and of the rights of small nations. Hence the United States, simultaneously with its own efforts and those of Mr. Hammarskjold to restore peace and some measure of stability, had to look to the graver danger of the expansion of Soviet power. Certain steps of an emergency nature were taken as the occasion demanded: the public and private warnings to Moscow that the sending of Soviet "volunteers" to Egypt would be met by force, and the warning that any threat to the territorial integrity or political independence of the states of the northern tier (Turkey, Iraq, Iran and Pakistan) would be viewed by the United States with "the utmost gravity." [1] These four states, however, and the situation itself, demanded a more comprehensive statement of American policy for the Middle East, one which would definitely commit the American people to its defense. Joining the Baghdad Pact, strongly urged by the northern tier states, might have been one way to do it, but for various reasons this course had been rejected, principally because it would further alienate Egypt and other Arab states. Other possible ways would have been a statement of policy in a public speech by the President, a formal communication to the United Nations, a series of diplomatic notes, or an increased aid program. The Administration wisely chose a method which would associate the Congress with the President in a solemn declaration of national intent.

The problem was one of a new public posture rather than of new policies, although policies could not be exactly the same because of the change in the context and the assumption of new responsibilities. It had been, after all, an American objective for some years to prevent the advance of Soviet power into the Middle East. That objective was implicit in the Truman Doctrine of 1947. It had been the basis for the programs of military and economic assistance carried on since that time. The State Department and other agencies concerned wished to keep on with the policies and programs they felt were achieving the basic objective. But to do so they needed more authority and more money, and they needed the assurance of backing by the Congress. The Administration chose the method of a public law which would combine a declaration of policy extending the "security frontiers" of the United States across the Middle Eastern gap between NATO and SEATO

[1] Department of State, *United States Policy in the Middle East, September 1956–June 1957, Documents* (Washington: G.P.O., 1957), pp. 419–420; John R. Beal, *John Foster Dulles* (New York: Harper, 1957), pp. 263, 287.

with a dramatization of the aid programs already in existence and increased flexibility in their future use.

The President's Proposals

President Eisenhower made the specific proposals in his special message to Congress on January 5, 1957. The United States, he said, must make more evident its willingness to support the sovereignty and independence of each and every nation of the Middle East against the predatory desires of "international communism," i.e., the Soviet Union. The proposed joint resolution would do three things: (1) authorize the President to employ as he deems necessary the armed forces of the United States to secure and protect the integrity and independence of any nation or group of nations in the general area of the Middle East requesting such aid against overt armed aggression from any nation controlled by international communism; (2) authorize the Executive to undertake programs of military assistance to any nation or group of nations in that area desiring such aid; (3) authorize cooperation with any nation or group of nations in the development of economic strength for the maintenance of national independence. The President also requested specific authority to spend $200 million of already appropriated funds for military and economic aid in the Middle East, free of the restrictions of existing legislation.

Although there was never much doubt that the resolution would be adopted by the Congress in substantially the form proposed—not to have passed it after the President had publicly placed it before the world as a necessity would have been a supreme gesture of irresponsibility—it ran into some rough weather in the Senate Foreign Relations Committee and was severely criticized by a number of prominent Democrats including a former Secretary of State, Dean Acheson. The hearings in both Houses brought out a variety of points on which the new "doctrine," as it came to be called, was seriously challenged. Some of the criticism had its origin in domestic politics or in general dissatisfaction with the way in which the Secretary of State had handled Middle Eastern affairs in the previous year or two. But most of the arguments went to the substance of the proposals and should be considered in any effort to evaluate the doctrine as national policy.

Debate on the Doctrine

It was said that the Soviet threat was not military and that it was therefore unwise to build a policy on the contingency of an "overt armed aggression" that probably would not take place. Another point was that the real danger was subversion, against which the doctrine offered no sure defense. Some critics objected to its unilateral character, in that it avoided a regional treaty arrangement or "bypassed" the United Nations. Others pointed out that in its limitation to "Communist aggression" it overlooked the more real danger arising from conflicts that arose in other ways, as recent events had shown. Perhaps the most justified criticism was that the new doctrine ignored the specific problems like Palestine and Suez that had made it possible for the Soviet Union to build up its influence in the area, not by force of arms but by well timed political moves.

Secretary Dulles vigorously defended the proposed doctrine against these criticisms. While an overt Soviet attack in the Middle East might not seem imminent, the Soviet Union had the means to attack and he preferred not to wait until an attack occurred in order to be sure it was going to occur; the important thing was to deter it by removing the danger of miscalculation. This end could not be achieved with the desired speed by the conclusion of security treaties "without involving ourselves in controversies which are of a local character, and do not involve international communism;" the Administration had seriously considered joining the Baghdad Pact but decided against it largely on those grounds. As for the United

Nations, the Administration's proposal had provided that the use of United States forces should be consonant with the Charter and with the actions and recommendations of the United Nations, and should not affect the authority and responsibility of the Security Council to take such action as it deemed necessary. While hoping that it would be possible to act through the United Nations, Mr. Dulles was not willing to be tied down by a requirement to do so: "We must have this alternative." As to the threat of subversion, the Secretary said that the United States could not intervene with force if there were no overt aggression. The way to deal with that threat was by the three-pronged policy of reducing the fear of armed attack, helping non-Communist governments to build adequate internal security forces, and fostering economic progress to remove the causes of popular discontent. Finally, Mr. Dulles rejected the proposal that the commitment should be expanded to cover aggression within the region, by the Arab states against Israel or vice versa, on the ground that in such a local controversy "international communism" would not be directly involved and the problem would be suitably handled by the United Nations.[2]

The official reasoning on all these points tended to dismiss too lightly the many complicating factors inherent in the Middle Eastern situation and to place too much value on declarations as effective policy. It overstressed the contingency of overt aggression and thus by implication slighted others. Still, the Administration made its case for a strong declaration of intent.

The Senate, concerned over the constitutional aspects

[2] *Economic and Military Cooperation with Nations in the General Area of the Middle East,* Hearings on H. J. Res. 117, U.S. House Committee on Foreign Affairs, 85th Cong., 1st sess., January 7-22, 1957 (Washington: G.P.O., 1957), pp. 13-17, 141, 152, and *passim.* (Hereafter referred to as House Hearings on the Eisenhower Doctrine.) *The President's Proposal on the Middle East,* Hearings on S. J. Res. 19 and H. J. Res. 117, U.S. Senate Committees on Foreign Relations and Armed Services, 85th Cong., 1st sess., January 14–February 4, 1957 (Washington: G.P.O., 1957), pp. 48-50, 256, 264-265, 334, and *passim.* (Hereafter referred to as Senate Hearings on the Eisenhower Doctrine.)

of a specific legislative grant of authority to the President to employ the armed forces, changed the resolution to read that the United States "is prepared to use its armed forces" to assist on request any Middle Eastern nation subjected to overt attack by a state controlled by international communism. With this change, and another one giving a little more recognition to the possibility of action through the United Nations, both houses passed the resolution and the Eisenhower Doctrine became law.[3]

Evaluation

The sharp criticisms of the doctrine in the course of the two months' discussion that preceded its adoption should not obscure the general agreement with its purposes. Even those Democratic Senators who were so caustic in pointing to its inadequacies were at one with the President and the Secretary of State in seeing the need for a public statement of policy that would place the authority of the Congress behind the President and thus express a national decision to keep the Middle East out of the Soviet orbit. Mr. Acheson found some features of the Administration's proposal unnecessary, others unwise, even reckless. Secretary Dulles found Mr. Acheson's proposed substitute, a concurrent resolution simply stating the sense of the Congress, to be dangerous, defective, and lacking in the grant of authority needed to deal with the situation. But there was no substantial difference as to the need for the United States to take on the role of leadership in the Middle East.

In terms of power, the United States had to fill the "vacuum" resulting from the British retreats and withdrawals. Arab leaders, obsessed by fears of a new colonialism replacing the old, took exception to that phrase, asserting that if there were any vacuum to fill, the Middle Eastern nations themselves would fill it. Secretary Dulles, extremely sensitive to such views and to Arab and Soviet propaganda based on them, took pains to avoid the phrase

[3] *Public Law* 85-7, 85th Cong., 1st sess., H. J. Res. 117 (March 9, 1957).

and to disclaim all intention to dominate other nations or to prolong or restore methods and policies associated with colonialism. Yet there was no disguising the fact that in the world balance of power between the Soviet-Communist world and the West a vacuum had been created, and that if American power did not fill it Soviet power would. No talk about the strength of the Middle Eastern nations themselves could have real meaning in terms of their ability to hold off Soviet power unaided. The United States, to provide the necessary counterweight, did not have to move into the Middle East in the sense of controlling the destiny of its peoples. But the presence of American power had to be felt there, through commitments and through the ability and the will to protect the area against Soviet encroachment.

These were not easy distinctions to make. British opinion took a certain wry satisfaction in the fact that the United States, so soon after taking Britain to task for unilateral intervention, found it necessary to proclaim what looked like a doctrine of unilateral intervention of its own. American officials took care to point out that the United States would act only on the request of a Middle Eastern government, and that going in to protect a state against Communist aggression was very different from going in with bombs to impose one's will. Be that as it may, there was no blinking the fact that the United States was now assuming virtually the entire responsibility, on behalf of the West, for the task of holding for the free world a huge area bristling with unsolved problems and too weak to provide for its own defense.

In the long view it may not be of great importance just what the Eisenhower Doctrine says on paper. The provision for the use of American armed forces was important in extending the "warning system" which in other regions takes the form of a series of regional and bilateral mutual assistance treaties. It may have helped somewhat in eliminating the danger of miscalculation by the Soviet leadership of the American reaction to an aggression, although the United States was already substantially committed through its special relationships with the Baghdad Pact countries, and we had no strong reason to expect the Soviet leaders would be any more inclined to embark on direct aggression in the absence of the doctrine than with it in existence. The provision covering aggression on the part of a Soviet satellite might prevent the spread of communism by force once it got a foothold in Syria or some other Middle Eastern state, but it would not prevent its being implanted there or elsewhere by means other than overt aggression. The provisions for military and economic aid involved no new departure. Such programs had not prevented the steady deterioration of the Western position or the solid gains of the Soviet Union in the area.[4] As many observers pointed out, however, the doctrine was not a policy or a complete program of action but only a beginning.

President Eisenhower's message, in what Dean Acheson called "conservatively speaking . . . the outstanding understatement of 1957," said: "This program will not solve all the problems of the Middle East." It might not solve any of them. It deliberately avoided such questions as Suez, the Arab-Israel conflict, and the future of the Baghdad Pact.

It is only fair to point out, however, that the Administration itself, judging by its conduct, did not regard the doctrine as an isolated step. It was part of a larger complex of moves which included strengthening (but not joining) the Baghdad Pact, continuing to supply arms to Arab states but not to Israel, and wooing certain Arab leaders

---

[4] The authority to spend $200 million in already appropriated funds without restrictions was useful in giving the Administration needed flexibility but of no new significance as a matter of basic policy, although the President's announced determination to ask in future aid programs for funds not limited to a particular fiscal year was an important indication of the intention to continue aid programs in the future. Secretary Dulles envisaged having to spend more money in the Middle East in the next few years than previously. (Senate Hearings on the Eisenhower Doctrine, cited, pp. 45-46, 375.)

such as King Saud as a means of counterbalancing the leadership of Egypt and Abdel Nasser.

If the Eisenhower Doctrine was not a policy, it supplied the framework for a policy. It made clear to potential enemies, to friends, and to all the peoples of the Middle East that the United States henceforth would take the lead in the defense of the whole Middle East. It established certain rules under which the game would be played. In highlighting the dangerous consequences of a resort to force by the Soviets or their satellites, it set the stage for a cold-war competition in which the United States would presumably use all the resources at its disposal. Furthermore, it offered to the Middle Eastern nations themselves more than the role of spectators, or victims, of such competition between great powers. To both allies and uncommitted states in the area it offered assistance in the task of consolidating and defending their own independence. It was a necessary and constructive step, though a belated one, in the development of an American policy for the Middle East. If interpreted rigidly, however, and if not completed and supplemented by a whole series of policies, it might prove largely irrelevant to the specific challenges of the future.

Part Two
PRESENT AND FUTURE

Chapter 10

THE MEANING OF DEFENSE

DEFENSE of the Middle East is a broad concept which cannot be profitably considered from the narrow angle of vision provided by any one of its many aspects. It must be considered in terms of the general objective, as a standard against which policies in this or that field may be tested and related to one another. We are not concerned merely with what to defend and how to defend it in the case of war. That is part of the problem, but what is required is a national strategy adequate to meet whatever situations develop, whether or not they involve military operations.

The aim of the Soviet leadership, stated in the simplest form, has been first to deny the Middle East to the West and ultimately to bring it under its own domination. While Stalin in his last years took no strong initiative to push forward toward those goals, his successors have now made this the main object of their cold-war strategy. They have appraised the Middle East correctly as probably the softest spot in the whole Western protective system, and in Western Europe's dependence on Middle Eastern oil they see its Achilles' heel. With remarkable swiftness they have capitalized on events, at no great cost or risk to themselves, to establish Soviet influence in the area more strongly than ever before.

Should the trend continue and the Middle East fall into Soviet hands, it would be a catastrophe for the United States and the Western world. The whole uncommitted world would see the writing on the wall. NATO would be outflanked. Once in control of Middle Eastern oil, Moscow would have its grip on Europe's jugular vein. It could hardly be long before our European allies would be forced into accommodation on Soviet terms, leaving the United States isolated. In the words of the President, Soviet control of the Middle East "would have the most adverse, if not disastrous, effect upon our own nation's economic life and political prospects."[1] He might have added, without exaggeration, upon our national security and our survival as a free nation.

The term "defense" to some may seem too passive or negative, indicative of a willingness to leave all initiative to the other side. It need not be so interpreted. The cold war is not one of fixed positions. There is inevitably a mixture of the offensive and the defensive in our whole policy toward the Soviet Union. Nevertheless, the military or football maxim that the best defense is a good offense does not really fit the situation at hand. We are trying to preserve the *status quo* in the sense of preventing an upset in the existing balance of power. The danger is that the Middle East will be lost to the free world. There may be various ways of countering that danger, some of them not confined to the geographic area of the Middle East itself. We are interested in the potential impact of the Middle East on the Soviet Union as well as in coping with the actual impact of the Soviet Union on the Middle East. Initiatives will have to be taken. Gains the Soviets have already made will have to be whittled down. But the problem remains, unless we are driven to the ultimate arbitrament of war, essentially one of defense.

What, then, are we trying to defend? First, we are defending territory of great strategic importance, which if it fell into the hands of a hostile great power would certainly be used against us. Second, we are defending resources, especially oil, essential to the economy of Western Europe and thus indirectly of great importance to the United States. Third, we are defending peoples against domination by outside powers. We recognize their right to be

[1] Message to Congress on the "Eisenhower Doctrine," January 5, 1957, Department of State, *United States Policy in the Middle East, September 1956–June 1957, Documents* (Washington: G.P.O., 1957), pp. 15-23.

independent and to run their own affairs. We cannot afford to see that independence taken from them or to see them, in ignorance or in recklessness, give it away. Fourth, we are defending certain principles, which are expressed in the Preamble and first two Articles of the Charter of the United Nations. Ideals are not always a practical guide for foreign policy, but they are nevertheless a part of our being as a nation and therefore an element in the defense of any part of the free world against forces dedicated to their destruction. The United States must seek the kind of world in which its own and other free societies can prosper.

No simple policy formula, such as "building a position of strength" or "partnership in collective security," provides the key to all four of these aspects of defense—nor indeed to any one of them. For the policies and methods which serve one purpose often handicap the pursuit of another, and the policy-maker is inevitably driven to the acceptance of compromises and half-measures. All policies, moreover, will depend in large degree on the cooperation of the peoples of the Middle East. While those peoples do, in general, want the same things the United States wants for them—security, independence, a better life—they do not always interpret them as we do, and like any group of national states they have conflicting interests and ambitions. They have territorial disputes and dynastic rivalries growing out of the distant or the recent past; their societies are wracked by the tensions of a revolutionary time that has seen the breakup of empires, the disintegration of old institutions, the rising expectations of the displaced and the disinherited, and the ominous spread of Communist propaganda and influence.

All this sets real limitations on what the United States can do in the Middle East, where it cannot simply impose its will but must try to attain its ends by persuasion. We may as well recognize that there will be no uniformly enthusiastic support on the part of the Middle Eastern nations for a common front against communism or for the maintenance of a strong military position against the Soviet Union. Governments and peoples are going to look at American proposals in the light of their own interests as they see them. Some of their leaders have sought Soviet support and will continue to do so if it suits their own purposes. The people will flirt with communism if they can find no more promising alternative. Oil-producing countries will see the oil industry from the viewpoint of what benefit they derive from it, not from that of the importance of oil to the West; that very importance, indeed, is a continuing temptation to raise their own demands. We shall find ourselves caught in the middle of the hatreds and conflicts of the area. Close ties with some nations will mean greater antagonism from others. Seeking stability or relief of pressures through the promotion of settlements of disputes, we shall find ourselves abused by both sides. Add to this the fact that, as a great power, more will be expected of the United States than it can possibly do. As a contestant in the cold war, its motives will often be suspect. As a representative of the West, allied with Western Europe both culturally and politically, it cannot avoid the charge of "imperialism."

Defense, then, is a complex and many-sided problem. In its first dimension it means maintaining a posture and pursuing a policy toward the Soviets that will influence their thinking and their policies. In its other dimensions it is a search for the cooperation of the Middle Eastern peoples, an attempt to bring them to a stable modus vivendi among themselves and with the West, and an effort to encourage trends which will reduce their vulnerability to attack or subversion. Thus we cannot ignore such questions as the nature of their governments, the impact of popular demands and political currents, their ignorance of Communist tactics, their willingness or unwillingness to take risks, their different sets of values. It is obvious that no simple concept or slogan such as "anti-communism," or "collective security," or "reliance on our friends," or "sympathy with rising nationalism" or "toughness" will suffice as a criterion for policy amid those complexities. On the other hand, the United States cannot just go along from day to day meeting crises as they arrive and trying to make the best of it. A certain amount of trial and error is inevitable; we cannot always be consistent. But we have to have some guidelines. To employ the terminology of the military, a strategy of defense has to have a strategic concept on which to rest and a general estimate of the situation in which it is to be applied.

A strategic concept for the Middle East must be a part of a global policy, as the Middle East does not exist for us in isolation. The global policy which the United States has developed since 1946 under both Democratic and Republican leadership is, briefly, to prevent further expansion of the Soviet-Communist empire (including its Chinese extension) and, while avoiding a major war which would in this nuclear age be a catastrophe for civilization, to compete with that empire, both in the free world and to the extent possible in the Communist world, to the end of shifting the world balance in favor of the free nations and ultimately dissipating the mortal threat to our security and freedom which the combined power and policies of the Soviet-Communist empire represent.

As a national strategy this policy seems sound. Advocates of a more "positive" policy that would eliminate the threat or "win the cold war" in some fixed period have been proponents, knowingly or unknowingly, of preventive war; those who have been inclined to a reduction of effort or a willingness to accept Communist terms at face value must be accounted as advocates of a policy of unjustified and intolerable risk. Yet, however sound the global policy may be in conception, its success will depend on its application in the critical areas of the world, among them the Middle East. The problem is to find the approach and to work out the policies in those areas which will support the grand strategy and at the same time take full account of the realities of the local scene.

Policy-making is a series of choices. Rarely is the choice

between one course bound to lead to success and another bound to bring failure. More often than not it is a choice between evils in a situation beyond our ability to control. Almost every decision involves the element of chance and of risk. All the more necessary then, amid the cross-currents of Middle Eastern politics, are such guidelines as will minimize the risks of failure by being based on a sound analysis of the forces at work there. When is consistency over the long run demanded, and when is it better to keep a free hand to exploit situations as they arise? What is the right balance, the right combination of policies that will take us where we want to go? It will have to be a combination, for the great problems that have to be faced—deterrence of war, alliances, the Arab-Israel conflict, oil, economic development, Soviet penetration—are all interrelated. What we do on one affects all the others. This truth will become evident as the various aspects of "defense" are analyzed. It is only by such an analysis, which recognizes the complexities of the Middle East environment and relates them to the objectives we seek, that we can reach conclusions that may be tenable and come to specific policy recommendations that may be sound.

Chapter 11

THE MILITARY PROBLEM:
STRATEGY

"So far as the sheer value of territory is concerned there is no more strategically important area in the world. . . ." These frequently quoted words of General Dwight Eisenhower with reference to the Middle East were spoken in 1951.[1] It is a conclusion which would seem to be the lesson of history. Over the centuries the great powers of the world have sought to establish themselves in this critically situated zone astride the communications linking three continents and two oceans. In and across it France, Britain and Russia struggled for positions of vantage throughout the 19th century. It was in the Middle East that the Western Allies in World War I first cracked the resistance of the Central Powers and opened the way for Germany's ultimate defeat. It was by holding the Middle East in World War II that they opened a vital supply route to Russia, prevented a junction of German and Japanese forces, and made possible the assault on Europe from the south. Its role in any future war between the West and the Soviet Union would seem to be crucial.

"Defense of the Middle East" has therefore been an accepted concept in Western military thinking. As we work out a military policy, however, it may not be sufficient to look only at the lessons of history or to be aware of the undoubted general strategic importance of the area in the world balance. We have to consider whether the great scientific and technological revolution which has changed the nature of weapons and of warfare has also

[1] *United States Foreign-Aid Programs in Europe,* Hearings before a subcommittee of the U.S. Senate Committee on Foreign Relations, 82nd Cong., 1st sess., July 7-23, 1951 (Washington: G.P.O., 1951), p. 277.

changed the nature of Middle Eastern geography, at least from the military viewpoint. We have to estimate the character of the military threat, the range of Soviet capabilities and intentions, and the various situations with which the United States may be confronted. Specifically, what kind of war is possible or probable in the Middle East, and how should we prepare for it? Finally, how can military policy play its part in the prevention of war and serve the national strategy in the cold war?

The United States cannot have a strategy for the Middle East separate from its world-wide defense problem. It faces Soviet-Communist power on a continuous front all the way round the world. In pursuit of the national strategy aimed at holding that line against further encroachment the United States has maintained a formidable military establishment, acquired strategic bases at various points on the world map, stationed armed forces in foreign countries, and concluded bilateral or multilateral alliances with forty-two other states. The Middle East has its place in this system, in the form of our understandings with a number of governments, association with the Baghdad Pact, bases, and the recently adopted Eisenhower Doctrine. A few comments on the military commitments involved in the new doctrine would be in order before we proceed to an analysis of the strategic problems involved in a military policy for the Middle East, a policy which should contribute to global strategy and at the same time be adequate to meet specific military situations likely to arise in that particular region.

The doctrine represents a general declaration of intent that can serve both purposes: to extend and strengthen the global security system by closing what was an obvious gap in it and to place the United States in a position to cope with crises arising from aggression in the Middle East itself. Without specifically committing the United States to take military action automatically, one of the three main points of the resolution states: ". . . the United States regards as vital to the national interest and world peace the preservation of the independence and integrity of the nations of the Middle East. To this end, if the President determines the necessity thereof, the United States is prepared to use its armed forces to assist any such nation or group of such nations requesting assistance against armed aggression from any country controlled by international communism." [2] The effect is publicly and formally, although not by treaty, to extend to the Middle East the diplomatic warning system already set up along other parts of the periphery of the Soviet-Communist bloc through NATO, SEATO and the series of alliances in the Western Pacific.

Henceforward, Secretary Dulles made quite clear in his testimony on the resolution, as did members of Congress in their discussion of it, any overt aggression in the Middle East by the Soviet Union or by a state which we chose to consider "controlled by international communism" would be met with armed force. The United States would act in accordance with U.N. resolutions if they were adequate to the situation; if not, it would be free to act in cooperation with the nations of the area in collective self-defense under Article 51 of the U.N. Charter.[3] Although limited to situations where aid is requested by the victim of aggression, and thus open to possible circumvention, insofar as the Soviet military threat is concerned the doctrine does represent a new and significant commitment. To give it meaning, however, we must devise effective military policies to back it up.

Soviet Capabilities and Intentions

The traditional military estimate of any situation includes an analysis of the enemy's capabilities and of his intentions. Now there is little doubt, if we look at the number of its divisions and its aircraft, of the Soviet Un-

[2] *Public Law* 85-7, 85th Cong., 1st sess., H. J. Res. 117 (March 9, 1957).
[3] House Hearings on the Eisenhower Doctrine, cited, pp. 5, 12; Senate Hearings on the Eisenhower Doctrine, cited, pp. 258, 284, 313, 335.

ion's capability of mounting an attack in the Middle East. Problems of supply would be difficult, but against any forces that could now be thrown into the field to oppose them, Soviet forces probably could reach the Mediterranean and the Persian Gulf within a few weeks. Of such possibilities our planning for defense or counterstrategy must take account, but planning makes sense only if it includes a weighing of the likelihood and circumstances of an attack, of the form it might take, and of what measures would dissuade the Soviet leadership from undertaking it at all. In other words, it rests on a careful consideration of Soviet intentions as affected by developments both within the Soviet bloc and in the Middle East and by the policies and posture of the United States and its allies.

We cannot, of course, have any feelings of assurance about Soviet intentions. Soviet history is replete with drastic and dramatic shifts not always foreseen by the outside world. Yet all the evidence of recent years points to the disinclination of the Moscow leadership to launch a major military attack on the Middle East alone. As we have seen, Stalin avoided any direct aggression,[4] and his successors have thus far chosen other ways of advancing Soviet power southward. The very fact that they have made impressive gains without resort to armed force, and are preaching sweet reason and peaceful coexistence throughout the world, makes a direct attack seem even more improbable. Furthermore, because they know the power of nuclear weapons, the Soviet leaders have every reason to be as cautious as ever in making decisions that could lead to all-out war and the resulting devastation of the Soviet Union itself. The threat of a conflict with the United States in case of an aggression in the Middle East has been present for the last decade. Now, although the Eisenhower Doctrine says nothing about the magnitude of the American reaction, its adoption should leave little doubt in the minds of the Soviet leaders that a decision to

[4] See above, Chapter 2, pp. 20-28.

launch an invasion of the Middle East in force would be the equivalent of a deliberate decision for general war.[5]

The Middle East in a General War

Thus the strategy for countering the risk of a major Soviet aggression in the Middle East resolves itself into the maintenance of the over-all deterrent to a Soviet decision for general war on any grounds, or for policies carrying an obvious risk of general war. It is safe to predict that the Soviet leaders will not take that decision unless at some time they should become convinced either that an American attack on the Soviet Union was imminent or that the United States lacked the capacity or the will to retaliate. On both counts it is up to the United States, by its words and by its conduct, to influence their decision against war.

The great deterrent, of course, resides in America's retaliatory striking power, so dispersed and defended that it can still overcome Soviet defenses and inflict unacceptable damage on the U.S.S.R. even if subjected to surprise attack. It does not rest on any specific military position in the Middle East itself, although there is no doubt that evidence of the seriousness of the American commitment there, in the form of a strong military position, may be a significant factor in Moscow's calculation of risks and thus in maintaining the deterrent.

Military planners, of course, have to consider the possibility that the deterrent will not deter. They must have plans to fight if war is forced upon us, including plans for the Middle East. Here there are two main possibilities: first, that Soviet forces attack, in the Middle East or elsewhere, and a situation of general war develops; second,

[5] According to Admiral Radford, any overt attack in force on the Middle East by Russian forces would start World War III. (House Hearings on the Eisenhower Doctrine, cited, pp. 80, 89.) It is a point on which conclusions cannot be categorical, for the American reaction would depend on the nature of the challenge as well as on the scope of the attack; but, without maintaining that "massive retaliation" would be instantaneous, one can still reasonably conclude that Admiral Radford's view is correct.

that they attack in the Middle East on a limited scale, and the United States finds itself unable or unwilling to reply by all-out war. These considerations bring us into the whole controversial question of the shape future wars will take and the strategic doctrine and military posture the United States should develop in order to ensure its security. It cannot be the purpose of a book on policy in the Middle East to go deeply into the many ramifications of that question. It is, nevertheless, necessary to make some general judgments on it, in order to talk at all about strategy in the Middle East. And it is possible that consideration of the nature of the military problems in that area may throw some light on the broader question of strategic doctrine.

With respect to the first possibility, general war, we can hardly do more than guess at the shape of such a war because of the revolutionary implications of missiles and nuclear weapons, to which both sides, in the absence of an effective agreement for their control, are becoming more and more committed. Any attempt to see beyond the vast destruction that would be inflicted with such weapons in the initial stages of an all-out war, probably smashing beyond recognition not only the Soviet Union but also our own society and Western civilization, tends to drive one's thinking back to President Eisenhower's dictum that "there is no alternative to peace." Perhaps the only sound conclusion is that once such a war breaks out all policies have failed and mankind is lost. Although we have a duty to contemplate that frightful holocaust and the possible later stages of such a war, the whole prospect lends an air of unreality to the traditional type of war planning for a theater like the Middle East.

That area would doubtless play a part in the exchange of nuclear blows so long as the West held bases there. We would use them as long as we could, which might not be for long. The Soviets would try to knock them out and might try to seize with airborne troops any they could not destroy with bombs or missiles. That much is more or less predictable. The speculation comes on whether Soviet armies would invade the Middle East in force and whether in that event the area could, and should, be defended. It is at least doubtful that the Soviets, while engaged in an all-out struggle to conquer Europe and to survive under a hail of nuclear destruction at home, would undertake a major invasion across rugged mountains and vast deserts in order to hold an area where their forces would be difficult to supply and the possession of which would not have any early decisive effect on the outcome of the war. Even the denial of Middle Eastern oil resources to the West would not cripple, though it would inconvenience, the Western military effort, and this could be more cheaply done by bombing than by a land campaign; moreover, the Soviets could turn the oil resources to their own use, if they needed them at all, only if they could capture the installations intact, protect them against counterbombing, and move the oil to where they needed it. If each side were aiming massive nuclear blows at the heartland of the other, would either be much concerned with the Middle Eastern theater?

The very horrors of a general nuclear war, however, might produce a situation in which events in that theater could be of great importance. Man's capacity for mass destruction may not be infinite. It is not impossible that, once a nuclear war started and the world had a taste of it, public pressure on all sides for surcease, on almost any terms, would be irresistible. Whoever controlled the Middle East at that particular juncture might well remain in control of it. If Soviet forces had been able to overrun it, or could do so while a nuclear armistice was under discussion or even after it had been concluded, the shift in the world balance might eventually be disastrous for the West. It is also within the realm of possibility that restraint in nuclear bombing would be shown on both sides and that a kind of lower-case general war would be carried on for a time with "conventional" forces and smaller types of nuclear weapons.

These are contingencies that lend some aura of reality to Western military planning that has concerned itself with such contingencies as a defense of the "Armenian knot" in eastern Turkey, the line of the Taurus and Zagros Mountains, the Persian Gulf oil region or the Suez area, with this number of ground divisions and that number of tactical air wings. Much of the thinking along these lines, both British and American, has been rooted in strategic concepts based on the experience of the two world wars, with the added ingredient of atomic weapons as a means of achieving more firepower with less manpower. This has been the basis for the planning that was to have been the function of the proposed Middle East defense organization and that which now occupies the military committee of the Baghdad Pact. Essentially, the idea is that the Middle East must be held in a world war because it is strategically too valuable to lose. It might also be the best invasion route to the heart of Russia itself, making it possible to avoid the need of fighting mile by mile across the northern European plain from the west. The Middle East, in any war with the Soviet Union, lends itself to "grand flanking operations" by one side or the other. At a minimum, according to this line of thought, the West should have a strategy for holding the key points of the area: the Turkish Straits, Iskenderun, Suez, and the oil-producing region near the Persian Gulf.[6]

It may be said that all strategic planning is useful. No great power can risk planning only for one type of war when it may be faced in the event with a quite different kind. But we do have an obligation to assess relative probabilities and to avoid military thinking that is based only on habit and the wars of the past. The real question in devising an adequate military policy for a variety of hypothetical contingencies is one of judgment, in which probabilities, availability of resources, and political factors

[6] See British Information Services, *Defence of the Middle East* (I.D. 1181) (London, 1953); E. J. Kingston-McCloughry, *Global Strategy* (New York: Praeger, 1957), pp. 85-88.

must all be weighed. We cannot reach a state of "total security" by any feasible measures of military preparedness. Consideration of the effort to be made in meeting the requirements for this particular contingency, that of a Middle East campaign in a general war, should therefore be made in the light of what seems to be a reasonable estimate of the probabilities that such a campaign will be fought, and in the light of what is required of us in the way of a military posture to meet threats other than that of general war.

It is a reasonable conclusion that a major campaign in the Middle East as part of a general war would take place only if the over-all deterrent failed, if the Soviets decided to make the effort to conquer the Middle East as part of their strategy for the conduct of a general war, and if the Western powers chose to meet the challenge, in force, in that theater and had the means available to do so. Looked at in that way, it seems but an outside possibility, anything but a probability.

Limited War

Let us turn now to the other possible consequences of a Soviet attack, a limited war. The improbability of general war and the implausibility of plans to wage such a war in the Middle East, unfortunately, do not relieve the United States of the risk of a test of military strength in that area. "No alternative to peace" is an apt phrase in describing the manifest unwillingness of both the United States and the Soviet Union to resort to all-out war or to take actions certain or likely to provoke it. It is also a deceptive phrase in seeming to ignore a range of possibilities between peace and total nuclear war. The very awfulness of total war raises doubts as to the will of either side to take a decision certain to bring devastation upon itself in response to a challenge that is something less than a direct attack on its own homeland or on adjacent territory vital to its security. May not the tacit agreement to rule out general nuclear war, it has often been asked, increase the prospects of local hostilities in which both sides attempt to hold within tolerable limits the risks of a resort to massive nuclear blows? This possibility may be minimal in Europe, where the stakes are so high and the commitments so rigid. In the Middle East and Asia it is surely greater.

Conceivably the Soviet leaders might embark on a military move, perhaps in the form of a "police action to restore order" in some country or of the sending of "volunteer" detachments to help "national liberation forces" install a pro-Soviet regime in another, on the calculation that the United States would not take the terrible decision to reply to such a minor aggression by unleashing general war. That this type of contingency represents the real military challenge of the future is the theme of a number of recent studies of strategy in the nuclear age.[7] There is much logic in the argument. Yet the element of speculation is bound to be large on two counts: first, in attempting to calculate the actions and reactions of both sides on the basis of their future estimates of the risks involved; and second, in attempting to judge how hostilities may be limited in a period when both sides possess in quantity the whole "family" of nuclear weapons. No formula will tell us just what combination of forces in being and declarations of intent will deter this or that type of Soviet aggression, or whether the nuclear stalemate will convince the Soviet leadership that it has a greater freedom of action for minor military adventures now than in the past. No "code of limited war" can guarantee that any specific limits, in weapons or in geography, will be observed in fact. Human factors on both sides can upset all calculations.

Stalemate or not, it will be desirable to keep the risk of general war in the forefront of Soviet thinking, to establish the conviction that any attack in the Middle East *could* bring devastating nuclear retaliation, and that, even

---

[7] For example, Henry A. Kissinger, *Nuclear Weapons and Foreign Policy* (New York: Harper, for the Council on Foreign Relations, 1957); Robert E. Osgood, *Limited War: The Challenge to American Strategy* (Chicago: University of Chicago Press, 1957).

if it did not, limited hostilities would not be likely to remain limited; at any rate, the decision to keep them limited would not be solely within Soviet control. The Soviet leaders have a healthy respect for America's strategic power, and one may doubt their inclination to start "little wars" here and there in the hope of picking up odd bits of real estate, with all the risk this would involve of the destruction of everything they have built up over a forty-year span. As the Soviet Union borders directly on the Middle East, they could not act with satellite troops (unless they first made a satellite of a Middle Eastern country) but would presumably have to commit Soviet forces, additional reason for them to exercise caution. All these considerations point to the fact that American strategic striking power should continue to be of some significance in deterring local Soviet aggression in the Middle East. The Soviet leaders have not shown themselves reckless in testing our willingness to employ it.

Of course, the temptation may still be there. The "massive" deterrent must be credible to be effective, and as an act that could only mean mutual destruction it simply might cease to be credible. Too great a dependence on it could deprive the United States of the flexibility needed to meet all aspects of the Soviet threat, from limited war to unlimited propaganda. We have every reason, therefore, to remove the temptation by developing and maintaining the means of meeting a "controlled" aggression successfully without resort to all-out war. The mere existence of those means should have the effect of discouraging Soviet adventures and lessening the risk that the Soviet leaders may come to count on a paralysis of American will.

The maximum deterrent effect, then, should come from creating in the minds of the Soviet leadership a mixture of uncertainty and certainty: uncertainty whether a local aggression might not result in general war, and certainty that even if it did not, the United States could and would react with such force locally that it would be clear in advance that aggression would not pay. The uncertainty, of course, has the disadvantage of working both ways: the creation of uncertainty in the mind of the enemy can also produce uncertainty in the minds of the American people.

These considerations, of course, apply to the contingency of limited war anywhere on the globe. While it is perhaps a more plausible eventuality on the borders of Communist China than on those of the Soviet Union, such experimentation on the part of the Soviet leaders is by no means to be ruled out, and the Middle East is the most likely scene of their choice. The many forms which the experiments might take necessarily complicate the task of finding a strategy adequate to all the possibilities. We cannot predict the locale and the circumstances with any certainty. Iran is a logical point of Soviet attack, but by no means the only one. The "limitations" of limited war, as to objectives, territory or weapons, might be quite different in different cases.

These uncertainties argue for powerful and flexible military capabilities on the part of the United States, so that the strategy found to be necessary or desirable at the time of crisis can be quickly carried out. That strategy almost certainly would require significant ground forces as well as sea and air power. If the fighting were of any duration, we should have to be sure of maintaining our own access to the region by sea, difficult as that might be under air attack, while exploiting the enemy's difficulties in moving his forces over the inhospitable terrain. These factors, less important in areas close to the Soviet borders, would apply increasingly as he attempted to move toward the Mediterranean and the Persian Gulf.

It is impossible to say in advance whether "tactical" nuclear weapons would be used; both political and military factors would bear on the decision made when the time came to make it. Insofar as possible the United States should put itself in a position of not being completely dependent on the use of nuclear weapons. Neither should it be handicapped by not being able to use them if they proved to be a necessary part of an effective military reply to an aggression. They may be particularly appropriate to the kind of military situation likely to arise in the Middle East—in which the enemy would be attempting to move forces through mountain passes or to seize, perhaps with airborne troops, certain key centers and routes of communication.

In general, the aim of the United States and its allies in a limited war would be to inflict such damage on the attacking forces as to deny them their objective—conquest of territory, the overthrow of a government, or whatever it might be—and to convince the Soviet leadership of the folly of the enterprise, while sparing the population of the victim country as much as possible and accepting no automatic ban on striking the enemy forces on their own territory. The possibility of a settlement, moreover, would always be held out as an alternative to further punishment and further risks.

One question will always be crucial: How big could a limited war in the Middle East become without inevitably casting off all limitations? The Soviet Government itself has warned that a little war would almost inevitably broaden into a big war.[8] If we could predict the interplay of currents making for the widening of any hostilities and those which impose caution based on mutual fear of all-out war, we would be better able to estimate the kind of strategy and the size of the military effort that might be required. Unfortunately, the question cannot be answered with any precision. It would seem wise, therefore, to take seriously the possibility that a "limited" war in the Middle East might reach a considerable scale without inevitably becoming general.

Other occasions for military action may arise from conflicts among the Middle Eastern states themselves. If the

[8] For example, see Premier Bulganin's letter to Premier Menderes of Turkey (*New York Times*, September 14, 1957). As the purposes of this and similar statements were to warn Turkey and the West of the dangers of intervening in Syria and to seek political gains through a war of nerves, one cannot be sure how much they represent a psychological tactic and how much a firm strategic conviction.

United States is determined to prevent any aggression by Israel or the Arab states across the armistice lines, or if it should guarantee newly agreed frontiers, it must have the means to give substance to that commitment. The existence of American forces, ready to act, would not derogate from the authority of the United Nations to uphold the Charter in the event of an outbreak of violence in the Middle East. Some American forces, indeed, might be part of a U.N. contingent or earmarked for it. The cardinal point is that they be available to support efforts "within and outside the United Nations," as the Tripartite Declaration of 1950 put it, to keep the peace. For such local "brush fires," if unchecked, tend to draw in outside powers backing one side or another and carry a real danger of bursting into general conflagration.

This is the real challenge to American military policy in the Middle East: to gain the flexibility necessary to cope with a variety of local military situations, whether they be the result of Soviet aggressive initiative or of intraregional conflicts which the Soviets hope to exploit. It is a question of having the kind of military power that can be applied in case of a movement of Soviet troops across the border into Iran, or the dispatch of Soviet "volunteers" to Syria, a clash between Syria and Turkey, or a new outbreak of war between Israel and its Arab neighbors.

Military Policy and the Cold War

Finally, if a small war is more likely than a big war, a continuation of the cold war is surely more likely than either. Many observers have pointed out, rightly, that there is no reason for the Kremlin to contemplate the use of force when it has made such great advances by other methods, such as diplomacy, propaganda and subversion. Local revolutionary situations, involving riots or civil war, may be clearly exploited and used for purposes of Communist penetration and ultimate control, all without resort to overt aggression. The Kurds, for example, who form a restive minority in Turkey, Iraq and Iran, might be used to further Soviet aims. Soviet agents have long been working among them.

Undoubtedly the main task of the West is to make more effective use of nonmilitary means in combating Soviet advances by such means. Secretary Dulles, in testifying on the Eisenhower Doctrine, pointed out that military force was not a proper weapon against Communist subversion of a Middle Eastern country. The United States could not, without violating the U.N. Charter, intervene with its armed forces to help a government deal with local Communists or to remove a group which had succeeded in taking over governmental authority.[9] Still, military policy does play a part in the cold war. It would be quite inadequate if it were directed only toward wars that do not take place and made no contribution to American objectives in existing and easily predictable situations short of war.

Many advantages, as events develop, will flow from having military force present in or near the area. It serves as a warning against intervention by others, as a stabilizing influence on local disputes, and as a means of showing the seriousness of the American interest. The very fact of a declared American policy of opposing armed aggression, with the means and will to back it up, should diminish the danger of subversion by giving confidence to local governments and depriving subversive forces of their strongest card, the threat of outside intervention on their behalf. And if a situation of virtual civil war should develop in some country, with Soviet military support of one kind or another available to one side, the United States should be in a position to support the other side with appropriate military measures. It is not a matter of overawing or coercing smaller nations, but of joining power and policy in a way that can make policy effective. In a region as volatile as the Middle East, with Soviet power poised menacingly in the north, the United States must have

[9] Senate Hearings on the Eisenhower Doctrine, cited, pp. 27-28; House Hearings on the Eisenhower Doctrine, cited, pp. 13-17.

some concentration of power as a counterbalance if it is to compete on equal terms in the cold war. Aside from discouraging Soviet adventures, the proximity of American power should also be useful as a restraint on the use or threat of force by Middle Eastern nations themselves in ways dangerous to peace. The situation in Jordan in April 1957 presented just such a possibility; Jordan's Arab neighbors and Israel might have been tempted to march into that strife-ridden kingdom had not the presence of the United States Sixth Fleet in the Eastern Mediterranean added emphasis to American diplomatic warnings.

It remains to be said, even though it will not be said officially, that an occasion may arise where the United States would be compelled, in order to prevent a disastrous shift in the world balance, to use force to prevent a Middle Eastern state from falling under Soviet control, whether there had been overt aggression or not. It might prove politically impossible to do so, and the consequences would have to be carefully weighed, but we should be alert to the dangers and to the possible need for the use of force in some form. One of the great perils of the coming years may be the gradual advance of Soviet power in such areas as the Middle East without resort to anything that international law or world opinion would call an act of overt aggression. It is well to remember that there is no accepted legal definition of aggression; and that the United States as a great power cannot allow its ultimate security to be compromised because its policies have been hamstrung by words like "aggression" and "sovereignty" which a rival power, the Soviet Union, always interprets to suit its own advantage, as it did in its reconquest of Hungary.

The United States cannot and should not try to emulate the full-blooded cynicism and disregard for principle that characterize the policies of the Soviet Union. But it must be able to see and to meet critical challenges when they come. Wise policies may avert the posing of the dilemma in its most disagreeable and difficult form, yet in the last analysis the United States should be prepared to react with force if the falling of a key country in the Middle East under Soviet control should be an imminent danger or an actuality. Its military planning, accordingly, should be directed first toward supplementing those policies intended to avert the dilemma, and, second, toward achieving the capacity to act quickly and decisively if the need for action should arise.

Chapter 12

THE MILITARY PROBLEM:
BASES, FORCES AND MILITARY AID

WE HAVE seen that not one but several military strategies
emerge from the estimate of the various situations and
threats which may confront the United States in the Middle East and of the tasks that devolve upon its military
power and resources. It is the job of military policy to
determine the ways and means of meeting the requirements which flow from those various strategies. The com-
plexity of the tasks requires a combination of over-all
strength and forces which is not tied to one strategy at the
sacrifice of all others and is suited to specific needs in
the area; a proper balance of Western and "indigenous"
forces; a proper balance of nuclear and "conventional"
power; and at least a "minimum position" in terms of
bases and other facilities. The result should be a total
military posture in the Middle East, a "position of
strength" if you will, adequate to the needs of the situation and consistent with our global strategy, while at the
same time realistic in terms of the political, material and
other considerations within which any policy must be
shaped.

Strategic Bases and Deterrence

The foremost consideration in military policy, the strategic deterrent to total war, consists at present of massive
striking power with nuclear capability, sufficiently secure
to withstand an initial attack upon it and still be able to
overcome enemy defenses and strike a lethal blow. It depends on a system of bases in the United States, in foreign
countries, and at sea. Because the Middle East is an area

from which vital parts of the Soviet Union can be reached by medium-range bombers, bases there form a useful part of the total complex of retaliatory power. We now have the right to use only a few: in Turkey, Saudi Arabia and, further back, Libya. The position would be stronger if others were available, for the mere existence of American strategic bases in the area complicates the Soviet problems both of offense and of defense, and the more of them there are the more difficulties they pose. Unfortunately, their nearness to Soviet bases makes them extremely vulnerable to attack by missiles or aircraft, even though they may be served by a warning system and are kept in a state of complete readiness; they might be "taken out" by Soviet bombers or missiles before they could be used at all. But if it were likely that they would in fact be available for launching that one crucial flight of aircraft with nuclear bombs, they would still serve their main purpose as a part of the general deterrent.[1] In any case they would cause a dispersal of the Soviet offensive effort.

The crucial question is whether strategic air bases in the Middle East, while undoubtedly useful, are an indispensable part of total American massive retaliatory power. This is a technical military question, the answer to which might conceivably change as various factors in the military and technological equation change. It can be plausibly argued, however, that no one base area is indispensable if there is no general or serious loss of bases elsewhere; the worldwide base system is extensive enough to take the loss of a few bases and still support a devastating blow at the Soviet Union. Furthermore, as the Strategic Air Command (SAC) develops "longer legs" in the form of longer-range bombers and extensive refueling capabilities, the need for overseas bases is reduced and the functions of the more vulnerable ones in the Middle East can be performed by others farther back (in Morocco or East Africa) and by the floating bases of the Navy. Therefore, the need

[1] Hanson W. Baldwin, "Strategy of the Middle East," *Foreign Affairs*, v. 35 (July 1957), p. 659.

for them seems less than absolute. Each case should be considered separately, taking into account the precise location of the base, its readiness for immediate strategic use, its vulnerability, and the political liabilities involved. Because a large strategic air base is extremely vulnerable not only to enemy attack but also to nationalist agitation, it may not be worth the cost to press for additional bases or to insist on holding those to which we already have access when to do so involves substantial political damage to our position in the country in question or in the Middle East generally. The experience of the British shows that bases cannot be held by force except at a price in harassment and antagonism that we are not prepared to pay.

A case worth careful scrutiny is Dhahran, often described as invaluable because it is our only base between Libya and the Philippines. The right to use Dhahran has been extended by agreement with Saudi Arabia until 1961. It will continue to be useful for a variety of purposes: as a convenient stopping-point for SAC training flights, a place for maintenance and repair of aircraft, and a distribution center for all our military and other missions throughout the Middle East. But the Dhahran airfield is not a full-fledged SAC base under complete American control, it is virtually undefended, its use in case of war is doubtful, and its continued availability depends on the good will of Saudi Arabia. It is important to keep both the base and the good will, but if it comes to a choice, let us be aware that the former has its limitations and the latter, in the long run, will be more important to us than any single air base.

If we look ahead to the age of guided and ballistic missiles, the value of good political relations with these states becomes all the more apparent. A multiplicity of fixed and mobile launching systems for intermediate-range missiles in the Middle East and in Europe, virtually impossible to knock out, would create something like an absolute deterrent to a deliberate Soviet choice for general war, even though the U.S.S.R. itself also possessed such missiles. The effect would be to guarantee the nuclear stalemate by ruling out any hope of launching a surprise attack without devastating retaliation.

The cooperation of Middle Eastern countries would not be easy to obtain. In general, we can hardly expect nations which object to American air bases to be more receptive to the idea of missile-launching sites on their territory. Soviet pressure on them is bound to be heavy; already Moscow has warned of the nuclear devastation certain to be meted out to any country which serves as a base for missile attacks on the Soviet Union. It will take strong nerves and a willingness to see their own interests in the context of the broader problem of security for the free world. We do not yet know whether the northern tier countries other than Turkey will see things that way. We know that the Arab states, except possibly Iraq, do not. All the more reason, then, for a long-range American policy which can establish, at least with some of the Middle Eastern nations, the kind of durable political relationship from which adequate arrangements for security will flow naturally with full consent.

Planning the Defense of the Middle East

The requirements for deterrence of general war, and for striking a lethal blow if it ever comes to that, rest almost entirely on United States forces alone. Contributions from others take the form of the provision of facilities for radar screens and for bases and a share in their protection. It is only when we look at the defense of the Middle East in a more traditional sense of a land and sea campaign that we run into the requirements for substantial forces from many nations and the difficult problems of raising, equipping and supplying them.

Western planning at the time of the first attempts to build a Middle East defense organization conceived of a defense resting primarily on the bases available by treaty

and on the forces provided or to be provided by Great
Britain, the Commonwealth (Australia, New Zealand and
South Africa), the United States, and such Middle Eastern
nations as could and would contribute. This strategic
thinking took as its key point the maintenance and continued use of the great Suez base, unique in its favorable
geographical position, its accessibility by sea, its supply
depots, power stations and workshops, and its proximity to
the population centers and food resources of Egypt. The
only deviation from the concepts of World War II was
the idea that Great Britain, pressed by its financial difficulties and by Middle Eastern nationalism, wished to be
relieved of the burden of keeping some 80,000 troops at
Suez and discharging alone, in Winston Churchill's words,
"the duty . . . of safeguarding the interests of the free nations in the Middle East, and also of preserving the international waterway of the Suez Canal." [2]

The unwillingness of Egypt and the other Arab states
to accept the "internationalization" of the Suez base under
a Middle East Command or defense organization forced a
revision of strategic thinking as well as of political approach.[3] The northern tier states took on greater importance, primarily because they were more willing than was
Egypt to cooperate but also because of the new factor of
nuclear weapons: Suez was especially vulnerable to nuclear attack, while new bases and added military strength
in the north would oblige the Soviets, if they chose to attack, to concentrate their forces for a break-through and
thus to present nuclear targets—"the same considerations,
in fact, as had determined the forms of organization for

[2] House of Commons, *Parliamentary Debates*, Weekly Hansard, no. 255,
col. 890 (May 11, 1953). See also British Information Services, *Defence of
the Middle East* (I.D. 1181) (London, 1953). Sir Winston had already suggested in a speech to the U.S. Congress on January 17, 1952, that America
share the burden with Britain (*New York Times*, January 18, 1952), without drawing any favorable response. The Congress was not looking for
new burdens of that type, and the State Department wished to avoid any
such involvement at a time when Egypt had not been brought into an
agreement on the future of the base.

[3] See above, pp. 42-46.

defence in Europe." [4] The Suez base was evacuated under the agreement reached with Egypt in 1954. Although in theory it was still to have a role in case of war, Egypt having agreed to British use of it in the event of an aggression against Turkey or any member of the Arab League, the emphasis henceforth was on the northern tier.

This was the basis on which further planning went forward, in Anglo-American military talks and within the framework of the Baghdad Pact, with which the United States established military liaison in April 1956. The forces of Turkey, Iraq, Iran and Pakistan were to be considerably strengthened through the provision of modern military equipment and training in its use. All four of these states were included in American military assistance programs, and Britain continued to provide arms and training to Iraq under the bilateral agreement made at the time the British gave up their bases at Habbaniya and Shu'aiba and joined the Baghdad Pact.[5] These "indigenous forces" were to have the principal initial role in meeting any Soviet attack on the ground, but they would be stiffened with Western (British) forces already based in the Middle East and supported by American and British air and sea power. In time, additional Western forces could be brought in. For practical purposes the plans were built around holding, as a minimum, eastern Turkey and the natural barrier of the Zagros Mountains.[6] The weak spot was the invasion route through northern Iran down into the plains of Iraq, by which a Soviet force could outflank Turkey. There the defense, especially of the mountain passes, might be suited to the use of tactical nuclear weapons.

[4] British Information Services, *The Security of the Middle East* (I.D. 1249) (London, 1956).
[5] See above, pp. 57-58.
[6] Planning based on defense of the Zagros rather than the Elburz Mountains would leave most of Iran on the undefended side of the line. The Iranian Government has therefore found it necessary to state the purpose of the pact as the defense of all the territory of its members, and thus to disavow a strategy not based on defense of the Elburz, at least initially.

Forces: Needs and Availabilities

In judging the soundness of the planning for a general military defense of the Middle East, it seems desirable, in addition to applying the test of probability mentioned in the preceding chapter, to weigh the possibilities that the requirements in men, resources, military facilities and political conditions to prepare for such a campaign could be met. It is not possible to state with precision what those requirements are. A conservative estimate would be ten Western army divisions, plus some twenty to thirty divisions of local ground troops, with adequate air strength for the bombing of communications and other targets and for tactical support of ground forces, plus naval forces and shipping tonnage sufficient to keep the forces in the field supplied and reinforced. It would make a difference, of course, whether nuclear or only "conventional" weapons were to be used. On the assumption that the Middle Eastern campaign would be but a phase of a general war, the use of nuclear weapons seems almost certain. Their use might reduce somewhat the number of ground troops required; on the other hand it would greatly increase the problems of training the local forces. No matter where or how the requirements are set, they are sure to seem unattainable when we measure against them the availability of Western forces, the capability of local forces, and the host of political problems bound to arise out of any efforts at military cooperation between West and Middle East and among the nations of the area themselves.

How can such a need for Western forces be squared with the global defense policies of the Western powers? Every recent development points to their inability, or reluctance, to commit any substantial ground forces to the Middle East, whether it is a question of maintaining them there in peacetime or of having them available for immediate participation in a major campaign against the Soviet Union in that area. It is scarcely conceivable that Britain will ever again maintain in the Middle East a force comparable to the 80,000 to 100,000 troops that were stationed at Suez a few years ago. The whole trend of British military policy, confirmed in the Defence White Paper of 1957, is toward the reduction of forces stationed abroad and a drastic curtailment of all ground forces. The Commonwealth can no longer be counted on to supply the manpower for campaigns in the Middle East. France is no longer a Middle Eastern power and its forces have been almost totally absorbed in trying to preserve what is left of French overseas territory. At a time when European NATO members are cutting their units in Western Europe below the level required for effective defense on the ground, nothing is available for the Middle East. As for the United States, the whole trend has been toward the reduction of ground forces stationed abroad, except in Europe, and an army with closer to fifteen than twenty divisions in all. One may deplore these developments. One may say that if the threat in the Middle East requires it, Western military policies should be revised to provide the necessary ground forces. But it is only realistic to accept the fact that both global strategy (especially the absolute necessity of maintaining the strategic deterrent and carrying on the ever more costly race for ever newer weapons) and the strains on the economy set limits beyond which defense budgets will not be stretched in peacetime.

What may be expected of the ground forces of the Middle Eastern nations, especially those of the Baghdad Pact? They, after all, would be counted on for most of the manpower. Here again abstract planning runs into unpleasant fact. Adequate trained divisions from Iran and the Arab states, able to fight in modern war, could not be brought into being for many years. The Iranian army has approximately ten divisions. Iraq has three. Jordan has at most two, Lebanon less than one, Saudi Arabia perhaps one plus some tribal forces. What of the future potential? The individual peasant or Bedouin soldier may be brave and a good fighter, but he is only the raw material. There is a formidable problem of training in mechanical techniques, both for officers and men, and in the qualities of leadership required of officers. These skills and abilities depend not just on instruction by foreign military experts but on the overcoming of ingrained habits and traditions and even on fundamental changes in the social order: an increase in literacy, a reorganization of political and social institutions, and a revolution in economic life.

Turkey, having begun to experience some of these changes, is better able to play a part in modern war. Israel has shown that it can fight and fight well. Yet the Turks, despite years of American training, do not yet have a force that could be expected to do more than fight defensively in their own mountains. Nor can Pakistan be expected to furnish military manpower for the Middle East as the old British Indian army did. Israel cannot be relied on as a bulwark of regional defense because it is so small, is not acceptable as a partner to other states in the Middle East, and must concentrate on averting the threat of its own destruction at the hands of the Arabs. One looks in vain for the military strength in the Middle East to carry on a major campaign in partnership with the West. One will look for it in vain for many years. The Republic of Korea is sometimes cited as an example for other Eastern nations. Its army was built up to a strength of twenty divisions and it learned to fight with the weapons of modern "conventional" warfare. But this was done in time of actual war, with American officers in positions of command and directly in control of the whole process. It is scarcely conceivable that the United States would be willing to make a similar effort in the Middle East in peacetime, or that any Middle Eastern state would permit it to do so.

If we consider the aspects of planning and preparation, the picture is no more hopeful. A common regional defense, to be immediately effective in case of war, requires a working alliance and preferably an agreement on a joint command and joint strategy as in NATO. These were the goals of the negotiations of 1951 for a Middle East Command, which the Western powers signally failed to achieve. The Baghdad Pact makes possible a certain amount of common planning in the northern tier. The pact members are anxious to build up their armies, and the United States is acting wisely in helping them to do so. But the pact does not in fact offer the means of defending the Middle East against a major Soviet attack, by reason of the weakness of its members, particularly Iran and Iraq, and because of the absence of cooperation on the part of the "southern tier" of Arab states. Unless the Western powers were successful in lining up Egypt and the rest of the Arab world along with the Baghdad Pact nations, they would lack the necessary ports, railway lines, and other necessary facilities for access to the area and for the conduct of defense in depth. The political climate in the Arab world, already unfavorable to military planning with the West, would only be made more unfavorable by Western efforts to press Arab governments for bases, facilities, transit rights and joint planning.

The conclusion to be drawn from this collection of negative considerations is that there is little point in trying to plan and prepare for an organized defense of the Middle East in a general war against the Soviet Union. It is quite apparent that the United States and its Western allies do not have ground forces for this purpose and are not likely to have them at such time as a general war broke out; that they cannot count on effective, organized "indigenous" forces now or for a long time in the future; and finally, that adequate planning on a regional basis is ruled out because of political conditions. Some planning may be necessary in order to satisfy the northern tier states, and could prove useful in case of war, but should not, in its lack of realism, be permitted to deceive the planners.

While the conclusion may seem discouraging, it should be accepted frankly and not tragically. There is no good reason to try to do the impossible in order to be ready for a military campaign which, as was indicated in the discussion on strategy, in all probability will never take place. The real defense against general war is the over-all strategic deterrent, and the real need for Middle East defense, in addition to that deterrent, grows out of the possibilities of limited war. If the United States were in a position to meet those two requirements, the chances are that it would have a good deal of power that could be brought to bear in the Middle East if it proved necessary in the event of general war. We should be able to make the area decidedly uncomfortable for the enemy even if it could not be held by the West.

Forces for Limited War

It is when we come to consider the question of limited war in the Middle East that we are dealing with the immediate and the pressing problems. The forces necessary to deter or to cope with limited aggression by the Soviet Union cannot be fixed with any certainty because of the wide range of variations in form, size and scope which an aggression might take. Two assumptions might be useful as guideposts: first, that there would be rather severe self-imposed limits, at least in the beginning, because of the danger of provoking massive retaliation and general war; second, that a substantial American capability to take counteraction on the spot would constitute a warning that any aggression up to a certain magnitude would meet certain and effective resistance and accordingly would not pay. It would thus be desirable to maintain a military posture that, in its effect on Soviet calculations, would narrow or eliminate any gap that might exist between an aggression too small to be worth the hard fighting required and one too large to be worth the mortal risk.

The precise composition of such a force is a matter for study by military experts, and it will change from time to time as weapons and other elements in the picture change. Nevertheless, it is possible to state the requirements in general terms. The United States Sixth Fleet in the Eastern

Mediterranean constitutes a basic element. A similar force in the Indian Ocean and Persian Gulf area is a necessary supplement to it. Each should have stronger forces of Marines than that now on duty with the Sixth Fleet. Beyond that, at least one division of ground forces with high mobility and firepower, able to use tactical nuclear weapons but also to fight without them if necessary, should be maintained either in the area or at points from which they could quickly be brought to it by air; not from Germany, where NATO strategy and European political considerations might not permit a withdrawal, but from other points where they would be stationed, to Moscow's knowledge, for the specific purpose of being ready in case of aggression in the Middle East. Tactical air power, which in these days can be brought quickly to the scene of action over vast distances, should be available for use when needed.

It may be asked whether one division would be of much use in a "limited war" like the one in Korea, which is the most recent historical example. Obviously it would not be adequate for a war of that size. But the following considerations may be relevant: the presence of one American division, prepared to fight, should remove any idea in Moscow (such as existed in 1950) that the United States would not resist an aggression; in the Middle East, where the Soviet Union's own forces would be engaged, it is doubtful whether an aggression on the Korean scale could be kept within limits, as Moscow must recognize; and even if the American forces on the spot were inadequate in the beginning, as the conflict developed and if it remained limited, additional forces could be sent to assist them. A central reserve of such forces should be kept in being, to be drawn on for that type of emergency, whether it should arise in the Middle East or elsewhere.

The United States, although it might have to act alone when a crisis came, would not assume to itself in advance the right and power to deal with any local aggression in the Middle East. Should the United Nations take a stand, action by various member states or even of an international U.N. force is a possibility. Great Britain might still have some forces in the area and could contribute the use of its remaining bases. The strength of the Middle Eastern nations, especially those most exposed to aggression, would be an important element: to keep order at home so as to discourage aggression in the first place, to resist it and thus clarify the situation to the world if and when it does occur, and to cooperate with American and other forces in repelling it. These are tasks, unlike that of defending the area in a general war, which are within the capacity of these nations to perform as they build up their forces.

Nevertheless, in the last analysis the core of resistance to Soviet aggression will be the power of the United States. That is the essence of the Eisenhower Doctrine: that the United States will use its armed forces, at the request of a Middle Eastern state, to resist Communist aggression. To carry out that pledge in a way that will not open the gates to general nuclear destruction, it must have the forces available to wage limited war successfully. Such warfare need not exclude tactical atomic weapons, nor need it be confined to the territory of the victim state, but the United States, so far as it has the choice, must have the statesmanship to keep prudent limitations on the weapons used, the territory involved, and the objectives sought.

The military forces capable of waging limited war with the Soviet Union in the Middle East would be entirely adequate to cope with any local conflicts, whether it be a recrudescence of fighting over Palestine or some other violent eruption of Middle Eastern quarrels. If the United Nations were prepared to take action in case of a breach of the peace, U.S. forces could back up U.N. efforts to restore peace; their mere presence would discourage resort to force and would strengthen the authority of the world organization; and in the last resort, in case U.N. action were blocked by a Soviet veto or by paralysis of the General Assembly, they could act alone.

The Need for Bases

The contemplated role for American military forces in the Middle East, both as to their stationing and their possible operations, raises the question of bases and also, inevitably, the question of "imperialism." With respect to strategic air power we have seen that Middle Eastern bases may be useful although not indispensable. With respect to limited war and local conflicts, bases in the area would be necessary both for ground forces and for tactical air power at such time as we had to conduct operations. But here we are faced with a dilemma. The United States, to back up the Eisenhower Doctrine and to perfect its military position, can seek to obtain and to hold the necessary key points for deterrence and defense despite political opposition and nationalist pressure. Or it can accept a less than complete defense posture until political conditions change. The first course would be the logical one were we at war or on the brink. Otherwise it would use up our political credit and jeopardize gains already made, embroiling us with the very nations we desire to protect.

Where Western bases or forces on Middle Eastern territory would only be points of friction and easy targets for nationalist and Communist propaganda, they are not worth a running controversy with states on whose territory they are located, if that is the price of keeping them. Turkey does not appear to fall into that category. We now have the use of Turkish airfields. It might be desirable also to station a small Army or Marine force, a battle group or reinforced battalion for example, somewhere in Turkey as a symbol of a strong American policy. A similar arrangement might be made in Iran. Turkey would probably agree to it now, Iran might not; but neither should be pushed into it, as such arrangements must rest on voluntary consent.

As for the Arab states, only Iraq through its Baghdad Pact association can be counted on at the moment to provide operating bases for American air power. Use of

Dhahran as a functioning base for tactical operations or as a stationing point for ground forces might not be possible, for Saudi Arabia remains balanced between its anti-Communist, pro-American inclinations on the one hand and its strong Arab nationalism and proclaimed "neutralism" on the other. It is a balance which, if one tries to tip it one way, may well end by tipping the other way.

To yield to these sensitivities and political factors involves a risk, but it is one that can be reduced to tolerable proportions by concentration on alternative bases and elements of military power. As the real question is how to show strength inconspicuously, to have military power present and taken into account in the calculations of all concerned but without raising political difficulties, it may resolve itself into one of location at points outside the area but with easy access to it. Naval task forces in the Mediterranean and the Indian Ocean are a large part of the answer. Wheelus Air Base in Libya is another natural choice, although too far away for tactical air operations and subject to possible political objections in the future. Bases in Ethiopia or in British East Africa might be useful. Not to be overlooked are the British base at Aden, for both naval and air units, and potential base areas in Muscat and other British protectorates on the Persian Gulf, although they would in due time come under the assaults of Arab nationalism, and there is no point in making that problem any more difficult than it is bound to be. Another base area, much better located, is Cyprus, presently under British sovereignty and control. Here the obstacles are political and call for a serious effort to bring about their removal.

Cyprus as a Base for the Middle East

It is not necessary to chronicle the long and tragic succession of events which have brought the so-called Cyprus question to the present pass where it has embittered relations among three NATO partners and enveloped the island itself in an atmosphere of fear and violence. Our purpose here is to assess the importance of Cyprus in a sound Western policy toward the Middle East and to see what steps may be indicated if it is to play a part in that policy.

Cyprus has limitations as a major base. Its harbors are not adequate for large ships. It has been a key head-quarters and communications center but was never a complete substitute for the Suez base. Its facilities cannot support large-scale land, sea and air operations. The British and French, in organizing and carrying out their attack on Egypt in 1956, could not do so from Cyprus alone. Nevertheless, Cyprus retains some military importance both to NATO strategy and to the Western position in the Middle East, which is vital to NATO. As to the former, it adds strength and flexibility by providing a base from which NATO operations in Turkey or elsewhere in the Eastern Mediterranean could be supported. As a base for tactical air power it might be difficult to replace, and it could be useful, though not essential, to the Sixth Fleet. So far as Middle Eastern strategy is concerned, Cyprus is one of the few remaining bases in Western hands. For use in dealing with situations of limited war it has many advantages. It is ideally located as a staging area on the doorstep of the Middle East but beyond reach of Arab nationalism and untouched by the conflicts of the Middle Eastern nations. The same clash between irreconcilable concepts of national rights and vital strategic interests is evident there and has complicated Western plans for defense. The basic conflict in Cyprus, however, involves the rival claims of two nations which have made their choice for the West and has worked to the detriment of the general interest, common to all parties concerned, in maintaining Western strength against the Soviet threat.

In defending his government's policy in Cyprus, Sir Anthony Eden made it clear that Britain was hanging onto the island so tenaciously for one reason alone: it was necessary for the protection of British interests in the

Middle East.[7] After the Suez base was given up, the British military authorities relied on Cyprus as their main base in the Middle East, the only one north of Aden that was under British sovereignty. They could not give it up, as they saw it, without giving up Britain's historic role and vital interests. Now, however, after the events of 1956, it is doubtful whether Britain is able to maintain an independent military position in the area, as guardian either of the general peace and security or, except for small-scale operations as in Oman or Aden, of the specific British territorial and economic interests which remain. For this reason, and because Cyprus as a political issue has already done far more damage to the Western cause than could be compensated by its strategic value, some new approach to the question of its future status is necessary. The basic problem, which London has failed to solve, is how to find a political solution tolerable to the two nationalities which inhabit Cyprus, and to Greece and to Turkey, and at the same time to protect the strategic Western interest in the availability of Cyprus as a military base.

That Cyprus has been allowed to poison the relations of three NATO powers and gravely to weaken the whole eastern flank of NATO is a sorry reflection on the diplomacy and statesmanship of the West. The years of delay, unfortunately, have only hardened positions and increased tensions. Now Britain, in the process of adapting itself to a new defense policy which involves cutting down overseas commitments, may be ready to be more flexible on Cyprus. While British sovereignty over the island has previously been considered essential to its full and free use as a base, London might be prepared to consider other arrangements that offered as much assurance at less cost in money and headaches. The United States, up to now, has been scrupulously "correct" in its position, avoiding comment on the merits of the dispute and expressing hope

[7] Speech at Norwich, June 1, 1956 (*The Times,* London, June 2, 1956). See also statement of the Prime Minister in House of Commons, *Parliamentary Debates,* Weekly Hansard, no. 347, cols. 420-421 (March 14, 1956).

that the parties directly concerned may come to some
agreement. A more active search for a solution would have
been more in keeping with this country's role as a leading
NATO partner and with its increasing commitments in
the Middle East.

Greece has insisted on the right of the majority of the
people of Cyprus to self-determination and thus to union
with Greece. This is a principle which in the long run the
Western world can hardly deny. Many of the difficulties
flow from the irresponsibility with which various Greek
governments, impelled by the pressures of domestic politics, have pursued it. It should not be impossible to give
Greece satisfaction in principle, limited by the need for
arrangements which will protect the interests of others
and for time to give the Cypriotes some experience in self-
government. The population of Cyprus, 80 per cent Greek
in language and culture, is weary of being ground between
the millstones of repression from above and terror from
below. Undoubtedly, the Greek Cypriotes, despite some
undeniable benefits from British rule, would like full self-
government. Presumably they desire eventual union with
Greece. But whether their will is accurately reflected by
the acts of murder and arson perpetrated by terrorist
leaders or by the pronouncements of Archbishop Makarios
is another question. What they need above all is a more
settled atmosphere in which they will have a chance to
work out their own political institutions.

Turkey, the other disputant, has taken a strong line in
opposition to any change in the *status quo*. Domestic
political considerations are not absent from the picture;
agitation of an issue with nationalistic appeal can be helpful to a government under pressure on the home front. It
would not do, however, to discount the intensity of Turkish feeling as to Cyprus. The Turks fear that in Greek
hands the island would be a potential menace to their
security; they feel no sense of assurance that Greece will
be immune to neutralism or to Communist influence. The
historic enmity between Turks and Greeks has not en-

tirely disappeared, despite the record of good relations
since 1930, and the Turks are naturally concerned over
the fate of the Turkish minority on Cyprus. Their arguments are not irrefutable. Turkey already has Greek
islands much nearer to its shores, and the existence of a
Communist Greece would raise far greater dangers for
Turkey and for the West than its possession of Cyprus.
To allow the indefinite deterioration of relations over the
Cyprus question is indeed one of the easiest ways to make
those dangers real. So long as the Turks show no sign of
willingness to compromise—except on the basis of a partition of the island, which would create more problems than
it would solve—it is not easy to make headway. But Turkey
can be given some guarantees against any use of Cyprus
by a hostile Greece. The Western powers and the whole
NATO coalition have an interest in the security of Turkey's southern coast and in keeping open its lines of communication to the West. In the last analysis Turkey should
not be allowed to veto an interim settlement that included
reasonable guarantees of Turkey's special interests.

What that settlement might be is a matter for careful
diplomacy, in which the United States should not avoid
direct participation. The population of Cyprus is entitled
to a recognition of its right to self-determination, with a
date set for its eventual decision on union with Greece or
some other international status for the island. Turkey is entitled to guarantees in regard to its own security and to the
rights of the Turkish inhabitants of Cyprus. The Western
powers are entitled to the use of certain areas for military
purposes. An interim settlement under which Cyprus
would enjoy full self-government, under either a British
protectorate, a United Nations strategic trusteeship with
Britain as administering power, or some kind of NATO
trusteeship, could include the necessary guarantees to
Turkey and the West. Given a time limit of ten or fifteen
years, it would meet the claim for eventual self-determination while providing a long enough period for the Cypriotes to learn something of the art of self-government,

and for all concerned, with their essential interests protected, to reassess the situation with greater detachment. Western diplomacy helped solve the Trieste controversy after it had for years seemed insoluble. The dispute over Cyprus, continuance of which benefits only the common enemy of all parties to it, need not be impossible of solution.

Like most bases, however, Cyprus is not so necessary that it must be retained at all costs. There and throughout the Middle East, good political relations are more important in the long run than a base held under siege. Increasingly intimate and cooperative relations with the Middle Eastern countries, indeed, are the best guarantee that their cooperation, including the use of bases and other facilities, will be forthcoming in time of crisis. The United States can be reasonably relaxed in its attitude on base rights, even if the paucity of good bases available to its forces makes military planning more difficult, so long as it maintains the essentials of a position of strength and so long as its diplomacy is successful in finding a basis of cooperation with a number of Middle Eastern nations. In those circumstances the Eisenhower Doctrine will have at least some chance of accomplishing its purpose of preventing any aggression in the Middle East.

Military Power and Subversion

The presence of American military power is also a necessary element in countering subversion and maintaining stability. Where the possibility of external aggression is minimized by the existence of visible counterforce, the chances for indirect aggression and subversion are correspondingly reduced, a point stressed by the President in his special message to Congress proposing the Eisenhower Doctrine. But here the main burden is not on outside military forces, except in the most exceptional circumstances, but on the capacity of the nations of the area to maintain internal security and guard their own independence. Adequate American help to strengthen them in that capacity means not merely the provision of arms and the usual training program, but also extraordinary and imaginative efforts to help create the kind of forces that can cope with subversion in the form of conspiracy, Communist-inspired riots, or insurrection and civil war. The police and gendarmerie may be as important as the regular armed forces, and weapons suitable for the control of mobs and for guerrilla warfare may be as important as tanks and planes.

While weapons appropriate to this purpose should be provided to Middle Eastern governments on a continuing basis, the exact location, character and magnitude of critical situations that will arise can never be foreseen without some margin of error. Accordingly, additional supplies should be kept under American control at points from which needed equipment can be moved rapidly to a country where a crisis has arisen. Whether, in some exceptional circumstances, advisers and trained men should go with it is a question that would probably depend for its answer on the extent of Soviet intervention. Delicate as the matter is in relation to our standing in the Middle East and elsewhere, it is one requiring some thought, and possibly some preparation, for the West cannot afford to concede to the Kremlin all the advantages of initiative and daring in this field.

The Provision of Arms

The strategies which determine our estimates of the forces necessary to support sound military policies for the defense of the Middle East should also provide the criteria for the nature and size of the military aid programs under which the United States dispenses arms and "defense support" to countries in that region. This is not an easy test to apply for the obvious reasons that the governments of these countries are not our satellites, they do not all see eye to eye with Washington on matters of strategy, and they often have motives of their own for wanting arms that have nothing to do with defense against the Soviet Union. Still, it is a goal toward which we should strive, for if a military aid program is nothing but an indiscriminate distribution of arms to governments who want them for one unrelated purpose or another, it is merely an expensive way to create more problems.

From the beginning of the Greek-Turkish aid program in 1947 to the end of 1956 the United States has provided $2,386 million in military equipment to the Middle East.[8] Additionally, it has provided substantial sums in economic aid related to the purposes of the military program, variously designated as "direct forces support" (non-military items for the use of armed forces) and "defense support" (economic aid to enable the governments to support a certain level of armed strength).[9] By far the greater part of these sums went to Greece and Turkey in support of NATO plans. Turkey's share, of course, contributes also to the defense of the Middle East. Pakistan and Iran have had smaller but still substantial shares in the past few years since the northen tier alignment took shape. Of the Arab states, only Iraq has been a regular recipient (since 1954). Jordan and Lebanon have received modest assistance since

[8] U.S. Department of Commerce, *Foreign Aid by the United States Government, Basic Data through December 31, 1952* (Washington, March 1953); *Foreign Grants and Credits of the United States Government, December 1953 Quarter* (Washington, April 1954), and subsequent issues through December 1956 Quarter. The totals given above include grants to Greece, considered officially for statistical purposes as part of the Near East; $530 million in military aid was granted under the Greek-Turkish aid program, of which $372 million went to Greece and $158 million to Turkey. For security reasons, published figures on military aid itself ("hardware") to "the Near East and Africa" are not broken down by country.

[9] The totals (in obligations) for defense support and direct forces support from July 1, 1951, through June 30, 1957, are as follows: Greece, $364 million; Turkey, $453 million; Iran, $102 million; Pakistan, $300 million. (U.S. Foreign Operations Administration, *Monthly Operations Report*, July 31, 1954; November 16, 1955; June 30, 1957.) The figures are somewhat deceptive as measuring the amount of money devoted to the military side of the program, for "defense support" was in many ways merely a way of saying "economic aid" with more chance of influencing the Congress.

the adoption of the Eisenhower Doctrine. Saudi Arabia has been permitted to buy military equipment, including tanks and aircraft, in the United States under license. Israel has been able to buy smaller items in this country but has not received any grant military aid. Egypt and Syria have found it easier or preferable to get their arms from the Soviet bloc.

The policy behind the American military aid program in the Middle East has not always been clear. Starting with the Greek-Turkish program in 1947, in many respects it "just growed," as the global aid program expanded and the interest of the United States in Middle East defense increased. When the first Mutual Defense Assistance Act was passed in 1949, as a result of the need to arm our allies in Europe, it was natural that requests should also come in from the Middle East. Iran, which had had American help in building up its gendarmerie, was then added to the list of regular recipients. Later, when American official hopes were placed on the "northern tier concept," the promise of military aid served as an inducement to Pakistan, Iraq and Iran to move ahead with the Baghdad Pact. While the Palestine conflict remained acute, Washington was reluctant to grant military aid to Israel or its Arab neighbors but was prepared to make an exception in the case of Egypt in 1955 when it was thought—erroneously, it turned out—that Abdel Nasser would cooperate in plans to defend the Middle East.

With the adoption of the Eisenhower Doctrine, one of the main points of which was the offer of military aid, any state which endorsed the doctrine apparently was eligible for it. The Baghdad Pact nations seem to be slated for increased aid, and Lebanon and Libya, which also endorsed the doctrine, will receive modest amounts. Jordan, which avoided a stand on it but whose king roundly denounced "international communism" (along with Syria and Israel and many of his own compatriots who were trying to push the country into the Egyptian-Syrian camp), has been granted some $20 million in arms in order to keep its army in existence—the British subsidy had come to an end with the British treaty connection and the promises of Egypt and Syria to contribute, along with Saudi Arabia, to its replacement had not been fulfilled. Israel's approval of the doctrine, however, was not followed by a grant of arms because, in the State Department's view, Israel was "quite substantially armed" and not in danger; [10] the real reason was that to provide Israel with arms would risk losing what gains the United States had made toward winning greater cooperation from several of the Arab states.

The stated general purposes behind the aid program, for the Middle East as for other parts of the world, have been to strengthen collective security and to enable threatened states better to defend themselves and to maintain internal security. These concepts cannot have much reality unless there is in fact an organization for collective security and an agreed strategy, unless the receiving states are really concerned about defending themselves against the Soviet Union, and unless the internal order being maintained is one which not only suppresses Communist subversion but also has some prospects of continuing stability and popular support. In the Middle East, in contrast to NATO, these conditions have been conspicuous largely by their absence, with Turkey a partial exception because of its membership in NATO and its concentration on the Soviet danger. Elsewhere it has been a case of a number of national governments wanting arms for a number of reasons of their own: to maintain the balance with a neighbor, to achieve a position of regional leadership, to prepare for settling the score with Israel, or to provide strength and prestige for the regime currently in power. And since no regional defense organization came into being and no common strategy was agreed, the several "country programs" could not be closely coordinated.

In those circumstances it was inevitable that the pro-

[10] Statement by Secretary Dulles at press conference, September 11, 1957, in *Department of State Bulletin*, v. 37 (September 30, 1957), p. 527.

gram as a whole should be spotty. What happened in practice was that governments which wanted aid, and to which it was considered to be in the national interest to provide it, generally had the idea of modernizing their armed forces with the newest equipment they could obtain. They wanted, above all, tanks and jet planes, the mark of an up-to-date military power. What they actually got was the subject of negotiation with the United States in which their requests were generally scaled down to fit what was available and what American advisers thought their military forces could use or could be trained to use. Once established, programs have tended to go along from year to year on momentum, on the assumption that what was done one year was about right, with a few alterations, for the next. Most of the country programs eventually included tanks and jet planes, along with other less spectacular items, for these were sovereign governments which had to be given at least something of what they wanted if one of the main purposes of American policy, keeping them well disposed toward the United States, was to be achieved. So far as the general purpose of the defense of the Middle East was concerned, no claims of notable accomplishment would seem justified.

At the same time, knowledge of the deficiencies of the past does not by any means light the way to much more impressive results in the future. It will help if we can have better guidance in clarity of strategic thinking and of military policy. Thus if we conclude that local forces have virtually nothing to contribute to the over-all strategic deterrent and that planning for a full-scale defense of the Middle East on the ground is all but unnecessary, then the role of "indigenous" forces will be confined to cooperation with United Nations or Western forces in meeting local aggression in limited war and to maintaining internal security. The United States Government, at least in its own thinking, should be able to have a fairly clear idea of what the military needs of Middle Eastern governments are or will be for these purposes.

Local political considerations, however, will not disappear from the scene. Middle Eastern governments will continue to want arms to increase their own prestige, to keep pace with their neighbors, and to overawe or crush their domestic enemies. So long as the United States is interested in keeping their good will, it will have to indulge some of these desires through its military aid program. For example, Saudi Arabia cooperates by allowing the use of Dhahran airfield partly because it is able to get in return the arms it wants from the United States. With Jordan it is a question of providing American arms or seeing the Jordanian army dissolve and anti-American elements take over the country. The military aid program has to continue to make provision for that sort of situation.

The question of arms for internal security is another delicate one. It is of the utmost importance that governments have the means of thwarting Communist attempts to incite to riot or to capture power by revolution and civil war. On the other hand, we do not like to see them using American weapons to shoot down those among their own people who, without any tie to communism or Soviet policy, think it is time for a change. The charge is often made that our grants of arms merely enable "feudal" regimes to fasten their oppressive rule on the people. It is the old problem we have long faced, and have never been able to solve, in Latin America. It seems no more easily soluble in the Middle East, and a doctrinaire approach will be the least helpful of any. On a country-by-country basis, using diplomatic persuasion and its control over the flow of arms, the United States can do something to reduce the misuse of American weapons for domestic political purposes, but it cannot lay down the law. It is often a question, too, whether in countries where it is the practice that one relatively undemocratic regime succeeds another it is as important to keep American arms from being used by the group in power as to keep the group in power friendly to the United States.

Another and more alarming by-product of the military

assistance program is its contribution to the local arms races in the Middle East. This is inevitable, as long as the United States is going to ship arms to any state in the region. Such shipments are bound to affect the local balance of power between rival states. Aid to Iraq has fortified its defiance of Egypt and caused alarm in Syria. Aid to Pakistan has led to further arming by India. Shipments to any Arab state will cause Israel to intensify its own quest for more and better weapons. Until 1955, however, the virtual monopoly of the sources of supply held by the Western powers permitted them to exercise some control over the arms race between the Arab states and Israel. The United States, indeed, refrained from providing grant aid in arms to Israel and to all adjacent Arab states, although it was prepared to supply Egypt after the agreement with Britain on Suez in 1954 if the terms could have been agreed. Then the Soviet-Egyptian arms deal removed all control and opened the door not only to a local arms race but to competition in supply between the great powers. The war of 1956, in which quantities of Soviet matériel were captured by Israel from Egypt, did not change the situation as the Soviets continued to pour more arms into Egypt.

The American reply to the new Soviet gains was the Eisenhower Doctrine, one tenet of which is the provision of arms to Middle Eastern states which wish to strengthen themselves against possible aggression. Thus we are now supplying five Arab countries (Iraq, Jordan, Lebanon, Saudi Arabia and Libya) in addition to the northern tier, and the Soviet Union is supplying Egypt and Syria, while Israel, alarmed over growing Arab strength, is looking for arms from every possible source and will get them from France and perhaps from the United States if the balance becomes too weighted on the Arab side. The result is that arms are being spread all over the Middle East, adding tinder to the explosiveness of the inter-Arab, Turkish-Arab and Israel-Arab disputes that could easily burst into flame.

This is not the kind of situation that should induce equanimity if we are serious about the objective of a more stable Middle East. Yet there are but two ways to arrest the arms race, neither one very promising: by preventing Soviet deliveries or by reaching an agreement to stop or to limit deliveries from all outside sources. The first might have been possible if the United States had taken immediate and decisive action in 1955 on the announcement of the Soviet-Egyptian arms deal, simultaneously proposing a plan of control to the United Nations. Now that Soviet deliveries are an established part of the scheme of things, it could hardly be done without acts of war, which world opinion would support the U.S.S.R. in resisting.

As for the second course, while attempts to negotiate a general settlement of Middle Eastern issues with the Soviet Union are likely to be pointless and even dangerous,[11] a negotiation limited to the supply of arms holds out at least the possibility of achieving something. The Soviet leaders even proposed it in 1956 and again in 1957.[12] The big difficulty is that they undoubtedly hope by such an agreement to cut off the supply of American arms to the states of the northern tier, a proposal to which we could agree only at our peril. Only if there is a global agreement on arms limitation could that be accepted. It is worth making a more restricted proposal, however, one which would place agreed limitations on the supply of arms to Israel and to Arab states bordering on Israel. If direct approaches to Moscow produced nothing, as is likely, such a proposal could be made to the United Nations, where support from many other states, even the Asian neutrals, might be forthcoming. Very few states can be looking with equanimity at the continuous piling up of modern arms in the hands of touchy and irresponsible governments in the Middle East. In any case, if no control

[11] See below, pp. 200-203.
[12] Statement of N. S. Khrushchev in London, April 27, 1956 (*New York Times*, April 28, 1956); Soviet note of February 12, 1957 (same, February 13, 1957).

is established and the United States finds itself compelled to keep on contributing to the arms race, it has an obligation to guarantee the peace, to make sure that the accumulation of weapons does not lead to the outbreak of local conflicts.

In summary, the United States should be prepared, barring the miracle of an agreement on arms limitation, to carry on indefinitely its military aid program to the Middle East. We should try to take the haphazardness out of it, to gear it as far as possible to a sound military strategy and thus to the tasks of limited war and internal security, and to minimize its effects on combustible local conflicts and rivalries. At the same time we should frankly recognize its political significance and use it where possible in the service of our own political strategy. Whether the United States can accomplish these purposes while keeping military aid at current levels or reducing it is an open question. In any event, no arbitrary upper or lower limit should be set.

The military aid program—like the decisions on raising forces and the use of bases—should be guided by more than the general idea of building military strength in the Middle East. It should be tied to a realistic military policy and to clear political purposes. The demands on American resources are such that we cannot afford to waste our efforts in trying to build military positions that are beyond the capabilities of the Middle Eastern nations and of the West or that ignore the political obstacles. The military effort must be adequate, but it must also be such as to meet the military threat with the minimum expenditure of resources without diverting attention and energies from the greater challenges and the demands that confront us in nonmilitary fields.

Chapter 13

COLD WAR AND DIPLOMACY

THE MAIN threat from the Soviet Union in the Middle East is not that of armed aggression, the less so as the nations of the West and of the Middle East develop an adequate military policy to meet it. The whole trend of Soviet strategy, despite recurrent threatening language in speeches and diplomatic notes, is one of conquest by cold war and diplomacy. A brief review of developments since the death of Stalin will confirm that conclusion.

Even Stalin, after the setbacks to his adventures in Iran and Greece in 1946–1947, did not pursue an aggressive or reckless policy in the Middle East. The continuing intransigent and menacing attitude of the Soviet Government during his last years, however, left no room for the growth of faith and confidence in its motives on the part of nearby states in the Middle East. Greece and Turkey joined NATO and moved toward cooperation with Yugoslavia, which was under still more severe Soviet pressure. Iran, even in the anti-Western frenzy of the Mosaddeq period, kept its military ties with the United States and did not turn to Moscow. Arab nationalists, generally distrustful of communism, still saw their future in a framework of relations with the West; and Israel, which in its first years had attempted a policy of neutrality between East and West, turned increasingly to the West as Stalin's regime, openly anti-Semitic in its last phase, broke diplomatic relations with Tel Aviv in February 1953.

The Turn in Soviet Policy after Stalin

The men who established a "collective" leadership on Stalin's death wasted no time in changing the tone of

Soviet relations with the outside world. As a part of their general campaign for "relaxation of tensions" they turned a smiling face to the nations of the Middle East, including those most closely associated with the West. Insisting on their own peaceful intentions, they expressed a desire for friendly cooperation, for more trade, for the settlement of troublesome questions still in dispute. Turkish and Iranian representatives were quietly informed that in some of his policies toward their countries Stalin had been wrong. The territorial claims on Turkey, put forward in 1945, were withdrawn. The fall of Mosaddeq in the summer of 1953, which must have caused the Soviet leaders acute discomfiture, did not bring any alteration of the new tactics toward Iran. On the contrary, negotiations for the demarcation of unsettled portions of the Soviet-Iranian border and for the return of Iranian gold long held in Moscow went right ahead.

Soviet policy seemed almost a throwback to the 1920's, when Chicherin had built a "security belt" of Middle Eastern states on Russia's southern border free of ties with the West and pledged to neutrality. As its first step the new Soviet diplomacy worked hard to put across to these neighbors the idea that, because there was no danger whatever of Soviet aggression, military ties with the West were therefore useless or, worse than that, were dangerous in that they kept up international tension. The governments of Turkey and Iran, however, while gratified at the easing of pressure from the north, remained extremely cautious and firm in their attachment to the policies they had chosen. The Turks had no intention of abandoning NATO. Iran stuck to its "neutrality," which had come to combine an absence of formal treaty alignments with reliance on the West for security and military aid. Both countries insisted that they alone could be the judges of what was necessary for their own defense.

The attention which Stalin's successors turned to the Middle East was no mere temporary tactic. Other signs of Soviet interest in that region, after years of concentration on Europe and the Far East, began to appear. The press called for increased interest in Oriental studies and for the training of many more scholars and experts. Academic institutes which had disappeared or relapsed into obscurity showed new signs of life at Moscow, Leningrad and especially Tashkent, the center of Moslem studies in Soviet Central Asia. Soviet scholars began to turn out books on the national struggles of Arab and African peoples against imperialism.[1] *Sovetskoye Vostokovedeniye* (Soviet Eastern Studies), a new periodical succeeding those of the 1920's, began to appear. All this activity, of course, was not for the sake of scholarly inquiry but to serve the purposes of the regime, primarily to train the body of diplomats, commercial negotiators, technical experts and secret agents in whose hands would rest the execution of a new and more active Soviet policy in the Middle East. Mounting evidence suggested that the new Soviet leadership had chosen that area as the scene of its next major offensive in the cold war.

Soviet Offensive in the Arab World

The offensive, when it came, was not aimed primarily at the Soviet Union's immediate neighbors, which refused to accept the new "line" at face value and were drawing together in the "northern tier" alignment promoted by the United States, nor at Israel, although the break in diplomatic relations was soon mended. The main target was the vast, restless Arab world, where the Western powers were already in deep trouble. In 1954 Soviet speeches, votes and vetoes in the United Nations gave a good indication of what was to come. The Soviet Union had decided to enter the Middle Eastern arena as the open partisan of the Arab cause, against Israel and against

[1] Walter Z. Laqueur, *Communism and Nationalism in the Middle East* (London: Routledge and Kegan Paul, 1956), p. 262; *idem,* "The Shifting Line in Soviet Orientalogy," *Problems of Communism,* v. 5 (March-April 1956), pp. 20-26.

the West. For several years the Western powers (the United Kingdom and the United States, with France as a junior partner on some occasions) had been acting as a sort of "concert" of great powers, in addition to their role in the United Nations, to control and stabilize the situation in the area and to promote the settlement of its pressing problems. The Tripartite Declaration of May 1950, under which they undertook to prevent armed aggression and to control the arms race in the Arab-Israel area, reflected that self-assumed responsibility. Unfortunately, the Western powers had not been able to bring about stability or to promote settlements by the time the Soviet Union appeared on the scene as the great friend of the Arabs. And it appeared with the great advantage that during the past few years, while the Western powers were trying to organize the Arabs into pacts and blocs, the Soviet Union had not apparently been trying to organize anything or to coerce anybody.

In April 1955, the Soviet Foreign Ministry published a significant policy statement to the effect that the situation in the Middle East had greatly deteriorated and that the Soviet Union proposed to develop closer relations with those countries in the interest of their independence and the cause of peace.[2] By that time it was becoming ever clearer what the Soviet strategy was, and that the point of concentration would be Egypt. Until then, Soviet propaganda had been calling Abdel Nasser a fascist dictator who persecuted "democratic" elements such as the Communists. Suddenly he became a patriot, a national leader fighting for his people's rights against the imperialists. The old question, much debated in the days of the Comintern, whether Communists should work together with bourgeois nationalists seemed to be resolved, at least for the current phase of Soviet strategy, in the affirmative. Indeed, having made their decision to use Arab nationalism as the path to penetration of the Middle

[2] *Pravda* and *Isvestia*, April 17, 1955 (*Current Digest of the Soviet Press,* v. 7, June 1, 1955, pp. 18-19).

East, the Soviet leaders followed the line of supporting all elements, even the most reactionary, whose weight could be thrown onto the scales against the West.

No Marxist interpretation of Middle Eastern society but only brazen opportunism could explain Soviet conduct. The Soviet leaders gauged the significance of Abdel Nasser in Egypt, and of Egypt under his leadership in the Arab world. They saw Egypt as the best means of blocking Western attempts to organize the Middle East, and they saw in the Egyptian leader one who had become a symbol and inspiration to Arab nationalists everywhere and who perhaps could be made to serve the Soviet cause as well as his own. This was the time of the Bandung conference, where Nasser was apparently much impressed with the virtues of neutralism, and where Communist strategists were in turn impressed with him. Both Moscow and Cairo were stung by the conclusion of the Baghdad Pact. The situation was ripe for both to exploit.

The great "break-through" was the Soviet arms deal with Egypt. Once Abdel Nasser declared his independence of the West, the Soviets made the most of the opportunity to prove to him and to the Arab world the benefits of what they had to offer: arms in quantities far greater than anything the Arabs had received or could expect to receive from the West; attractive offers for cotton and other crops for which they desperately needed an assured market; and strong diplomatic support. In this way the Soviet Union established itself as a "Middle Eastern power" to a degree it had never succeeded in doing before, and began to act the part. It had cracked the virtual monopoly over arms deliveries to the area by which the Western powers had tried to keep some control over developments. It denounced the Tripartite Declaration of 1950, which was the symbol of that Western monopoly, and helped to bury it as an effective instrument of Western policy. It began to build what looked very much like an old-fashioned "sphere of influence" of its own, including Egypt, Syria, and possibly Yemen and Jordan too.

After refusing to discuss with the Western powers the Egyptian arms deal, a "purely commercial transaction," the Soviet Government then made offers to the Western powers to negotiate on the whole Middle Eastern question. On the eve of the Khrushchev-Bulganin visit to England in April 1956 it issued a statement of willingness to cooperate for peace and stability in the area. At London Khrushchev broached the possibility of an agreement to restrict arms deliveries to the Middle East (apparently including the Baghdad Pact nations as well as Israel and its Arab neighbors). During the November crisis Moscow proposed joint Soviet-American intervention to "stop the aggression," a suggestion that seemed to be based on the concept that those two powers alone could and should keep order in the Middle East and settle its problems. Then in February 1957 came a return to the idea of a four-power conference and an over-all settlement in the Middle East, followed by a number of proposals that the four great powers agree to renounce the use of force in that area.[3]

These manifold diplomatic initiatives are open to several interpretations as to the nature of Soviet aims and ambitions. Are the Soviet leaders merely trying to cause a maximum of embarrassment and trouble for the Western powers? Are they seeking the right to be consulted, to be a member of the club, to make the Middle East, like Germany or Korea, a subject of negotiation in which the U.S.S.R. would participate as a major interested power (and thus exercise a veto on what the West might want to do)? Or are these diplomatic moves but steps in a predetermined plan to establish the Soviet Union as the dominant power in the Middle East and reduce the nations there to the status of satellites?

The evidence of recent Soviet actions, against the background of past policies, suggests that all three suppositions are valid. The desire of the Soviet Union to be con-

[3] For unofficial texts of these several proposals, see *New York Times,* April 18, 28, and November 6, 1956; February 13, April 21, 1957.

sulted, to be one of the "concert of powers" dealing with
the Middle East, is obvious, though the reason for wanting such a status is surely to consolidate Soviet gains and
to keep things in ferment rather than to work sincerely
for settlements. We may discount all the asseverations of
concern for the rights and sovereignty of the Arab nations
and for the peace and security of the area. The underlying
purpose, no matter how those who draft Soviet diplomatic
notes choose to phrase it, is always to push Western influence out and Soviet influence in. Yet this purpose, so far
as we can tell, is not set to any timetable. The Soviet leaders would like to negotiate the West out of the military
position it holds. Failing that, they will use diplomatic
proposals and offers to negotiate as a means of winning
favor among the Arabs and putting psychological pressure
on the West. They will not precipitate matters if to do so
would spoil the game by bringing on war or opening the
eyes of those now bemused.

It would not do to exaggerate the idea that Soviet strategy proceeds according to a specific or detailed "master
plan." Many Soviet moves in the Middle East have been
reactions to those of other powers or the product of circumstances, favorable or unfavorable, as they arose. At this
particular juncture in history, from 1955 to 1958, the circumstances were especially favorable. Khrushchev and his
colleagues have found themselves at a point much further
advanced toward domination of the Middle East than
Stalin or the Czars had ever reached.

The Soviet Union has won these successes chiefly by
identifying itself with a popular cause, and without any
great expenditure of resources. Politically, all it has had to
do is to take sides on current issues. It has meant alienat-
ing some to win the friendship of others, but this is a matter of easy calculation. Unpopularity in Israel is a cheap
price to pay for the cooperation of key Arab countries, just
as the resentment of Pakistan is bearable if the pronouncements which cause it mean great gains for Soviet influence
in Afghanistan and in India. Nor has the economic price

been high. Surplus obsolescent arms could be put to no more useful purpose than to supply Middle Eastern states hungry for them and, henceforward, dependent on the same source for more. Trade relations, in general, have been mutually beneficial, as the Soviet bloc has been able to absorb those exports from the Arab countries for which no markets could be found in the West. Financial aid has been modest (although substantial credits have been granted to Afghanistan and India, only Syria and Egypt among the Arab states have been so favored thus far), and despite the strains on their own economy the Soviets probably could provide much more if the promise of political gains made it worthwhile.[4]

On the propaganda side, the Soviet Government undoubtedly puts considerable effort into its press and radio services to the Middle East, but the most effective work of all on behalf of Soviet aims is done by Cairo's "Voice of the Arabs." A perusal of Moscow and Cairo broadcasts since 1955 reveals striking parallels in content and tone. They have the same themes of peaceful coexistence, national liberation and respect for sovereignty, interlarded with violent attacks on Western imperialism, the oil monopolies, the policy of military blocs, and the West's alleged preparations for war. The main difference is that Cairo has much more to say about "Zionist imperialism." Both convey roughly the same picture of the United States, a land of grasping capitalists and oppressed masses, of considerable wealth but no culture, interested in the Middle East only for the purpose of substituting its own domination for that of England and France.

Finally, there is the field of political penetration and covert operations, where we have no sure means of measuring the magnitude of the Soviet effort. Here the Kremlin has a weapon of great flexibility useful for varied purposes. The growing volume of traffic in persons between the Soviet bloc and the Middle East—political leaders and

---

[4] See below, pp. 254-258, for data on the Soviet economic relations with the Middle Eastern states.

officials, military officers, technical experts, professors, students, journalists, athletes, religious dignitaries—has contributed to the rise of Soviet prestige and influence. The atmosphere of friendly cooperation, too, opens the doors of office and the channels of influence to those citizens of Middle Eastern countries who follow the Soviet line, now indistinguishable in many respects from the official line of the local regime.

It is by this means that the Kremlin can work secretly against, as well as openly with, the government of the day in certain of the Arab states. By placing men of confidence, whether they be technically Communists or not, in key positions in government, army, schools, press and radio, it acquires not only an influence on governmental policy and public opinion but also a series of vantage points from which it might, at the desired time, bring down a government or destroy the independence of a country. The Communist parties in the Middle East have never had a mass basis, with the one exception of the Tudeh Party in Iran before 1953. They have generally lived outside the law, split into factions, ineffective and without a popular following. They have played their part in organizing conspiracies and in fomenting riots, but as an instrument of revolution they suffer, as the Kremlin knows, under serious handicaps. As bearers of an ideology dedicated to the overthrow of the social order and established religion they accomplished almost nothing.

Under the new dispensation, however, the Communist danger becomes more serious. The Communists have taken to preaching nationalism and not social revolution. In Syria they have become the respectable allies of other parties in an ominous parallel to the "national liberation fronts" by which the Communists won their way to power in Eastern Europe. In Jordan, Communists have been in the forefront of the "nationalist" efforts to put the country into the Egyptian camp. In Egypt itself Communists and their sympathizers have found their way into key spots in public life with the full tolerance of the regime.

Communist moderation and respectability have put a new face on the problem of subversion. In countries where the Soviet Union is accepted as the nation's greatest friend, where Communist propaganda repeats that of the regime and the "fellow-traveler" basks in the sun of official benevolence, it is almost subversion by consent. This is no matter of plots and revolution but of gradual change in which the point of no return may be passed almost without notice. Indeed, the Soviet strategy may well be to refrain from asserting control and installing a patently puppet regime or Middle Eastern model of a "people's democracy" even when it could easily be done. A pliant "nationalist" regime may serve Soviet purposes of the moment more effectively and with less risk. The current pattern is not uniform, of course, throughout the Arab world. In some countries like Iraq the nationalist-communist front may be in opposition to the existing regime, but there also the tie with nationalism opens up vistas of power that Communists could not hope to attain by themselves; and at such time as a bid for power might be made the Soviet Union could step forward in the role of benevolent supporter of the sacred cause of nationalism.

The Western world has tended to underestimate the force of the Soviet appeal. The Arab view of what Soviet policy represents is very different from that of a European or an American. Arab opinion, in general, is not disturbed about the nature of the Soviet system or worried about the Soviet military threat, which is widely regarded as an invention of Western propaganda. Moscow's espousal of the Arab cause against Israel is what clinches the argument. The myth of the disinterested Russian friend is widely believed; and even those who are skeptical will regard Russia's appearance on the scene not as a menace but as a great opportunity. It enables Middle Eastern nations to face the West on far better bargaining terms than before; it opens up possibilities of having the best of both worlds by playing the two contending forces against one another.

The American Response

The Soviet challenge comes on many levels and therefore has to be met on many levels. On some it is a case of direct relations with the Soviet Union, calling for communication of a warning, a movement of armed forces, a diplomatic *démarche*, or the handling of a Middle Eastern dispute in the United Nations. On most others the American response centers on the relations with the Middle Eastern nations themselves, involving us unavoidably in their hopes and hates, their politics and economics, and their unsolved problems. In the simplest terms, so long as the use of force can be held off, the cold war is a competition in which each side is trying to bring about and maintain attitudes and policies on the part of Middle Eastern governments and peoples that are favorable, or at least not harmful, to its own aims and interests. It is not just a popularity contest, or a question of how much effort each side is willing to put into propaganda or money into foreign aid. It is a whole complex of shifting currents in which internal and external influences interact.

The course of events is never wholly under the control of one outside power or the other, although it is perhaps still less under the control of those who at a given time happen to be the ruling elements in the countries of the Middle East. In recent years it has become customary, though none the less salutary, to drive home to the American public the fact that we cannot deal with affairs abroad as we can with those under our own jurisdiction.[5] And an American diplomat with long experience in the Middle East has noted that we confront a variety of forces there which we can meet head-on, yield to, or try to deflect.[6] We may often have to settle for half a loaf or less. At the same time we may, with wise policies, have some influence

[5] The theme is expanded in C. B. Marshall, *The Limits of Foreign Policy* (New York: Holt, 1954), and Louis J. Halle, Jr., *Civilization and Foreign Policy* (New York: Harper, 1955).
[6] Raymond A. Hare, "Capability and Foreign Policy," *Department of State Bulletin*, v. 37 (July 1, 1957), pp. 22-25.

on the content of those forces and the course which they take.

The strategy of the cold war must be, in a sense, internally inconsistent in that it must serve both expediency and principle, both the needs of the moment and the goals of the future. In the short term we are engaged in a world struggle which is with us here and now. The need is for emergency measures to meet current crises: to encourage the friendship of governments that are well disposed and temper the mistrust of those that are not; to help a friendly government to hold the line against a riot or a *coup d'état*; or even to encourage, by means that are suitable, an opposition movement when the shoe is on the other foot.

There are always the crises of today that could not be or were not anticipated yesterday. All that we can do is to prepare for them as best we can, with alert diplomatic representatives, a good intelligence service, and flexible means of action at hand. It may be necessary, at any given moment, to support an individual or a regime, representative or not, democratic or not, so long as the urgent immediate purpose is served. Swift action may be required to avert disaster or to take advantage of a momentarily favorable situation. That is why it was necessary to woo King Saud and make the most of the possibility that he could rally conservative elements in the Arab world to check the advance of "Nasserism" and Soviet influence. That is also why it made sense to support King Hussein in the Jordanian crisis of April 1957, for he was the only one who could still prevent the country's falling under Egyptian and possibly Soviet domination. The role of the United States may not have been decisive, but the movements of the Sixth Fleet and the quick offer of economic aid surely helped the King to take the bold stand he did and then hold on successfully until loyal units of his army could bring the situation under control.

Let us look at a concrete case, Syria. By mid-1957 Soviet subversion seemed to have come very close to the point of domination despite loud denials on the part of the Syrian Government and other Arab governments that this was so; in any event, the U.S.S.R. among the great powers had acquired a position of exclusive patronage, and Syria's official voice had become its faithful echo on all international questions. Soviet arms were pouring in. Every declaration of policy in Damascus, every change in governmental personnel, seemed to confirm the inexorable trend away from the West, away from any real neutrality, and toward an exclusive relationship with Russia.

The specter of a Soviet-controlled Syria is a frightening one: to Turkey, which sees itself being hemmed in on all sides by Soviet power and fears for its port of Iskenderun, a vital link with the West in case of war and the object of Syrian claims ever since Turkey retook it in 1939; to Lebanon, Jordan and Iraq, already shaky enough without having to cope with a dynamic Sovietized Arab state on their borders; to King Saud of Saudi Arabia, fearful of communism and concerned about Arab unity; to Israel, whose very existence is at stake; to the Western powers, as they see the northern tier overleaped and perhaps neutralized, control of the oil pipelines falling into Soviet hands, and a Soviet military and political base being built up in the heart of the Middle East.

What can the United States do about such a situation if it has not found at some earlier stage the means of preventing matters from coming to that pass? It is likely to find that the use of force or other action carrying considerable risks of war is simply not politically possible because of the restraints of world opinion, the effects in the Middle East itself, or its own concern for international law and the principle of nonintervention. Being thus thrown back on nonmilitary means, the U.S. Government should avoid committing itself publicly to the overthrow of a regime it finds offensive, determined as it may be to bring about that very result, for success cannot be guaranteed within any given period and will depend also on the will and actions of others.

Nor does it do much good to look to the Eisenhower Doctrine, which requires overt armed aggression by a Communist-controlled state and a request from the state attacked before the United States can take action under it. The doctrine, contrary to Secretary Dulles's publicly stated belief at the time it was proposed, did not prevent the kind of situation which arose in Syria—for Syria, by early 1957 when the doctrine came into being, was already too strongly neutralist to be interested in American military and economic aid or pledges of armed support—but even Mr. Dulles did not claim that the doctrine would save the situation after subversion was successful. It could be called into play if Syria should embark on armed aggression against its neighbors, but to make much of this threat unless it is a real possibility, or sufficiently credible to make preventive action by Turkey or other neighboring states politically feasible, tends to enlarge rather than reduce the difficulties.

The Syrian crisis of the autumn of 1957 illustrated how the lines are ostensibly drawn on the issue of military aggression, when actually the real question was the establishment of Soviet influence in Syria. The United States felt compelled to stress the possibility of aggression by Syria against its neighbors as a means of mobilizing Middle Eastern support against the regime in Damascus, and to consider the specific conditions that would call for action under the Eisenhower Doctrine. Only if the Syrians had chosen, or had been provoked into, a resort to force against a neighbor, however, could anything rapid and effective be done about what Washington was publicly calling an extremely serious situation. Meanwhile the Soviet Government, with support from Damascus, took the occasion to whip up a war scare based on the alleged intentions of the United States, Turkey and other states to attack Syria. With the eyes of the world on the scene, all parties were careful not to be provoked into action that could set off a world war. As a result, Soviet influence was more firmly entrenched in Syria than ever, and Moscow was reaping more Arab plaudits as defender of the Arabs against the nefarious designs of the United States.

What can be done in such a situation does not come within the definition of any doctrine. It involves general lines of action and a certain amount of experimentation, rather than any set of acts which can be determined in advance. It involves continuing consultation with other governments in the area, though they may have quite divergent views, for example, Turkey and Saudi Arabia on the subject of Syria; the use of every promising channel to influence officials of the country in question, both those who are committed to the Soviets and those who are not; indirect contacts with persons or groups within that country; varying combinations of political and economic pressure; and appropriate use of propaganda, both "black" and "white." It may involve helping to create conditions where anti-Communist forces will have a freer hand to take action on their own. It is likely in any case to require a willingness to take some risks. If the West must remain impotent while the Soviet Union deals in its own way with "subversion" in Eastern Europe, it cannot afford to have its hands tied when the Soviet Union moves into the free world, or it will be at an intolerable disadvantage.

In no case, however, is a singlehanded crusade by the United States, conducted in full public view, likely to produce results. If the events leading to the situation of dominance or near-dominance by Russia were played out ostensibly through the workings of internal politics, then concrete action to reverse that situation, except in the most desperate circumstances, will have to take the same route.

Once a pro-Soviet regime is established, its dislodgement is not easy, but it is not impossible, particularly in a country having no direct territorial connection with the Soviet bloc and where, as in Syria, political instability is endemic and abrupt change a common occurrence. As no precise course can be charted, it is pointless to demand one. As long as the United States Government is aware of the seriousness of the situation and may be assumed to be alert and resourceful, it is best left to move quietly ahead without the goad of public agitation.

Expediency, of course, has its limits and anti-communism is not an adequate long-range policy. Strategy for a period of several years ahead allows more room for principle and for planning. The requirement here is to look beyond the government or immediate issue of the day in order to estimate what groups are gathering strength, where popular aspirations lie, and how and when the political picture is likely to change. Once sound estimates are reached, some of the questions of policy can be more easily answered. But it is not always easy. To take one case where the estimate was faulty, the advent of the Nagib-Nasser regime in Egypt seemed to presage an era of practical cooperation with the West both in carrying out overdue reforms in Egypt and in finding a modus vivendi on outstanding international issues. In actual fact it has not worked out that way. Even so, while assessing the future must involve a certain margin of error, it provides the only basis for sound long-range strategy, without which the Middle East almost surely will be lost.

How long the cold war will last we do not know, if only because we can only guess what will happen inside the Soviet Union in the next decade or two. Any developments which help to take Soviet pressure off the Middle East, without unduly intensifying it elsewhere, will be welcome, and it is incumbent upon the West to encourage such developments: by maintaining military strength while seeking an acceptable agreement on disarmament; by building a healthy and unassailable community in Western Europe; by opening up channels of communication to the peoples of the Soviet bloc; and by holding out to them and their leaders the prospect of a real "peaceful coexistence" with no room for domination of one nation by another.

So far as the Middle East itself is concerned, long-range American strategy should be aimed at the building of stable and fruitful relations with the peoples of the Middle East. Even a modest degree of success will supply a solid basis for taking the necessary tactical measures to deal with specific cold-war challenges as they develop. In formulating such a strategy we must attempt to draw in broad lines the kind of Middle East with which we shall be dealing. If the region is now in flux, as all observers say, what appears to be emerging from the flux? We must at least seek tentative answers to such questions as what will be the impact of outside ideas and techniques on Islam and on the societies of the Middle East; what kinds of governments will emerge in that area; whether and how the tremendous social gap between the privileged and the disinherited will be bridged; what paths economic development may take, especially as the age of petroleum gives way to that of atomic energy, and what basis for economic cooperation will exist with the West; where nationalism will lead, to struggle and chaos or to some broader unity; and what future Israel can have if Arab hostility is permanent.

The United States Government does not have to make up its mind and establish a "party line" on all these difficult and speculative questions now or at any one given moment. What it should do is to keep them in mind, to have a continuing estimate as a basis for day-to-day judgment. Sound American policy and leadership require giving some direction to the course of events, but to do so they must be attuned to the forces at work in the Middle East or they will wind up in the blind alleys of history.

Perhaps the most valid criticism of American policy in the Middle East has been that too little attention has been paid to the longer-term aspects; not that it has overlooked any infallible formulas with guaranteed success in application, but it has seemed to lack guidelines for the long term which will permit planning ahead without losing the flexibility necessary to cope successfully with the crises of the day.

The chapters which follow will take up the main fields in which the challenge comes: first, that of relationships

with the states of the Middle East, alliances and alignments; second, that of economic development and changing society; third, that of emerging political leadership
and how to deal with it; fourth, the Arab-Israel conflict,
the touchstone of our relations with the Arab world and
nerve point of the entire Middle East.

The Challenge to American Diplomacy

The great burden of the effort in all these fields falls on
our diplomacy, once the use of force is, by an adequate
military policy, reduced to a minor or at least a controlled
element in the picture. The diplomacy is of two kinds:
first, negotiation with other outside powers and especially
the Soviet Union, on the affairs of the Middle East, in a
contemporary version of the historic "Eastern Question"
with which the powers of Europe occupied themselves for
more than a century; and, second, dealing with the nations
of the Middle East itself, most of them newly independent
and glorying in their sovereignty.

No one can be sure that we shall not come at some time
to the point where the settlement of major issues outstanding between the Soviet Union and the West may be possible. Those responsible for American policy should,
therefore—on disarmament, reunification of Germany,
freedom for Eastern Europe, Far Eastern matters, the Middle East, or a combination of several of these—work out
in their own minds what are the elements of an acceptable settlement. Recent spectacular advances in scientific
achievement and in the making of new destructive weapons add urgency to the quest for basic agreements. There
is, however, no urgency to surrender or to compromise the
free world's future. Nor is there any gain in self-deception
as to Soviet aims and the character of Soviet diplomacy.
We have had experience of agreements "in principle"
which worked out only to Soviet advantage in practice, of
bargains in which concrete positions were gained on one

side and empty promises on the other.[7] Despite changes in the composition of the ruling group in the Kremlin, basic attitudes toward the non-Soviet world and the nature of Soviet diplomacy have not undergone such changes as would offer the hope of real settlements which would end the cold war.

In Middle Eastern affairs we have extra reason for caution. It is a region which has been free of Soviet control, and one in which the West cannot afford to permit a Soviet break-through to vital communication routes and sources of oil supply. The Soviet leaders, nettled by Western success in building the barrier of the "northern tier," would like nothing better than to destroy it under the guise of negotiating "settlements" which might seem to offer the West some relief from Soviet pressure in the Arab area. They have called many times for four-power negotiations. A negotiation which implicitly or explicitly recognizes anything like a Soviet "sphere of influence," however, would have only disadvantages and dangers; it would only provide a recognition of positions won, from which the Soviets could jump off to others. The United States would have nothing to gain by such a deal except in the unlikely circumstance that it was part of a world settlement including substantial Soviet concessions elsewhere.

This is not to say that an active diplomacy is not desirable, even necessary, in the effort to counter the Soviet threat in the Middle East. The United States has to be willing to take positions and defend them, in diplomatic notes as in the halls of the United Nations. It should be prepared to invite Soviet cooperation in certain proposals for stabilizing Middle Eastern conditions such as regional limitation of armaments. We need not be blind to the fact that the U.S.S.R. already is a Middle Eastern power

[7] See especially Raymond Dennett and Joseph E. Johnson, eds., *Negotiating with the Russians* (Boston: World Peace Foundation, 1951); Stephen Kertesz, "Soviet and American Diplomacy," *Review of Politics*, v. 19 (January 1957), pp. 3-36; John C. Campbell, "Negotiation with the Soviets: Some Lessons of the War Period," *Foreign Affairs*, v. 34 (January 1956), pp. 305-319.

with its own "sphere of influence" in the shape of at least two Arab states whose policies are closer to those of Moscow than to those of the West. Some say that since the Russians are there, it is foolish not to seek a settlement with them. This thesis presupposes a desire on their part for a settlement, when all the evidence is to the contrary. What they want is continued unrest, not stabilization, in the Middle East. Their influence is growing. Can we expect that a willingness on our part to talk will induce them to halt that process?

Soviet proposals give no scope for fruitful negotiation unless the Kremlin is prepared either to negotiate a retreat from present positions or to agree to joint action by the great powers to stabilize the area, settle its most explosive disputes, and remove it as an area of possible conflict leading to a major war. There is no evidence of either intention on the part of the Soviet leaders. If we consider the various proposals they have made for four-power agreement, the suggested principles to guide the policies of the powers and the proposed agreement ruling out the use of force, it seems plain enough that the intent is to get the Western powers committed to a set of generalities which can be used to embarrass them and upset their plans while the Soviet Union merrily pursues its own.

The United States should of course be ready to seize any hopeful opening for active diplomatic efforts with the Soviets as the scene changes within the Soviet bloc itself and elsewhere in the world. If the problems in other areas become sufficiently acute, Soviet concentration on the Middle East may lose some of its intensity. Opportunities for serious negotiation with the Soviet Government may well arise. Negotiation must also be called into play to keep the necessary ties of unity with our Western partners, so dangerously strained in the past year. But the real opportunities for American diplomacy, so far as one can judge today, are in the field of relations with the governments and peoples of the Middle East. It will be a stern test not only of the soundness of planning and policies, but also of the ability of the United States to use the new methods and techniques of diplomacy that are needed to meet the conditions that have developed in the world since the second World War, conditions which have brought information programs, foreign aid, and technical cooperation into the picture as adjuncts to traditional diplomacy in the age-old game in which nations attempt to influence the conduct of other nations.

American diplomacy can play this game with success only if the various instruments of public action, and some of private, are coordinated with each other and put to the service of soundly conceived policies. The mere fact of being a great power dealing with small nations means that the voice of America will be heard, but it means also that it will often be suspect or disbelieved. Since methods of domination are ruled out and the United States does not propose to use force in the Middle East except as it may be necessary to keep the peace, it must find policies and methods which elicit the necessary degree of consent from those nations and which reconcile their national aspirations with the vital interests of the United States and the Western world. It must find policies which help the nations of the Middle East to develop the will and the strength to meet the challenges of the modern world and to maintain their freedom without menacing that of others. This is a tall order. Certain critical major decisions may have to be taken by the American nation as a whole. But for the most part it will fall to those who are or will be our professionals in diplomacy, in the broadest sense, both to conceive what is to be done and to decide how to do it.

Chapter 14

ALLIANCES AND REGIONALISM

MUCH of the Western effort to defend the Middle East has gone into the building of alliances and treaty systems. To obtain the necessary cooperation from Middle Eastern governments, it seemed logical to seek commitments from them to help in defense of the region in time of crisis, or at least provide needed facilities so that the Western powers could defend it. Turkey, an ally of Britain and France since 1939 though it remained neutral until almost the very end of the second World War, made its choice after the war in favor of formal alignment with the West through NATO and was ready to participate in a treaty organization for the Middle East. Iran at first stuck to its historic policy of balance between Britain and Russia, wishing to provoke neither by too close ties with the other, but after the fall of Mosaddeq in 1953 the Shah began to consider alignment with the West. In the Arab countries two treaty systems were already in existence at the close of the war, one of British origin and the other the Arab League.

Great Britain had for some time been building a treaty system intended to replace the direct control as the sovereign, protecting or mandatory power it knew it would eventually relinquish. London had concluded treaties with Iraq (1930) and Egypt (1936), and after the war added similar arrangements with Transjordan (1946) and Libya (1951) as those states gained their independence. These treaties generally provided for the stationing of British forces and the use of bases and other facilities in return for a British guarantee of the integrity of the country in question. It was an ingenious system, but it could not withstand the pressure of rising nationalism. These were still regarded as "unequal" treaties, and those Arab leaders who tried to negotiate new arrangements that would prolong the relationship did so at the risk of their political posts and of their lives. Premiers Sidky of Egypt in 1946 and Salih Jabr of Iraq in 1948, on their return from "successful" negotiations in London, were met with protests and street riots to which their governments and their new treaties fell victim. The Anglo-Egyptian treaty finally was denounced by Egypt in 1951 and liquidated by consent in the agreement of 1954; its pale substitute, which gave Britain the right to return to Suez in case of an aggression against Turkey or an Arab League state, did not survive the crisis of 1956, when Egypt denounced it (although the British say it is still in force). The Anglo-Iraqi treaty was canceled by mutual consent when Britain joined the Baghdad Pact in 1955. The Anglo-Jordanian treaty was marked for liquidation by the Jordan Government after the nationalist victory in the elections of October 1956 and was annulled by agreement in March 1957. Only Libya, weak and quite dependent on outside aid, remained in a relationship of bilateral alliance with Great Britain.

The British Government had already seen during World War II that it would have to make more of a compromise with Arab nationalism in order to make the system work, and had given its blessing to the League of Arab States, established in 1945. But basically the League was the result of Arab self-assertion, not of British diplomacy. The fact of British sponsorship did not dispose of the questions at issue or bound to arise between London and the Arab states, and because these issues were not resolved the League came to be an instrument not of British policy but of anti-British policy, largely under the guidance of Egypt. In 1950 its members concluded an Arab Collective Security Pact pledging military action in case of an attack on any one of them.[1]

[1] J. C. Hurewitz, *Diplomacy in the Near and Middle East, A Documentary Record*, v. 2, pp. 245-249, 311-314.

The entrance of the United States onto the scene raised new questions: Would it become a partner in the British system, or try to replace Britain, or would it attempt to work out some new relationship with the local governments? In Greece and Turkey the United States simply replaced Britain as the provider of funds and thus as the chief protector; then the entry of those two states into NATO associated them formally with the whole Western community. Elsewhere in the Middle East the American approach was guided by three concepts: the strategy of air power with its requirement for bases near the Soviet Union, the principle of collective security, and the desire for friendly relations with all concerned.

The first concept was largely responsible for the special relationships which the United States developed with Saudi Arabia and with Libya providing for use of Dhahran and Wheelus respectively; these arrangements were not so different from those of the British treaty system, though less comprehensive and sugared with larger economic benefits to the local countries. The second factor, the principle of collective security, was part dogma and part practical calculation. The Department of State was wedded to the principle of regional arrangements as a necessary supplement to the United Nations. NATO and the Organization of American States stood as examples of what could be done. It seemed logical to extend the principle of collective security, if not NATO itself, further eastward. Thus by a collective organization, with small and large states as nominally equal partners, the means might be found to bring a number of disparate arrangements into a harmonious whole and to "internationalize" a British system no longer able to stand by itself.

We have reviewed the abortive efforts of the United States and the United Kingdom to build a military command or alliance system linking Turkey and the Arab states with the West. We have also traced the course of the more limited and more successful attempts to create an alliance of states on the "northern tier" of the Middle

East, and their result: the Baghdad Pact, joined by Britain but not by the United States.[2] And we have seen how Iraq's "defection" to the West nearly broke up the Arab League through the refusal of others to follow Iraq's example and the attempts of Abdel Nasser to build his own alliance system through bilateral treaties with Syria, Saudi Arabia and Yemen. The treaties provided for a common (Egyptian) command, which Jordan, although without signing a treaty, also accepted in October 1956. This Egyptian system was not long in showing signs of wear and tear owing to conflicts of interest among its members and did not even function when one of its members, Egypt, was attacked by Israel.[3] Thus the Arab states fell into a number of different and conflicting alignments, although all still proclaimed loyalty to the Arab League and its Collective Security Pact of 1950.

On top of this patchwork quilt came the Eisenhower Doctrine. Although not a proposal for a new treaty system, it did pose the question of alignment when Ambassador James P. Richards traveled about the Middle East "explaining" the doctrine and in effect soliciting responses to it. A public alignment with the United States against "international communism" was a stand some Middle Eastern nations, though friendly, wished to avoid and which others less friendly found easy to reject. Some governments reacted favorably, others merely listened to Mr. Richards; still others refrained from inviting him at all. Nevertheless, the new initiative represented by the doctrine was encouraging to many in the Middle East who had hoped for a stronger American policy and for increased political and material support. The total result was a perceptible shift in the line-up: the northern tier

[2] See above, Chapters 4 and 5.
[3] Abdel Nasser has stated that Egypt's allies offered to come to its support but that he told them their military help was not needed; Egypt's policy was to keep other Arab states out of it. (Speech at Al Azhar, November 9, 1956, *New York Times*, November 10, 1956.) A more plausible explanation is that Israel was obviously strong enough to take care of any Arab armies that might have chosen to join the fighting.

states were still solidly with the West; Saudi Arabia,
Lebanon and Jordan were more inclined than before to-
ward association with the United States (though of these
three only Lebanon formally welcomed the doctrine); and
Egypt and Syria were increasingly isolated in their pro-
Soviet orientation.

Thus, in considering the future we do not start with a
clear slate. The Baghdad Pact, the Arab League and the
Eisenhower Doctrine, unlike the Allied Middle East Command and the British treaty structure, are existing political facts that must be taken as conditioning any theoretical
regional system, or lack of system, which might recommend itself. Nevertheless, we should attempt some general
assessment of the value of alliances and regional security
systems for the Middle East without any sense of commitment to what already exists. Do the relationships we
would like to see established between the United States
and nations of the Middle East require formal alliances or
international organizations? Do the present alliances and
organizations fill the bill? Can we work with those which
have no Western participation, such as the Arab League?

From the standpoint of military policy, both for deterrence and for coping with the most likely military challenges, we have seen that certain minimum contributions,
in facilities and in the maintenance of modest levels of
armed strength, are required from a number of Middle
Eastern states. Moreover, certain attitudes and policies,
preferably on the part of all of them, are necessary if we
are to succeeed in preventing subversion and meeting
various cold-war threats. The basic political problem,
then, is one of obtaining the necessary degree of practical
cooperation, while strengthening the will and the capacity
of those nations to maintain and defend their independence against Soviet efforts, direct or indirect, to destroy it.
Past experience points to the compelling need to seek cooperation and to strengthen the forces of resistance to the
advance of Soviet influence in ways which are not self-
defeating in running afoul of the other interests, the sen-

sibilities and the prejudices of the nations of the Middle East.

Because those interests and prejudices are many and are often in conflict with each other, the American approach must have the utmost flexibility. The method of alliances, precise commitments and formal organizations is in many ways quite unsuitable. An alliance represents the formal recognition by two or more states of the existence of a common threat, and the assumption of an obligation to fight together if one of them is attacked; more broadly it represents a common willingness to coordinate policies in facing the common threat. So far as many states in the Middle East are concerned, the very proposal of an alliance with a Western power generates antagonism. It is also an unavoidable fact that some recognize the Soviet threat while others do not. The mere existence of so many separate sovereignties, each with its own problems and national interests, has the effect of ruling out any broad, inclusive alliance or security organization or any comprehensive cooperation for regional defense. This is the inevitable result of the "Balkanization" of the Middle East.[4] Great Britain, in the old days, had only one government in Constantinople with which to deal. Now, in place of the Ottoman Empire, there are a dozen different governments.

Any attempt on the part of the United States to build an alliance system, to have any chance of success, must be limited to a part of the region. This is likely to be so for a long time to come, for we cannot set a date when Arab governments will cease to be subject to their real or alleged complex on the subject of alliances, when Arab leaders will no longer try to play Russia against the West, or when the presence of Israel will cease to inflame Arab spirits with thoughts of revenge. A primary question to be answered is whether the advantages of a limited alliance system (with which the United States is associated, like the Baghdad Pact, or in which it actually participates,

[4] Majid Khadduri, "The Problem of Regional Security in the Middle East: An Appraisal," *Middle East Journal*, v. 11 (Winter 1957), pp. 12-22.

like SEATO) outweigh the adverse effect on American interests elsewhere in the region. Another is whether those advantages may be gained in some other equally feasible but less costly way.

Turkey, Iran, and the Baghdad Pact

Let us apply these tests specifically to the Baghdad Pact. The questions may best be answered if generalities are dropped in favor of more specific consideration of the individual nations concerned. Turkey, like Greece a member of NATO, is a special case, for it is already an ally for the defense of the "North Atlantic area," which stretches from Alaska to the Caucasus. What concerns us here is Turkey's role as an ally in the Middle East. Since 1951 it has been willing to play such a role in association with the West. Its joint sponsorship of the Middle East Command was intended to give the proposal a native as well as a Western flavor. Its active diplomacy had much to do with the formation of the Baghdad Pact. However, although Turkish officials did have some influence in persuading those of other northern tier states that alignment with the West was the best guarantee of security and the surest means of getting modern military equipment, Turkey has not had the closest of natural ties with those states. And the influence of Turkey on the foreign policies of the Arab states other than Iraq has been negligible. Arab memories of the era of Turkish rule remain, and Turkish contempt for the "backwardness" of the Arabs is not hidden.

Militarily, Turkey's importance for the defense of the Middle East lies in its geographical position and in the strength of its armed forces, not in treaty commitments. Turkish political leadership in the Middle East has yet to develop, despite a certain amount of admiration for what Turkey has accomplished; indeed, the completeness of Turkey's turn to the West gave rise to doubts and hesitations elsewhere. These considerations at least raise some questions as to how much is gained by trying to build a Middle Eastern alliance around Turkey. What we expect from Turkey and what Turkey expects from the United States are available to each through the connection with NATO and through long-established programs of military and economic aid.

Iran's choice of a Western alignment, in joining the Baghdad Pact in November 1955, was the choice of the Shah, made primarily as a means of getting more support from the United States but also from a conviction that Russia was the natural enemy, and America the logical protector, of Iran's independence. It was a daring move, very welcome when the West was still smarting under the sting of Abdel Nasser's arms deal with Russia, and a historic break with the country's tradition of neutrality. The United States did not put pressure on Iran to take the step, but it had long made clear its belief in the value of regional cooperation for collective security. The Iranian Government knew perfectly well that to join the Baghdad Pact was the best way to get what it wanted from the United States: some kind of guarantee against attack, more military equipment, and continued assistance to Iran's effort to move forward into the modern world and to maintain its independence in the process.

There was no strong desire on Iran's part to ally with Turkey, Iraq, Pakistan or Great Britain. Without American adherence, which it continued to urge, the pact had limited significance in the eyes of the Iranian Government. Actually, with the cooperation of the United States, Iran's aims might have been as well or better attained without joining. The equivalent of an American guarantee, if it did not already exist in the deterrent effect of Washington's long-expressed interest in Iran on the Soviet leadership, was later provided by the Eisenhower Doctrine. The desired increase in U.S. military and economic aid could have been provided without a formal treaty tying Iran to the West or to other states in the Middle East.

From the standpoint of the United States the essential

point is Iran's determination and ability to strengthen itself against any attempts to undermine or overthrow its independence. Iran is much weaker and more unstable than Turkey. It adds no significant military strength to the defense of the Middle East. It gives little solid assurance of continuity either in internal or foreign policies. Membership in an alliance or organization such as the Baghdad Pact is significant only as the end of greater stability and strength is served; it is harmful if it tends to generate internal conflict and gives pro-Soviet or other anti-Western elements new opportunities to make trouble. More than formal allies Iran needs encouragement, help and time. It needs time to settle down to build sound institutions, to surmount the dangers of a period in which the country's future has rested so dangerously on the wisdom and the life of one man, as it has since 1953.

Pakistan, India and Afghanistan

Pakistan, Iran's neighbor, is on the outer edge of the Middle East. Its decision to seek alliance with nations of the northern tier was the result of a particular set of circumstances in which the United States was looking for allies wherever it could find them in Asia, while Pakistan was seeking consolidation of its independence and, above all, arms to hold its own against India. Washington found in Pakistan a country with a military potential, a dislike of communism, and a willingness to stand up and be counted. Pakistan's willingness to ally with Turkey (1954) and later to join the Baghdad Pact (1955), like its participation in SEATO, may be explained in part by the conviction of the country's leaders that collective security was the best answer to the Soviet or Chinese Communist threat to the independence of free nations. This was the argument that was being put forward by the United States, and this was the road that meant support from the United States. But the military, economic and diplomatic assistance which Pakistan expected by taking that road was desired primarily for more immediate reasons than the general strengthening of the free world against possible Soviet aggression or any specific Soviet threat to Pakistan itself. Those reasons flowed from the conflicts in which Pakistan found itself engaged with its two neighbors, India and Afghanistan. Prime Minister Suhrawardy, later defending the decision before his own National Assembly, stated it was the only way Pakistan could get aid against the threat from India and avoid an isolation that might have been fatal.[5]

An evaluation of the wisdom of Pakistan's participation in a Middle East alliance or formal regional security system involves several considerations: from the standpoint of the other Middle Eastern nations, whether it contributes to their interests and security; from the standpoint of Pakistan itself, whether it contributes to what it regards as its own vital interests; and from the standpoint of the United States, whether the advantages of having a committed ally offset the dangers of losing the sympathy, cooperation and even the continued independence of other states currently at odds with Pakistan.

Pakistan's army retains many of the traditions and the personnel of the Indian Army as it existed before partition. These troops could conceivably be used in the Middle East, yet how real is this prospect? Pakistan is a comparatively poor, geographically divided country which has not yet attained political stability despite undeniable advances made in the decade since independence was won. It cannot support a large modern military establishment. And it will not, in building up and training its forces with American help, divert its planning toward the defense of the Middle East, which is far removed from the concerns of the eastern half of the country while the attention even of West Pakistan is riveted on Kashmir and the possibility of war with India. These facts color the whole military picture.

[5] Statement of February 22, 1957, reprinted as H. S. Suhrawardy, "Foreign Relations and Defence," *Pakistan Quarterly*, v. 7 (Spring 1957), pp. 5-12.

On the political and economic side also, Pakistan has few ties with the countries of the Middle East. Its connections run rather to South Asia and overseas. As an Islamic state it aspires to some kind of solidarity with other Moslem nations; but secular Turkey is distrustful of this element in Pakistan's approach, and "neutral" Arab states like Egypt see it as a device by which Pakistan may try to divert them from their chosen policies. It happens that the four Asian members of the Baghdad Pact are Moslem states, but Islam is not the cement that binds them together.

Whether American military aid to Pakistan and the latter's joining the Baghdad Pact, though vigorously denounced by Moscow, have had any real effect on deterring Soviet aggression in the Middle East is doubtful. The firm pro-Western policies of Pakistan may have had some favorable influence in other countries, such as Iran, where Soviet pressures have been greater and the choices more difficult. The more immediate effects on America's position and prestige in the area, however, have been seen in connection with India and with Afghanistan.

American relations with India have been put under great strain by a number of issues, but by none more than this one. While the United States is under no obligation to allow its national interests in Asia to be defined by Mr. Nehru, it does have to take account of the fact that India is one of the most important countries in determining the future of Asia, and of the additional fact that the growth of Soviet influence there has been aided considerably by Pakistan's participation in military alliances sponsored by the West. India's annoyance, despite all the assurances given by the United States with the intention of holding it within bounds, was expected. What was not so precisely calculated was the extent to which these moves, to use Mr. Nehru's phrase, would bring the cold war to the Indian subcontinent. Moscow adroitly seized on India's mood of hostility to the United States to adopt a new line toward India, praising its efforts for peace and instructing the Indian Communist Party to support Nehru.[6] Soviet-Indian relations became increasingly cordial.

Another disadvantage to the United States has been the equivocal position in which it has been placed on the issues dividing India and Pakistan. Obviously it cannot compete with the Kremlin in support for India's case on Kashmir, but it could perhaps, in the absence of the ties of alliance with Pakistan, gain more credence in India for the impartial stand it has taken. On the other hand, we find that on such an issue we cannot give Pakistan the support to which it feels entitled. Pakistanis ask themselves what the alliance is worth.

With respect to Afghanistan the stakes may not be so high, but the situation has been even more critical. Afghanistan lays claim to the areas of Pakistan inhabited by Pathan or Pushtu-speaking tribesmen, sometimes to even more. These claims may have little substance either in law or on grounds of national self-determination, but they are taken seriously in Afghanistan and underlie the Afghan-Pakistani tension that led to rioting on both sides of the border and to the rupture of diplomatic relations in 1955. The subsequent cutting off of Afghanistan's access to the outside world through the port of Karachi had the practical effect of leaving open only the routes to and through the U.S.S.R.

Traditionally a neutral buffer state, Afghanistan had not committed itself to either side in the cold war and had received economic aid from both—that from the Soviet bloc being somewhat more showy and immediately useful and therefore of greater political effect. Now, with Pakistan tied formally to the West, Afghanistan has been all the more open to Soviet blandishments and penetration. The most spectacular step was the dramatic offer, on the occasion of the visit of Khrushchev and Bulganin to Kabul at the end of 1955, of $100 million in credits,

[6] G. F. Hudson, "Soviet Policy in Asia," *Soviet Survey,* no. 16/17 (June-July 1957), pp. 3-4.

accompanied by the words of sympathy for Afghanistan's territorial claims on Pakistan.

The Afghan leaders, a small group exercising control over a society still largely tribal in character, are certainly not desirous of seeing their country reduced to the status of a Soviet satellite. They have soft-pedaled the agitation for Pushtunistan and temporarily patched up the quarrel with Karachi. Still they have been taking the Soviet bait, and it is a question whether they can check the ominous trend without being able to depend on some counter-balancing influence from outside. That can only be the influence of the United States, which has seemed reluctant or unable to exert it. A partial explanation lies in the fact that, as in the case of India, the United States has found the closeness of its ties to Pakistan a handicap to carrying out policies that seem to be called for as a consequence of Soviet penetration.

The Soviet offensive in Afghanistan, in one sense, was a reply to Pakistan's accession to the Baghdad Pact. It may not have been the intention of those who conceived and organized the pact to consign an independent country of the Middle East to the Soviet bloc. But they have found themselves facing a serious problem in how to prevent it.

The Arab States and Israel

The Arab world reserves its greatest hatred for Israel. Except in Iraq, the whole idea of alliance with the West against the Soviet threat has had little appeal and tends to raise the old specter of Western imperialism. It has been demonstrated again and again that the Arab world as a whole will not be drawn into any regional organization of Western inspiration or with Western participation. Iraq's decision to conclude the Baghdad Pact flowed from the honest conviction of its leaders that this was the best way to strengthen the country's security and its international position. But the aftermath of that decision, as we have seen, raised two serious questions: whether the Government of Iraq could make it stick for a long period in the absence of the adherence of any other Arab state, and whether the reaction of Egypt and the rest of the Arab world did not outweigh any gains for Iraq and the West. For Cairo's new Arab alliances, ostensibly directed against Israel, were also aimed at Iraq and the West, and they were accompanied by Egyptian moves toward close partnership with the Soviet Union.[7] Perhaps these developments would have taken place anyway. It seems at least possible that they might have been delayed or partially avoided if the United States had merely extended military and economic aid to Iraq under the mutual security program without following so relentlessly the fetish of what some critics have called "pactomania."

Israel, because it presents a special case, is left out of all consideration of a regional alliance or security organization. No other state in the Middle East will enter into an alliance with it. Turkey might be inclined to do so, for they are the two strongest states in the immediate vicinity, but would not wish to break its ties with the Arab world, which would be the inevitable result. Israel has looked to the United States for a treaty which would guarantee its security and integrity, but does not get it because the United States will not thus jeopardize its position in the Arab states or give formal recognition to the armistice lines as permanent legal boundaries. Israel has, by official action of its Government and the Knesset, welcomed the Eisenhower Doctrine and affirmed its own · stand against any aggression (not Communist aggression alone). This formal approval of the doctrine was "noted" in Washington, but elicited no promises of support.

It is ironic, but understandable, that a state which is willing and anxious to play its part with the West in the collective defense of the region, and has the military capabilities to match its willingness, has been left out of consideration while pleas are made to reluctant and militarily feeble Arab states to join. Some critics of American

[7] See above, pp. 52-62.

policy, mainly those already committed to Israel's cause, have urged an alliance with Israel as the only friendly and dependable nation in the area except Turkey. The reasons against such a move are compelling, for it could bring in its train the certain loss of the whole Arab world.

American official thinking has taken the line that regional defense should be organized throughout the rest of the Middle East, Israel being left aside until its boundaries and other disputes with neighboring Arab states are settled. In other words, Israel would be left out indefinitely. But that has not meant that Israel would not have certain assurances against attack—those which existed by virtue of the United Nations Charter and the Tripartite Declaration of 1950. The latter fell victim to the Anglo-French attack on Egypt in 1956, but the United States Government later announced that, so far as it was concerned, the obligations were still in force, and on several occasions it has publicly called attention to the President's statement of April 1956 that the United States would aid the victim of an aggression, whether Israel or an Arab state.[8]

Alliances and Long-Range Aims

If we try to look ahead, we find no reason to believe that the Soviet threat will be uniformly felt or judged throughout the Middle East, or that at some point all states of the region will be prepared to come together in an alliance for the common defense. Despite their common religion, the Arab world and the non-Arab states of the northern tier do not feel a sense of common purpose. Their attitudes toward the West vary sharply. Iraq is hardly a strong enough link between them to warrant reliance on some early merger or cooperation of the two groups for collective defense. The Arab states seem incapable, for some time to come, of any effective cooperation even among

---

[8] *Documents on American Foreign Relations, 1956* (New York: Harper, for the Council on Foreign Relations, 1957), pp. 282-283.

themselves. And the Arab-Israel conflict, so long as it remains unresolved, will continue to poison Arab relations with the West. In such a situation do alliances and pacts offer an answer to the main problems of defense of the Middle East?

If it be true that the danger is not armed attack but Soviet subversion and enticement, success in combating it will depend principally on the internal strength of each country or area under threat. As a whole the Middle East will continue to be a "soft" region, with too much weakness and instability and too many internal and intra-regional conflicts to permit building the kind of community that NATO represents. The attempt to build such a community by persuasion from outside has the effect of forcing a showdown which divides the states into those willing to join it and those intent on not doing so. The advantages of securing the commitment of one's "friends" have to be weighed against what is lost by the increase of tensions within the area and by the alienation of those nations which choose not to commit themselves.

Conditions in the Middle East, conditions likely to endure for some time, indicate that the tensions and divisions heightened by outside attempts to organize security through alliances could jeopardize our long-range objectives. Those states brought into the alliance system will increasingly look to it as a means of getting preferential treatment and pursuing their own national aims within the region. Those outside it will tend to be pushed further away, and therefore more into the danger zone of close ties with the Soviet Union. The Middle East will then become what the Balkans used to be, an arena where local rivalries magnify, and in turn are magnified by, those of the great powers. Those who are not with us, as allies, will be against us. If the objective is to keep the entire Middle East in the free world, we cannot afford to see soft spots develop where the Soviets will have an open invitation to walk in. What has happened in Egypt, Syria and Afghanistan is enough to give pause.

Baghdad Pact and Eisenhower Doctrine

In the light of these prospects the Baghdad Pact has serious deficiencies as a principal instrument of policy for the defense of the Middle East. True, it brings together with the West those states of the Middle East which have many points of strength and, in contrast to the Arab world, greater stability and traditions of statecraft. To some in the West the Baghdad Pact has seemed to offer a new fulcrum for Western policy, now that Suez and the British treaty structure in the Arab area are gone.[9] It is, however, a rather artificial combination of four Middle Eastern states which have few natural ties with each other but whose governments joined together for various reasons: to get more support from the United States, or to pursue local interests of their own, transient or permanent, and only partly because of the Soviet menace. The combination has no military strength which the members do not have as individual states, and its effectiveness for military defense is gravely prejudiced by the nonparticipation of the "southern tier" of Arab states through which run most of the communications and lines of supply from the West. It adds little enough to a "position of strength," whether the viewpoint be military, economic or political. The inclusion of Great Britain in the pact has been a source of embarrassment since the Suez affair, when the four Asian members felt compelled to denounce the resort to force by their ally.

The ambiguous position of the United States, which has joined the committees of the Pact Organization without signing the pact itself illustrates some of the anomalies and difficulties inherent in the situation. Despite the embarrassment of not claiming its own child and the urgings of all the members, the United States has stayed out for fear of increasing the difficulties of its relations with other Middle Eastern states, especially Saudi Arabia on whose

[9] "The Baghdad Pact," *The Round Table*, no. 187 (June 1957), pp. 215-224.

good will continued access to oil and to the Dhahran airfield depends. Formal adherence by the United States would give the Baghdad Pact more strength and prestige and might in time attract additional Middle Eastern states to it. Still, why should a miracle be expected where so many obstacles, already evident, will continue to stand in the way?

To recognize these prospects is not to conclude that the pact should be abandoned or American support for it withdrawn. That would be merely to present Moscow and Cairo with a political victory of major proportions and provoke the resentment of all who were encouraged to form the northern tier alliance in the first place. Whatever is done by way of taking emphasis away from the pact should be matched by providing the member states with the equivalent, or more, of what they were getting by virtue of their association with it. Where the pact is a symbol of solidarity with the West, it should be replaced by other symbols which preserve the gains in the northern tier states while reducing the difficulties elsewhere.

The Eisenhower Doctrine, although denounced as loudly as the Baghdad Pact by Egypt and Syria, holds more promise if it can be developed into coherent policy. It has the virtue of covering the whole "general area of the Middle East." It is flexible. It implies a military commitment to the northern tier states that is as firm as the vague commitments of the Baghdad Pact, even should the United States join it. It makes it possible for Iraq to continue to get heavy American support, which is what it has sought through the pact, while keeping the door open to reconciliation with the other Arab states. At the same time it provides Arab countries like Lebanon, Jordan and Saudi Arabia, which could not be induced to join the pact, with the opportunity to cooperate with and receive aid from the United States to strengthen their own independence, without need of formal commitment on their part. It leaves to the decision of the individual Middle Eastern states whether they want to combine in alliances among themselves. The principal drawback is that the doctrine, like the pact, poses the question of open alignment with the West in the cold war and presents an easy target for Soviet, neutralist and nationalist propaganda, which has had some success in attaching the adjective "imperialist" to it in the public mind.

The Baghdad Pact, like the Arab League, might well be left to find its own level as a Middle Eastern organization. Perhaps it will gently fade into obscurity like its predecessor, the Saadabad Pact of 1937, which linked Turkey, Iraq, Iran and Afghanistan. Perhaps it will develop a real political and economic unity it does not now have. Such a trend should have some help, but not leadership and direction, from Western powers. Much of the trouble the Western powers have harvested in the Middle East has grown out of the impression, justified or not, that they were trying to dragoon nations into alliances against their will. Soviet propaganda has made inroads in the Middle East by playing upon this very theme. Not that the United States should allow Soviet propaganda, successful or unsuccessful, to dictate American policy, but the problem has grown out of the history of the area, not out of the fertility of Russian minds. The nations of the northern tier should continue to get the strongest support. The note of caution applies only to the nature of the arrangements by which it is provided.

The Arab League

The Arab League, deprecated as it has been in the West, irresponsible and divided as it has been in its own counsels, is worth a more searching and sympathetic look by the United States, without the illusions that colored British attitudes when the League was created and without taking at face value the extravagant claims of Arab leaders. Unquestionably anti-Western and anti-Israel in its thought and action so far—these being the lines which its preponderantly Egyptian leadership has tended to stress

—the League has established itself as something bigger than an instrument of Egyptian policy or a purely negative and destructive force. It gives concrete form, however imperfect, to the nearly universal Arab yearning for national unity. For better or worse it is regarded by Arabs as their own.

Arab governments have frequently put forward the idea that if the West is really interested in promoting security and welfare in the Middle East, it can do no better than to support the Arab League. The dangers have been obvious—support which only fed Arab ambitions against Western interests or Israel would not help the cause of peace or that of containing Soviet expansion—but those dangers may not always be of the same magnitude as they are today. The Arab League will be likely, no matter how conditions change, to continue to reflect the balance among Arab governments and the prevailing opinions in the Arab world. Despite their divisions the Arabs themselves recognize it as an enduring institution. It survived the disasters of the Palestine war of 1948 and Abdullah of Jordan's "disloyal" conduct in annexing a large part of Palestine. Iraq, when it signed the Baghdad Pact, made much of its continued loyalty to the Arab League. And Egypt, despite threats to withdraw, never carried them out. In the long run, so far as Iraq is concerned, the Arab League is likely to have more staying power than the Baghdad Pact.

It may be wise, by a more tolerant attitude toward the League, to help it develop a moderation of its own and to strengthen the tendencies which Iraq now represents while weakening those which turn the Arabs against the West. It is not suggested that the United States should shift support from the Baghdad Pact to the League—that would be folly—but rather that the pact cannot serve as the chosen instrument of American policy without risking the alienation of the Arab world; and that the League may be a rallying point for Arab nationalism when the time comes that it will assert itself against the Soviet imperialism of the present instead of against a Western imperialism that no longer exists. A strengthened Arab unity need not, if we are clear and firm about it, mean the destruction of Israel or the weakening of Western support for the states of the northern tier.

It is important to understand the political importance of illusions. When the West has talked of the need for regional alliances for defense and of filling the vacuum of power in the Middle East, the stock Arab reply has been that a regional alliance already existed: the Arab Collective Security Pact of 1950, which the West could support if it were really interested in security. The argument could not be taken seriously. Divisions among the Arab states, military weakness, political instability, economic backwardness, lack of organization and the manifest desire to fall upon the State of Israel made of that pact anything but an anchor of Middle Eastern security. Yet real political risks lie in ignoring the fact that, weak or strong, it still has, and will have, significance in the minds of the great mass of the Arabs.

The United States would do well to give some recognition to the Arab League's possibilities, to be moderate in judgment of its faults, sympathetic toward it as an expression of Arab aspirations for greater unity, and more willing to give ear to it as spokesman for the Arab world. This is not a matter of concrete political and military support—obviously out of the question at this stage—but of general attitude, of storing up good will we may sorely need in the future.

The United States, in pursuing its objectives in the Middle East, must seek cooperative and friendly relationships, in varying degrees, with all Middle Eastern countries. As the struggle is likely to unfold, it is not the search for active allies in war that will be our guiding purpose—although that is not something to be ignored—but the search for political and economic conditions which will prevent a weakening anywhere in the Middle East. American policy must take account of the "neutrals," so long as their neutrality is genuine and not a disguise for serving Soviet ends, as well as those nations which choose to be allies. Efforts to form or to encourage regional alliances or organizations may or may not be helpful to the general purpose. As easy generalization is not justified, perhaps it is enough to point out that the military advantages (which may in many instances be obtained in other ways) and the benefits of having a number of declared allies may be outweighed by the loss of freedom of action and the risks of accentuating tensions and divisions within the area and of driving other states into the arms of Russia. Where regional groupings are of local inspiration and represent genuine unifying forces in the area, they are likely to have more staying power and should enter into our calculations for the future, dangerous or disruptive though they may be in the present. All in all, while it may be a good rule of thumb that the value of a policy for the United States varies directly with the loudness of the protests which Mr. Khrushchev, Mr. Nehru and Colonel Nasser raise against it, it would seem that conditions in the Middle East make a policy of "pacts and blocs" scarcely more suited to our objectives than to theirs.

Chapter 15

ECONOMICS AND POLICY

ECONOMIC factors explain much of what is happening today in the Middle East, a region notable for the wealth
of its oil resources and the poverty of its people. The
problems are of such magnitude—relentless population
pressure on limited resources in some areas, dependence
on a single-crop economy in some, need for land reform,
limited possibilities for industrialization—that local governments, despite brave words, are nearly all beyond their
depth in their attempts to cope with them. It is not possible here to attempt a comprehensive survey and analysis
of the problems themselves or of what various governments have done about them. Our more narrow concern
is with the bearing of economics on international relations
and on the objectives of American policy. Economic factors may not determine the policy, but unless properly
handled they can wreck it.

One set of problems flows from the location in the
Middle East of over two-thirds of the world's proven reserves of petroleum.[1] What is its importance in case of war,
and in the absence of war? How do the West's requirements for oil limit or affect relations with the nations
under whose soil it lies and through whose territory it

[1] *Petroleum Survey*, Hearings before the U.S. House Committee on Interstate and Foreign Commerce, February 4-March 22, 1957, 85th Cong., 1st
sess. (Washington: G.P.O., 1957), pp. 24-27. The estimated percentage has
been revised, always upward, a number of times during the last two decades
as new fields have been discovered. In 1957 Mr. Felix Wormser, Assistant
Secretary of the Interior, gave the current estimate as "about three-quarters"
of the world's known reserves (*Emergency Oil Lift Program and Related
Oil Problems*, Joint Hearings before U.S. Senate Subcommittees of the
Committee on the Judiciary and the Committee on Interior and Insular
Affairs, February 5-21, 1957, 85th Cong., 1st sess., pt. 1, Washington: G.P.O.,
1957, p. 62).

must move to reach its markets? Does oil promise us new opportunities in the Middle East, or certain failure? Another set of problems arises from the scarcity of water and of good land in the Middle East and the poverty and backwardness of its people, together with their ardent wish for economic progress and a better material life. Will an expanded program of outside assistance bring an appreciable rise in living standards? Will it help to solve the political problems?

The challenge to the West, and especially to the United States, is to fit together the answers to these two sets of questions in a way that will protect the vital Western interest in oil on terms satisfactory to the Middle Eastern nations, while giving them some prospect of a more abundant life in generally friendly and cooperative relations (but not necessarily in alliance) with the West. American policies on trade, foreign aid, investment and the protection of American commercial interests should fit into the general strategy of establishing this necessary cooperation. Much of our foreign economic policy is, of course, global in character for the obvious reason that international trade and finance are global and can only flourish on that basis. In the Middle East, however, we encounter situations where economic measures are the most suitable or perhaps the only easily available instruments of national policy. Although the general principles of U.S. commercial and financial policy are not to be lightly ignored or broken, they may perhaps be bent to fit the urgent requirements of political strategy.

The Need for Middle Eastern Oil

The domestic economy of the United States is not dependent on Middle Eastern oil. More political pressure, indeed, has been generated to keep it out than to bring it in. In 1956 imports from the Middle East amounted to 19.7 per cent of all petroleum imports and equaled only

4 per cent of domestic crude oil production.[2] It can be argued that the use of imported oil conserves our own national resources against early depletion, but the U.S. Government has accepted as a more compelling argument on grounds of national security the thesis, put forward chiefly by the independent producing companies, that unless domestic producers have a sufficient share of the domestic market they will not undertake the necessary exploration for new resources needed in time of crisis. The President, acting under legislative authority, has called for voluntary limitation of oil imports, setting quotas for each company, and has indicated that direct import controls will be enforced if the voluntary scheme does not work.[3]

Whether one interprets such measures as reflecting the requirements of national security or domestic political pressures, they illustrate the American economy's independence, for as far ahead as we need look, of Middle Eastern oil. It may be that sharply rising costs of exploration and development at home will bring demands for increased imports of the much cheaper oil of the Middle East, but not as a matter of national necessity. Should supplies from the Middle East be cut off altogether, the United States would still have access to ample alternative supplies, in proved reserves and predictable new discoveries, in the Western Hemisphere.[4]

On the use of the oil of the Middle East in the event of

[2] U.S. Bureau of the Census, *United States Imports of Merchandise for Consumption,* Report no. FT 110 (Washington: G.P.O., 1957), p. 88; U.S. Bureau of Mines, "Crude Petroleum and Petroleum Products," *Mineral Industry Surveys* (Washington: Author, 1957). The proportion was roughly the same in 1954 and 1955.

[3] Report of the Special Committee to Investigate Crude Oil Imports (Secretary of Commerce Weeks, Chairman), submitted to and approved by the President, July 29, 1957 (mimeographed).

[4] *Emergency Oil Lift Program and Related Oil Problems,* pt. 1, cited, p. 62. A study put out by the Chase Manhattan Bank, however, forecasts a steeply rising demand in the United States and a threefold increase in imports (to some 3.3 million barrels daily) by 1966 (Kenneth E. Hill, Harold D. Hammar and John G. Winger, *Future Growth of the World Petroleum Industry,* New York: Chase Manhattan Bank, 1957, pp. 19, 33).

war, we can do little more than speculate. In a limited war it could be tremendously useful if the installations were held more or less intact. In a general war of any duration it is at least open to grave doubt whether the oil would be available to anybody. Even if the Western powers could hold the Middle East for an extended period, the oil installations and pipelines would be primary targets for missiles, bombing and sabotage. If it be assumed that Soviet forces could overrun the Middle East, the chances that they would find the installations intact would be minimal, and even if they did they could not get the oil back over the mountains into the Soviet Union.

The great danger is not the loss of the oil in the hypothetical case of war, but its loss in time of peace if the countries which produce it, or through which it moves to Western markets, should pass under Soviet control or should themselves decide to cut off the supplies. Control of Middle Eastern oil, which the Soviets do not need for their own economy (they export oil now and apparently have plentiful reserves), would give them an inestimable advantage in the cold war, for though the United States can get along without Middle Eastern oil, Western Europe cannot. A few figures will illustrate the extent of Europe's dependence, and thus of its vulnerability. Western European requirements in 1956 were about 3,000,000 barrels daily, amounting to some 20 per cent of the total energy used. Seventy per cent of this oil came from the Middle East.[5]

The crisis of 1956, when the Suez Canal was blocked and the pipelines from Iraq to the Mediterranean were cut, showed how vulnerable the Western European economy was to the interruption or sharp diminution of these supplies. They were not entirely cut off: some 200,000 barrels still moved to Europe daily by pipeline from Saudi Arabia, and some of the tankers which had previously gone through Suez delivered oil by the longer

[5] Walter J. Levy, "Issues in International Oil Policy," *Foreign Affairs,* v. 35 (April 1957), p. 454.

route around the Cape. With the increase of supplies from
the Western Hemisphere to meet the emergency, Western
Europe was able to maintain total oil consumption at
about 80 per cent of normal, with a higher figure for basic
transportation and the most urgent industrial requirements. The immediate crisis was surmounted without
causing a disastrous drop in industrial production, although the impact on trade balances and on the gold and
dollar reserves of some Western European countries was
severe, and the fact of vulnerability was brought home to
every citizen deprived of gasoline for his automobile or
fuel oil for his home.

The crisis was surmounted because the loss of Middle
Eastern oil was not total, was not lasting (the canal was
open again in May 1957 and the pipelines from Iraq were
in partial operation by March of that year), and was almost
matched by added supplies from the Western Hemisphere.
Suppose that in some future crisis the whole supply from
the Middle East were unavailable. Suppose that the Soviet rulers had it under their control, to turn the faucet
on or off at their whim. Some adjustments could be made,
including rationing on both sides of the Atlantic. Still,
Europe could not possibly meet the financial strain of
meeting its requirements indefinitely from the Americas.
As a matter of fact, we cannot be sure that sources in the
United States and Venezuela could stand the strain of
indefinitely meeting Europe's requirements as well as
those of this hemisphere.

The dependence of the Western European economy on
oil, moreover, is increasing. As coal production will have
no spectacular rise, oil is expected by 1965 to account for
more than 25 per cent of the total supply of energy. Projected import requirements for 1965 come to some 4,300,-
000 barrels daily, well above the present level. Production
of nuclear energy, even if rushed at top speed, cannot
be expected to do more than reduce the rate of increase
of the need for oil. Over the next decade Western Europe
will need more and more oil, and unless there are un-

foreseen developments it can only be Middle Eastern oil.[6]

So long as Western Europe's strength and stability is important to the United States, the latter must accept the oil problem as its own. If Middle Eastern oil does not flow westward, if Europe's economy is placed at the mercy of the Soviet Union or of local potentates willing to cut off Europe's lifeblood for whatever purpose, the whole structure of Western security on which American policy has been based will be threatened with collapse. We may set it down as a vital American interest, then, that Middle Eastern oil supplies continue to be available to Europe.

Yet merely to state the proposition is not enough. Much depends on what shape the threat takes and what means of defense can be used. The main danger is not a Soviet attempt to seize the oil resources by force, presenting the United States with a clear choice of using counterforce at the request of a Middle Eastern country. It is that a Middle Eastern country may come gradually under Soviet influence to the point that it exercises its "sovereignty" over producing or transit facilities in the service of Soviet interests; or that its relations with the Western powers may so deteriorate that it chooses to seize installations or interrupt transit as an act of pique or reprisal; or that the oil companies may become the natural target for virulent nationalism, leading to their expropriation. To be faced only with the alternatives of losing access to the oil or of using force against a Middle Eastern state to maintain it is to lose out no matter which choice is made, for the use of force cannot provide a permanent answer and would destroy the prospects for even that minimum of respect and good will without which the Middle East cannot be held in the free world.

The main task, then, is to forestall the incipient crises, to prevent matters from coming to such a pass that nationalization or the cutting of pipelines seem to Middle Eastern governments and peoples to be necessary measures of defense or of national self-expression. As for the means,

---

[6] Levy, article, cited, pp. 455-456.

the building up of bargaining power provides a partial answer; for the rest, it is a matter of creating favorable political and economic relationships among the Western governments, the oil companies, and the governments and peoples of the Middle East.

A Search for Alternative Sources and Routes

One reason for the precariousness of the present position is that most of the bargaining power is in the hands of sovereign rulers and governments whose conduct, by Western standards, may be quite irresponsible. When a Mosaddeq can close down oil production in Iran, an Abdel Nasser can block all passage through the Suez Canal, and a Syrian army clique can blow up the pipelines crossing that country, the Western governments and companies are without recourse except to diplomacy and can hardly exercise much suasion as long as Europe's dependence is so extreme. That dependence has to be lessened by finding and developing alternatives: new sources of energy other than oil, new oil supplies in other areas, and new routes of transport less subject to arbitrary interruption.

The lesson of the Suez crisis has stimulated the British and other Western European governments to redouble their efforts toward the development of nuclear energy for industrial purposes. They may be expected to make the most of coal and hydroelectric resources. Whatever they do, however, barring some scientific "break-through," does not hold out the promise of making an appreciable dent on the growing requirements for oil over the next ten or fifteen years.

Can any large proportion of the oil come from sources outside the Middle East? Western Europe itself (Italy, for example) can raise its own production, although at best the total will only reach a few hundred thousand barrels daily, a mere fraction of the requirements. Algeria is a great hope, but will it be available? New resources may be developed in the Western Hemisphere, especially in

Canada, which can serve Europe as a partial alternative to Middle Eastern oil in time of crisis. Whether they could supplant it over a long period would depend on the ability to work out financial arrangements which would not place an intolerable burden on the dollar reserves and the economies of the Western European countries.

Another desirable measure of insurance is the accumulation of reserve supplies in Europe to provide a cushion for several months or even longer in case of emergency. Perhaps the most hopeful and practical possibilities of increased bargaining power lie in establishing new means and routes for the transport of petroleum products from the Middle East to Western Europe. The Suez route, shorter by far than the route round the Cape, will continue to be more economical for tankers up to the largest size (30,000 tons) that can pass through the canal. The costs of the Cape route can be sharply reduced, however, by the use of "supertankers" of the type recently built, reaching 80,000 and even 100,000 tons in size. So long as the Suez Canal remains open, private enterprise may not have the incentive to build them. In that case public policy would appear to demand that they be built, either through subsidy or by Western governments themselves. Nothing would put the Suez Canal issue in better perspective than to loosen the stranglehold on Western Europe's life which the present government of Egypt, or any government of Egypt, will have so long as over one million barrels of oil must pass daily through the canal on their way to Europe, with no economically acceptable alternative.

Other possibilities of lessening dependence on local governments lie in increasing the number of pipelines. At present all the lines from the Persian Gulf area to the Mediterranean run through Syria, which of all the Arab states has been the most unfriendly to the West, the most open to Soviet penetration, and the least stable politically. The lines of the Iraq Petroleum Company (I.P.C.) all traverse Syria, and some cross Lebanon as well (the line to Haifa in Israel has been cut since 1948). The Tapline, which carries the Arabian American Oil Company's oil from the Saudi Arabian fields to Sidon on the Mediterranean, crosses the territory of four countries: Saudi Arabia, Jordan, Syria and Lebanon. That this line was not cut in the Suez crisis, as were the I.P.C. lines through the simple means of blowing up the pumping stations, was due to a forbearance on the part of Arab governments that they might or might not show in some future crisis.

Alternative routes through countries less hostile to Western interests have been considered, and even surveyed. One is a line from Iraq northwestward through Turkey to Iskenderun on the Mediterranean, an expensive but apparently feasible project. Lines from the Iranian fields could be tied into it; or a separate line could be built from the Qum field in Iran to Iskenderun, without crossing Iraq. Another project is a line across Israel from the Gulf of Aqaba to the Mediterranean, a much shorter route but one requiring tanker haulage at both ends. Bearing in mind the long-term interest, the Western nations would do well to see that some new pipelines are built, for they cannot be improvised overnight in time of crisis. The other purpose to be served is that of proving to countries like Egypt and Syria that they do not hold a noose around Europe's neck, and that to interrupt the transit of oil will merely cut their own revenues without putting great pressure on Europe. The mere demonstration of a serious intention to go ahead with such new pipelines should strengthen the hand of the Western powers in dealing with certain Arab governments. Again, if private enterprise finds the obstacles too great, it is up to governments to see that means are found to get the job done.

Measures like the building of large tankers can be taken by the West on its own initiative and without undue concern over the reactions of Arab governments. Much more ticklish from the latter viewpoint are some of the pipeline projects. Iraq, for example, may hesitate to go along with the line through Turkey for fear of being charged with disloyalty to Arab interests. The line across Israel, already laid with 8-inch pipe, would undoubtedly arouse Arab ire and possible reprisals against the West; some of the oil-producing countries could be expected to try to prevent shippers of their oil from using it. Arab governments are talking about an "all-Arab" pipeline system, to consist of new pipelines (and confiscated old ones?) owned and operated by the Arab states. It is hard to imagine an economic enterprise, if it ever came into being, more likely to be used for political purposes.

As these illustrations indicate, measures to provide alternative routes of transport and thus to reduce dependence will be most effective if their construction and use have an international flavor and are not solely the enterprise of Western governments and companies, and if they are linked with policies which conciliate rather than antagonize the Middle Eastern nations concerned. The main idea, after all, is to continue to have Middle Eastern oil available, moving to Western Europe in ways most economical for all concerned, chiefly through the Suez Canal and the existing pipelines. Alternatives are a necessary hedge against what the future may bring. Even so, they are no guarantee against nationalization of the oil companies or the interruption of the lines of supply. Those contingencies are real enough to warrant the most serious effort to find a basis for relations with the Arab governments that will reduce to a minimum the possibilities of their occurrence.

Oil and the Pressures of Nationalism

Abdel Nasser's political victory in the Suez crisis has posed the question whether other Arab governments may be tempted to seize Western oil companies operating under their jurisdiction. Egypt's own influence seems certain to be asserted in that direction, and so long as Abdel Nasser's brand of anti-Western Arab nationalism continues to win converts in the other countries, the oil companies are natural targets of agitation. The Egyptian approach is to speak of all the oil in the Arab world as "our Arab oil" now in the hands of the imperialists. Several times the Egyptian Government has called for an Arab oil conference to be held in Cairo. Whether the aim is to carve out an oil empire for Egypt, itself poor in proved oil resources and unable even to supply its own needs, or to enhance Egypt's position by embroiling the oil-producing countries with the West, the appeal is a powerful one. Communist propaganda on the iniquities of the oil monopolies helps it along. Any ambitious Arab politician must be attracted by the temptation to seek popularity on the issue of Arab national rights to the resources which lie under Arab soil and are now making handsome profits for foreigners. Nationalist fervor could crystallize on the oil question as easily as it did on Suez. Mosaddeq in Iran showed how it can be done.

The pattern of the oil industry in the Middle East is the product of a half-century of history, in which Western enterprise, with some official pushing and support, has scrambled for concessions, taken great risks, and made huge profits in countries at a lower stage of economic and technological development. By its size alone and the monopolistic nature of the concessions, not to speak of its impact on the local society, the oil industry inevitably became a special problem, not just a business enterprise like any other. The companies have had to concern themselves with local and international politics, to arm themselves with experts on "government relations," and to perform many of the functions ordinarily associated with governments. As the Middle Eastern countries advance, the question arises whether these particular types of concessions and relationships will endure.

The oil companies have attempted to ward off the threat of nationalization by keeping the governments satisfied. In Iran, where concessions to local demands might have averted the nationalization law of 1951, the Anglo-Iranian

Oil Company did not make them in time. Elsewhere the companies have taken the edge off nationalist demands through the now generally applied formula for division of profits on a 50-50 basis between oil company and local government, plus arrangements for the training of local citizens, the provision of public services like roads and hospitals, and many concessions to local pride and sensitivity. Even in Iran, after two years of crisis demonstrated the inability of the Iranian Government to produce and market the oil without the cooperation of the Western companies, an acceptable *modus operandi* was worked out in 1954 by which the company remains nationalized, management of production and marketing are in the hands of an international consortium, and profits are divided on a 50-50 basis.

The stake which local governments have acquired in the continuing profitable operations of the companies is a considerable one, which must give them pause when they think what nationalization would mean in economic terms. The Mosaddeq experiment carried a lesson for the Arabs as well as for the West. What happened in 1956 is instructive. The wave of anti-British feeling that swept across the Moslem and especially the Arab Middle East after the Anglo-French move into Egypt found expression in outbreaks of sabotage here and there against oil installations, and in a Saudi Arabian prohibition on the direct export of oil to Britain and France, in addition to the Syrian interruption of the I.P.C. pipelines. That was all. There was no general assault on the British oil companies. The ruler of Kuwait, the biggest producer, had every reason not to disturb a relationship which had made him and his country fabulously wealthy under British protection. The governing group in Iraq did not want to court further losses in oil revenue beyond those caused by interruption of the pipelines. Saudi Arabia saw no reason to take action against Aramco, an American company and the sole concessionnaire in that country, as punishment for the sins of Britain and France. Iran, slowly benefiting

from its gradual return to the ranks of the major producing countries, had never been sympathetic with Nasser's challenge to the West and had no interest in helping
Egypt at Iran's own expense. In general, the oil companies
survived the test of a critical time very well.

The bonds of mutual economic interest are and should
continue to be strong. As long as production continues
to rise, royalties under the 50-50 arrangements rise also.
In the past few years the producing countries have taken
in nearly one billion dollars annually in royalties and
other direct payments. The 1956 figures for the three big
producers were approximately $280 million for Saudi
Arabia, $300 million for Kuwait and $193 million for
Iraq.[7] The rulers of these three countries are not likely,
by emotional and ill-considered political action, to place
in jeopardy the development plans and the style of living
to which, by virtue of revenues of this magnitude, they
have become accustomed. That is, however, no cause for
complacency on the part of the companies. Already they are
circumscribed in their operations by a variety of requirements affecting the terms of the concessions, the location
of headquarters, management decisions and control of exports. The growth of nationalism seems almost certain to
put increasing pressure on the governments and to bring
demands for a greater share of the profits and a larger role
in management. Eventually, as confidence in local ability
to run the machinery of production grows, the demands
will include nationalization of foreign companies and
reservation to national companies of rights to future development of oil resources. The decision of the Iranian
Government to put development of the new field at Qum

[7] The total was about $880 million in 1955 and $940 million in 1956.
While Iraq's royalties fell from $207 million to $193 million owing to the
cutting of the pipelines in Syria at the time of the Suez crisis, Iran's oil
revenue rose from $90 million in 1955 to $146 million in 1956. See U.N.,
Department of Economic and Social Affairs, *Economic Developments in
the Middle East, 1955–1956* (New York, 1957), p. 58; *Emergency Oil Lift
Program and Related Oil Problems*, pt. 2, cited, p. 1420; Senate Hearings
on the Eisenhower Doctrine, pt. 1, cited, p. 33.

in the hands of the national oil company and not those of the international consortium illustrates the trend.

Demands for a larger share of the profits are only natural. Any government with a chance of increasing its "take" by holding out for more can be expected to do so, nationalism or no nationalism. In negotiations which Tapline and I.P.C. have carried on with Syria and Lebanon on payments or "rental" for the pipelines it has been perfectly evident that the motive purpose on the side of those two governments was simply to sell at the highest possible price their consent to the flow of oil across their territory. Similarly, Saudi Arabia and other Arab states may see possibilities in demanding for themselves a greater share of the profits on the production and sale of oil. Is there anything sacred about the 50-50 formula? Might it not just as well be 60-40 or 75-25, with the local government taking the bigger share, so long as the goose will keep on laying the golden eggs? How high will the companies pay for the privilege of staying in business? From the viewpoint of the companies, what assurance do they have of continuance on a basis they can accept?

As far as the public interests of the Western nations are concerned, the important point is not the margin of profit of the companies but their continuing ability to produce oil and move it to Europe. If the alternative is to see their expropriation and the subsequent drying up of production as happened in Mexico in 1938 and in Iran in 1951, the Western governments have a duty to do all they legitimately can to keep the companies in business. Over the next decade the problem will be a three-cornered one, with the companies under pressure from governments and nationalist forces in the Middle East, the local governments caught between popular pressures and fears of losing the Midas touch, and the Western governments trying to keep the companies operating and the oil flowing on terms that will not unduly disturb political relations with the Middle East. Should the companies and the Western governments seek new arrangements to cushion the shocks to come? Such arrangements might include changes in the character of the companies, new intergovernmental relationships, or some form of "internationalization" of the industry.

It is difficult to see what internationalization could mean in practical terms. Local nationalism is not likely to be more tolerant of an international agency representing foreign governments than it is of the private companies, and the industry certainly would not run as efficiently under such an agency. International agreements to assure uninterrupted access by all consuming states to the Middle East's oil might be useful if the producing states could be induced to sign them, but they would not really work unless effective redress could be taken against a state choosing to exercise its sovereignty by some action that would in fact interrupt or shut off that access. Would the existence of a treaty prevent Syria, in a time of political stress, from cutting the pipelines again? And if that happened, would world conditions permit the injured parties to apply sanctions? The experience of the Suez crisis would indicate a negative reply on both counts.

Similarly, an attempt to bring the United Nations into the picture holds no great promise. It would tend to throw the whole oil question into the framework of the Arab-Western disputes perennially before the United Nations and also of the controversies over "colonialism," in which the Communist states and the Asian-African bloc could have a field day at the expense of the "oil monopolies" and "Western imperialism." If, by some remote chance, agreement could be reached on acceptable terms for a U.N. authority or commission to oversee the oil industry in the Middle East and protect both producers and consumers, the West might have some further assurance of continuance of its supplies, although the possibilities of deadlock in such a commission would be infinite and the possibilities of enforcement of its decisions against a Middle Eastern government intent on exerting its rights of sovereignty would be strictly limited.

These considerations merely reinforce the importance of the future relationships involving the companies and the governments directly concerned. The Western governments should do what they can to improve the political atmosphere, so that the operations of the companies do not suffer merely because they are convenient targets of a general antagonism to the West. The industry itself must be conducted in such a way as to create and fortify in the minds of the Middle Eastern peoples two convictions: that these enterprises are not wholly foreign but are partly their own, and that the wealth which their oil represents is producing returns for them in terms of broad economic development.

The first point the companies may meet successfully if they continue to anticipate demands in providing an expanding role for local governments and local citizens in management and operations. This is an especially difficult proposition for the companies in that they cannot continue to function efficiently if the process goes too fast, or to function at all if vital decisions are taken out of their own hands. It tends to make them, in practice, national companies in each Middle Eastern country where they operate, whereas they are in fact international companies (of American, British or mixed ownership) with world-wide interests. They are also naturally concerned with whether appeasement of local pressures can be brought to a stop short of expropriation. Several countervailing factors exist, however. Local governments and most local nationalist leaders are aware of some of the limits beyond which it is unwise to push. If one government alone pushes too far, as Iran did in 1951, it may find it has no market for its oil and that other producing countries are expanding their output to make up the difference.[8]

The best hope, surely, is to give the producing nations a sense of partnership in a successful enterprise that

[8] When Iran lost its markets, production in millions of metric tons in Kuwait rose from 17.3 (1950) to 47.3 (1954), and in Saudi Arabia from 26.6 (1950) to 46.5 (1954).

would cease to be successful if the partnership broke down; and it should be a sense shared by popular opinion as well as governments. It may be possible to achieve this partnership within the framework of the present system. If not, the companies and the Western governments should attempt to forestall the crisis by timely negotiation. If it comes to nationalization, the best response may well be the Iranian solution, a national company operating through an international consortium; but it should be reached before instead of after a crisis like Iran's, which held up production for over three years.[9]

The second point, the use of oil revenues for economic development, also presents the companies and the Western governments with difficult decisions. The principal producing countries already have vast sums at their disposal from royalties and taxes on Western oil operations. Iraq has used its oil revenues wisely, devoting 70 per cent of them to a development program planned and administered by a nonpolitical Development Board. Iran is also moving ahead with a development plan, though it is still more plan than development, owing partly to the drop in oil production during the Mosaddeq period and the need to use subsequent oil revenues to cover the regular budget. Saudi Arabia gives no public accounting of its expenditures of oil revenues, and there is no question that much of it goes abroad and into palaces and other forms of conspicuous consumption on the part of the King, his relatives and principal supporters. Some, however, goes into roads, schools and welfare projects, and the national economy generally derives benefit from it. In tiny Kuwait it is a case of more oil money than the ruling Sheikh

[9] Iran's present policies hold the door open to equitable and practical arrangements between the national company and foreign concerns, and an agreement has already been concluded with the Italian state oil entity covering an area outside the territory of the consortium. (Text in *Bank Melli Iran Bulletin*, no. 185-186, August-September 1957, pp. 316-325; also "Persia's Petroleum Policy," *Petroleum Press Service*, v. 24, October 1957, pp. 359-362.) This agreement and a recent one between Saudi Arabia and a Japanese concern, however, provide a higher than 50 per cent "take" for the government and thus may tend to unhinge the 50-50 pattern.

knows what to do with; so, after providing his subjects with all the public services they can absorb, he banks the rest of it in London. How the local governments have spent their oil revenues has been their own decision, and the pattern has had wide variations. The Western governments and the oil companies have followed a "correct" line of not attempting to influence those decisions, but they are involved with them in the public mind for the obvious reason that the companies are the source of the revenues.

Here again the idea of partnership is a useful one. The oil companies have an interest in proving that their activities represent not the exploitation of Eastern peoples by Western capitalists, but the exploitation of natural resources to mutual advantage; and that, besides the benefits that accrue to the people living in the vicinity of the main installations, these activities produce general benefits to the whole country. It is also in the interest of the United States and British Governments that the use of the oil revenues be such as to promote economic and social progress and to help in the process of peaceful transition toward new political institutions consonant with popular aspirations. Middle Eastern governments are understandably touchy about being told how to run their own countries. This is, however, a field in which much can be done cautiously and tactfully by way of exchange of information and advice.

The U.S. technical assistance program and that of the United Nations provide means of extending help in planning as well as in techniques. The oil companies, with men who know these countries and their problems, may make an even greater contribution. They might employ such a device as earmarking a certain percentage of profits, before the 50-50 split is calculated, for a development fund to be administered jointly with the local government. Such projects may sound quixotic. They would cost something. But the danger represented by the contrast between a backward country with meager signs of general economic

and social advance and a prosperous foreign company
paying large sums to a government that does little or
nothing to promote the livelihood of the people is worth
some extra thought and some extra expenditure.

The Urge for Development

Except for oil, the Middle East is ill endowed with
natural resources, and of those that it has, many are still
to be developed. Vast expanses of desert press in upon
the limited arable areas where a backward peasantry
struggles in want against the handicaps of inadequate
water, primitive techniques, and a myriad of pests and
diseases affecting crops, farm animals and people. In recent years some improvement has resulted from irrigation
and drainage projects, increased use of chemical fertilizers,
better tools, pest control and general health measures.
Nevertheless, as the annual United Nations economic
survey notes, "these improvements have not, as yet, fundamentally changed the character of agriculture in by far
the greater part of the region." [10]
Industry, though expanding, is subject to serious limitations in the shortage or lack of domestic raw materials,
not to mention capital, management skills, and a trained
industrial labor force. Several countries are so dependent
on one or two crops as to be a prey to developments beyond their control. If Turkey's wheat crop is ruined by
drought, or if Egypt's cotton crop finds no market at an
acceptable price, the foreign exchange position of those
countries is hit disastrously. Amid all the talk of modernization, new projects, seven-year plans and the like, the
standard of living remains abysmally low. Annual per
capita income in every country of the area, except Israel
and Lebanon, is under $250, and in some it is under $100. [11]

[10] Economic Developments in the Middle East, 1955–56 (New York, 1957),
cited, p. 5.
[11] U.N. Statistical Office, National and Per Capita Incomes, Seventy
Countries—1949, Statistical Papers, Series E, no. 1 (New York, 1950), p. 28;
and also Per Capita National Product of Fifty-five Countries, 1952–1954,

Poverty has long been the lot of the Middle Eastern peasant and nomad. In itself this fact has had not extraordinary political significance except for an occasional outbreak of violent protest. Even today the masses in the Middle East are not organized as a political force. They are gradually awakening, however, and they are listening to the words of local political leaders and to those which come over the air from foreign lands. The appeals of nationalism, of communism and of democracy all offer them a higher status and a better material life. The articulate political demand for progress, for social reform and for economic development comes primarily from the new middle-class intelligentsia. They may be interested mainly in better jobs and status for themselves, but their demands reflect a much broader feeling on the part of great numbers of people that they are entitled to something better than they have. It is an expectation which colors the attitude of peoples toward their governments, and of both peoples and governments toward foreign powers which are trying to win their favor.

Such expectations are not peculiar to the Middle East. They are present throughout the many underdeveloped areas of the world. American policies which have evolved over the past ten years in response to this situation are, in their main outlines, general rather than based on a specific political strategy for the Middle East. The approach has followed the theory that steady economic development will create stability, or at least minimize instability, and will thus reduce vulnerability to communism. It is a theory impossible to prove. Many times in history instability and revolution have appeared not when conditions were at their worst but when they had begun to get a little better; partial satisfaction of wants

Statistical Papers, Series E, no. 4 (New York, 1957), p. 7. The higher figures are: Israel $470; Lebanon $260; Turkey $210. For Egypt and Syria the figure is between $100 and $200. For Afghanistan, Pakistan, Iran, Iraq, Jordan, Saudi Arabia and Yemen it is under $100. These statistics are not and cannot be precise, as statistical methods in most of the Middle Eastern countries are rudimentary, but they give the approximate picture.

has proved to be a certain stimulus to pressure for something more. Vulnerability to communism cannot be mathematically measured by the standard of living. Nevertheless, we really have had no choice. For the wealthiest country in the world to ignore the insistent desire of the underdeveloped countries for help in developing their economies would destroy all faith in American leadership in the free world, turning allies into neutrals and neutrals into enemies. A foreign aid program, long labeled as temporary for home consumption, has come to be an accepted concomitant of leadership of the free world.

The U.S. Aid Program

American economic and technical aid to the Middle East has been spread rather widely, with some variation of the pattern because of differing needs and political attitudes. Turkey, besides getting considerable economic benefits from military aid, has been granted substantial economic aid for years, recently at an annual level of over $100 million. Iraq, needing no outside capital because of its own substantial oil royalties, has received technical aid only. Iran has had substantial economic aid since 1953, chiefly to keep the government solvent, in addition to a large program of technical assistance. Modest amounts have been granted to Lebanon and Jordan for specific public works and industries. Syria has refused all aid on the ground that the conditions attached to it (the same as for all other recipients) were unacceptable. Saudi Arabia accepted technical assistance for a while, then arbitrarily terminated it in 1954. Egypt has had very little, and since the grant of $40 million in 1954 made at the time of early faith and hope in the Nasser regime, nothing. Israel has received, since 1948, $266 million in grants and $206 million in loans, more than all the Arab states combined, in addition to considerable sums from private American sources. The table on the following page shows the totals through the middle of 1957.

U.S. NONMILITARY AID TO THE MIDDLE EAST, JULY 1945–JUNE 1957 [12]

(millions of dollars)

	Grants				Loans (net)
	Mutual Security Program (Economic & Technical)	Extraordinary Relief	Agricul- tural Surplus Through Private Agencies	Total Grants	(from 1940)
Turkey	400.2	12.2	0.9	413.3	205.3
Iran	232.4	2.8	2.1	238.0	153.6
Pakistan	150.3	108.0	17.5	275.8	103.1
Afghanistan	8.1	—	0.1	8.2	51.7
Iraq	11.0	—	0.5	11.5	1.4
Saudi Arabia	2.7	—	—	4.3	31.8
Syria	0.1	0.2	0.8	1.1	0.1
Lebanon	19.8	0.3	1.9	22.0	1.6
Jordan	33.9	1.1	2.9	37.9	—
Egypt	33.9	1.0	28.5	63.8	25.5
Libya	26.3	9.7	1.0	50.0*	3.5
Israel	226.8	—	39.0	265.8	206.3
	1,145.5	135.3	95.2	1,391.4	783.9

* Includes $13 million "special purpose funds."

Source: U.S. Department of Commerce, *Foreign Grants and Credits by the United States Government, June 1957 Quarter* (Washington, October 1957).

It is difficult to draw up a balance sheet. American aid has enabled Turkey to maintain an army it could not

[12] The figures on different kinds of grants do not always add up precisely to those for total grants, owing to the inclusion in the totals of certain minor items (U.N.R.R.A. to Egypt and lend-lease to Saudi Arabia and Iran). The table does not include sales of agricultural surpluses for local currencies; where these currencies are returned to local governments as loans or grants, they are included under the general headings above. Agreements concluded by June 30, 1957, provided for sales of agricultural surplus with market value as follows: Turkey, $111.6 million; Iran, $12.9 million; Pakistan, $120.5 million; Israel, $52 million. See *Sixth Semiannnal Report on Activities under Public Law 480* (83rd Cong., as amended), U.S. House Document no. 212, 85th Cong., 1st sess., July 22, 1957 (Washington: G.P.O., 1957), p. 25.

otherwise afford. It has helped Iran over the difficult period before its oil resources could again begin earning substantial revenues. It has made it possible for Israel's economy to keep going even though imports were running three to five times as high as exports. And it has saved Jordan from bankruptcy. The political gains are undeniable, although not subject to measurement in terms of the money spent. On the other hand, in many countries political stability is still as far away as ever. American aid has not stabilized Jordan; indeed, the U.S. economic mission and its works have been the target of nationalist rioting and abuse. And general economic progress in the area has been disappointingly slow.

Some critics have maintained that what has been given has been merely wasted, citing the continued absence of sound development, the recent Soviet gains, the "ingratitude" of some recipients, and the unwillingness of others to commit themselves to the Western side in the cold war. Others have argued for a much larger program, one which would make a real impact both on the minds of the peoples of the Middle East and on the economic problems themselves. What the U.S. Congress and the American people will support in the way of an aid program in the future is a controlling factor, and also an unknown one. It will depend in large degree on how clearly the Executive analyzes the possibilities and defines its purposes, and on how persuasively it then presents its recommendations to the Congress and to the people. Special studies of existing programs were in fact made in 1957 at the behest of the Senate in connection with a general review of the global program then in progress.[13] Bearing in mind their recommendations, which generally favored continuing or increasing current programs, it is worthwhile reassessing the

---

[13] *Greece, Turkey, and Iran; Report on the United States Foreign Assistance Programs* (Survey no. 1), prepared at the request of the U.S. Senate Special Committee to Study the Foreign Aid Program, 85th Cong., 1st sess., February 1957 (Washington: G.P.O., 1957); and also, *Lebanon, Jordan, and Iraq; Report on United States Foreign Assistance Programs* (Survey no. 2), same.

entire role of foreign aid and economic policy as it relates to long-term objectives in the Middle East.

The general strategy of thwarting Soviet advances and establishing or strengthening common interests with the nations of the Middle East has been discussed in other chapters. Here the question is how economic measures can serve that strategy. The following might be listed as the general aims such measures should seek to accomplish: (1) to have an immediate impact on decisions by Middle Eastern governments and on the views of important segments of the population; (2) to encourage those who cooperate with us; (3) to counter and frustrate moves by the Soviet Union, both political and economic; (4) to promote stability and strengthen the capacity of Middle Eastern nations to uphold their independence; (5) to establish habits of cooperation and mutual confidence between the West and the Middle East; and (6) to help build a more prosperous Middle East as a means of promoting trade and general economic progress throughout the free world. It seems evident that the first three of these aims call for one kind of program, which should be short-range and eclectic, and that the last three require a different kind of program, one of longer range and greater consistency.

Certain things have to be done in the economic field to surmount critical situations, to help friendly states, or to demonstrate American interest and generosity. In this category is the economic aid to Turkey, Iran or Pakistan, which has helped them to survive the effects of a series of bad crops, to cope with critical shortages, or to restore order to public finances. In this category also would fall emergency aid to Jordan or to some other state to meet a demonstrable immediate need; support of a spectacular project important to a Middle Eastern government or likely to impress local public opinion at a critical juncture; or measures to forestall or counteract Soviet moves in the economic field, including unorthodox trade practices if necessary, to prevent a Middle Eastern country's mortgaging its economic future to the Soviet Union.

In a sense this is economic warfare, in which the economic cost is accepted because of the political gain. For a policy of this nature to be successful, the Administration should have a free hand to use appropriated funds as the occasion demands, without being bound by fixed country programs, restrictive criteria, or the requirement to refer decisions to the Congress. How much money would be necessary will depend on how events in the Middle East develop.

By these criteria much of our past aid to the Middle East, either because of the character of the projects or because of the methods used, has been aimless and sometimes politically harmful. The Point Four operations in Saudi Arabia, for example, aroused resentment without producing any compensatory favorable results. It is always wise to look closely at the pattern of leadership, upon which so much in the Middle East depends, so that specific programs and projects may be weighed according to whether they will strengthen the position of those leaders who are, actually or potentially, favorably inclined toward objectives similar or parallel to those of the United States.

Long-Term Development

For the longer term the needs and the requirements of policy are different. Here we run into questions which go beyond the bounds of the Middle East. The whole subject of American aid for economic development abroad is a matter of considerable controversy, official and unofficial. With respect to global policy, it is not the purpose here to go into the arguments on such questions as the relative roles of private investment and public aid, the virtues of loans as against grants, the merits of multilateral and unilateral channels in providing and administering aid, or the desirability of a large-scale new program aimed at a general steady rise in living standards throughout the underdeveloped areas. In the conviction, however, that aid for development should be a continuing part of the foreign policy of the United States, and on the assumption that it will in fact be continued, a number of pertinent observations may be made regarding the use of such aid in the Middle East.

How much capital will be necessary, and what portion of it should be provided out of United States public funds, it is impossible to say. This will depend partly on what other governments and the World Bank will provide, and partly on the rate of private investment, domestic and foreign. The World Bank, because of the restrictions of its charter and its practices, is not likely to make sufficient loans to assure a rate of progress in development that will be adequate in terms of both local economic possibilities and political tolerances.[14] It is a bank and not an "aid fund." Investment of foreign private capital is not likely to be significant outside the oil industry. The scope of an additional program of public loans or grants would depend both on the goal set (in terms of a steady rise in national income or of completion of certain big projects) and on the ability of the local society to absorb outside capital and technical aid, taking into account both the economic and the cultural or human limitations.[15]

The mutual security legislation approved by the Congress in the summer of 1957 provided for a global Development Loan Fund, capitalized at $300 million for the next fiscal year, in addition to the regular mutual security funds, of which the Administration planned to devote some $236 million in "defense support" and technical

[14] The Bank has loaned $246.4 million to Middle Eastern countries (Iran, Iraq, Lebanon, Pakistan, Turkey). See International Bank for Reconstruction and Development, *Twelfth Annual Report, 1956–1957* (Washington, September 1957).

[15] The studies of the World Bank on the economies of Syria, Jordan, Turkey and Iraq are useful in this regard. See International Bank for Reconstruction and Development, *The Economic Development of Syria* (Baltimore: Johns Hopkins Press, 1955); and also, *The Economic Development of Jordan* (Baltimore: Johns Hopkins Press, 1957); *The Economy of Turkey* (Washington: Author, 1951); *The Economic Development of Iraq* (Baltimore: Johns Hopkins Press, 1952).

assistance to the Middle East.[16] Whether, over the years, this level of aid will provide an adequate program cannot be judged arbitrarily. On the basis of past experience and assuming that the program is expected to show some solid results, it is a reasonable guess that the level will have to be higher, possibly twice as high.

The first consideration in regard to method is that a program of development aid (both economic and technical) should be based on criteria that are primarily economic rather than military or political, although military and political benefits may flow from it in due course. Simultaneous efforts, moreover, should be made to attack the political problems, to which economic aid may contribute; for example, it could be called into play to help reduce the proportions of the Arab refugee problem. But the guiding purpose should be to foster sound and steady economic development, based on the best available estimates of what is feasible in each country and in the region as a whole.

A second and related consideration is impartiality. It involves the assumption that the basic purpose is to strengthen the Middle East generally; that the United States wishes to see progress, rather than stagnation and unrest, in all states of the area: allies, neutrals and even those whose "neutrality" leans to the Soviet side. The aim would be to support a program that would reach and serve the peoples of the Middle East, not necessarily over the heads of their governments but, insofar as possible

[16] *Mutual Security Appropriations for 1948,* Hearings before the U.S. House Subcommittee of the Committee on Appropriations, 85th Cong., 1st sess. (Washington: G.P.O., 1957), p. 547. The figure of $202 million for defense support, however, is for the whole of "the Near East, South Asia and Africa," including Greece, Libya, Morocco and Ethiopia. That of $34 million for technical assistance excludes those countries, but includes Afghanistan and Pakistan. In view of the cuts made in the Administration's bill by the Congress, actual expenditures in the Middle East may not be as high as these figures indicate, although previously appropriated unexpended funds were still available. Ambassador Richards committed $118.7 million of these funds in his trip to 15 countries explaining the Eisenhower Doctrine (see "Promoting Peace and Stability in the Middle East," *Department of State Bulletin,* v. 37, August 26, 1957, pp. 339-343).

and reasonable, without regard to the political views of governments. It is a worthwhile investment in human values and in present or future good will. Thus there should be no requirement for endorsement of the Eisenhower Doctrine or other commitment to the Western side in the cold war.

A third set of considerations concerns organization. The reluctance of the U.S. Congress to vote money to be dispensed by an international agency is a political fact. The experience with U.N.R.R.A. after World War II, necessary as the work of that agency was, left no happy memories with the Congress. Subsequent attempts of underdeveloped countries to have the United Nations set up a special multilateral fund or agency for development have encountered the opposition of the United States which has yielded only to the extent of proposing (in 1957) a small "technical development fund" tied to the U.N. technical aid program. The American position has been that no multilateral capital fund is practicable until international disarmament makes resources available. Accordingly, it may be unrealistic to suggest anything but a unilateral American program, which we should have in any case. Nevertheless, it is worth considering, if only for a part of the total program, the arguments for a multilateral approach, such as a U.N. development fund or an adaptation of the Marshall Plan in which the recipients would have a collective voice in the allotment of the funds.

What the United States wants from a long-range economic program is results: economic, social and, with luck, political. It does not want the headaches and special responsibilities involved in identification with specific projects that may turn out well or badly. Suppose, for example, that the construction of the High Aswan Dam should again be considered to be a feasible and desirable project, both on economic grounds (the World Bank approved it once and only withdrew because the United States and Britain did) and, applying the criterion of impartiality, on grounds of acceptance by interested states.

The dam remains a necessity for Egypt, if only to stay even in the race against overpopulation.[17] It could hardly be done on the previously contemplated basis: the past could not be so easily forgotten on either side; besides, the United States would not want the troubles that would go with trying to make Egypt toe the mark in its economic policies in order to do its part on the dam. These difficulties for the United States would be avoided if the World Bank, working with a special international development agency, were carrying out the project with Egypt.

The whole question of "political strings," so successfully exploited by Soviet and nationalist propaganda, should be eliminated, wherever possible, from long-term aid. The people of the receiving states would probably know well enough where the help came from, although it might bear the label of the United Nations or some other international agency. The United States inevitably would be the chief provider, but not necessarily the only one. Other industrialized countries, particularly the German Federal Republic, could contribute, as could the oil-producing countries in the Middle East itself. An international program, moreover, seems the best answer to the Soviet economic offensive in the Middle East. The Soviet Union could be asked to contribute to the program. If it agreed, although it could create plenty of difficulties from within, the sharp teeth of its own economic assault would be drawn. In the more likely contingency of its refusal, it would be up against a competitor without specific national ulterior aims and with greater resources at its disposal.

The Soviet Economic Offensive

When the propaganda is stripped away and the economic data are examined, the Soviet offensive looks less formidable than it has seemed. As to trade, the U.S.S.R.

[17] Doreen Warriner, *Land Reform and Development in the Middle East* (London and New York: Oxford University Press, for the Royal Institute of International Affairs, 1957), pp. 16-24.

and its satellites have negotiated many new commercial agreements with Middle Eastern states, but as the following table shows, up to the end of 1956 they had not greatly increased their share in the trade of any of them except Turkey and Egypt. Later statistics, when available, should show also a sharp rise in the Soviet bloc's share of Syria's foreign trade in 1957 as well as a further increase in that of Egypt.[18]

TRADE WITH THE SOVIET BLOC (INCLUDING COMMUNIST CHINA) AS PERCENTAGE OF TOTAL TRADE

	1953		1954		1955		1956	
	Im-ports	Ex-ports	Im-ports	Ex-ports	Im-ports	Ex-ports	Im-ports	Ex-ports
Turkey	5.5	7.4	9.4	16.5	18.4	21.8	14.6	19.7
Iran	9.7	12.5	9.5	18.3	9.4	15.2	10.0	16.7
Pakistan	5.1	1.6	2.0	9.4	1.2	9.2	0.6	6.5*
Iraq	—	—	—	—	—	—	—	—
Syria	3.2	—	2.5	0.5	2.8	1.2	3.2*	4.6*
Lebanon	2.1	2.0	2.3	2.3	2.6	5.3	3.0*	2.5*
Egypt	7.7	12.2	5.9	14.1	6.8	26.7	14.4	34.4
Jordan	—	—	—	—	—	—	—	—
Israel	0.8	3.4	4.1	5.2	1.7	3.8	1.0	4.6

* Incomplete figures.

Source: U.S. International Cooperation Administration, *The Strategic Trade Control System, 1948–1956*, 9th Report to Congress on Operations under the Mutual Defense Assistance Control Act of 1951 (Washington: G.P.O., 1957), pp. 94-101. These totals do not include arms shipments to Egypt and Syria, but presumably do include goods exported to the Soviet bloc in payment for arms. Figures for Afghanistan are not available.

The case of Turkey is one of economic necessity for the Turks, because of their lack of foreign exchange and of credit in the West. They have taken the step with their eyes open and are on guard against an economic dependence that could give Moscow the ability to exert significant pressure. As for Syria and Egypt, although both

[18] In the first half of 1957 the U.S.S.R. led all other countries in its share of Egypt's exports and imports (National Bank of Egypt, *Economic Bulletin*, v. 10, no. 3, 1957, p. 281). Unofficial reports indicate a rise in the Soviet bloc's share in Syrian exports, in the first half of 1957, to 23 per cent, and in Egypt's to 47 per cent (*New York Times*, January 7, 1958, p. 68).

governments have proclaimed their desire to trade with the West, they have become increasingly dependent on the continued willingness of the Soviet bloc to take their principal exports and to supply in return what the local economies need. They have, furthermore, obligated themselves to pay for large quantities of arms with commercial exports over future years. Data are not available on these agreements and transactions which have played so large a part in entrenching Soviet influence in Egypt and Syria. If estimates of the value of the arms shipments in the hundreds of millions of dollars are correct, then Egypt and Syria are likely to be without the means of preserving their traditional trade with the West at more than a very low level.

The other side of the Soviet offensive is the extension of loans on easy terms, usually at 2 or 2½ per cent and "without strings." In 1955 Afghanistan was promised, and apparently is receiving, credits totaling $100 million. In 1957 Syria was granted credits the amount of which was not officially divulged but appeared, from the list of projects, to run to several hundred millions of dollars, to be used for equipment and services provided by the Soviet Union. Late in the same year, on the occasion of General Abdul Hakim Amer's visit to Moscow, the official Egyptian news agency announced a Soviet offer to extend Egypt credits in the amount of 700 million rubles ($175 million); but again, as in the Syrian case, the actual total would be determined by later agreements on individual projects. Those were the only known large Soviet loans to Middle Eastern countries reported up to the end of 1957.[19] The Soviet practice is to choose a country where the economy is vulnerable and the political atmosphere favorable, then move in with an offer to finance projects the local govern-

[19] According to the U.S. Department of State, total credits extended by Communist bloc countries to Middle Eastern states, from January 1955 through December 1957, including military, were as follows (in millions): to Afghanistan $145; Egypt $480 (including $5 million in grant aid); Syria $280; Yemen $10 (*New York Times*, January 4, 1958). Smaller credits went to Lebanon and Sudan.

ment particularly wishes to undertake. In the case of Syria, where the World Bank had already made a study and questioned the economic desirability of certain projects favored by the Syrian Government, the U.S.S.R. offered to finance those very projects.

It is impossible to say whether in the long run Moscow will make good on its promises. The fine print in the agreement with Syria and the practical working out of the program may contain many a string not apparent to Syrians dazzled by the amount of the loan and the signs of effusive and disinterested friendship. For Russia the value of the agreement lies in the opportunities to put its experts in all key spots, to direct Syria's economic policies, and to monopolize its trade. The prime objective is to gain control of Syria. The complementary objective may be to use Syria as an example to attract other Middle Eastern states into the Soviet orbit. Future offers to other states may be very attractive. When the political stakes are high enough, the Soviet Union somehow manages to "afford" the economic policies that help to win them.

The American response to the Soviet economic offensive should not be a response at all, but a series of policies which stand on their own feet in terms of the Middle East's needs and aspirations. In the economic field there is every opportunity for initiative and very little reason specifically to match or outbid Soviet offers or to copy Soviet methods. The challenge will be met if the United States and other nations can develop sound and continuing policies and programs, which offer to Middle Eastern nations an attractive alternative to exclusive economic ties with the Soviet Union. The latter might be able by spectacular moves to upset such a program here and there, but the opportunities should diminish as it gains momentum.

Participation by the U.S.S.R. and its satellites in the trade of the Middle East, or in its economic development, should be no cause of undue concern to the West. The danger lies in situations which allow the Soviet Union to acquire positions of excessive influence, by well-timed offers or bargains or by building up a dominating position as a provider of capital and technical help. The best insurance against that danger lies in keeping open all the channels for the Middle Eastern nations (including Egypt and Syria) to trade within the free world, in averting serious payment problems which force them to turn to the Soviet bloc, and in seeing that their economies develop with help from non-Soviet sources.

American policy should be double-barreled: flexible enough to permit governmental decisions and rapid action to meet situations of urgency or to support individual Middle Eastern countries as may be necessary; and steady enough, through a long-term and preferably international program, covering investment and technical aid, to produce the results and the atmosphere of cooperation that will immunize the Middle East to serious Soviet economic penetration.

Prospects for Regional Development

Several serious proposals have been made for a "bold new program" of regional economic development in the Middle East.[20] The idea may be helpful in stimulating public interest and in galvanizing the West into constructive action. It also has merit economically in that some of the great basic projects of harnessing rivers and irrigating deserts should not be restricted by national frontiers. The Euphrates runs through Turkey, Syria and Iraq; the waters of the Jordan should serve Syria, Jordan and Israel; projected new pipelines, like the old ones, will cross a number of international boundaries. Projects of this nature will require a high degree of international cooperation.

[20] *The Middle East and Southern Europe*, Report of Senator Hubert H. Humphrey on a Study Mission for the U.S. Senate Committee on Foreign Relations, July 1, 1957, 85th Cong., 1st sess. (Washington: G.P.O., 1957), pp. 2-4; *Regional Development for Regional Peace, A New Policy and Program to Counter the Soviet Menace in the Middle East* (Washington: Public Affairs Institute, 1957), pp. 10-37.

Similarly, with other problems which are obstacles to economic progress—the inadequacy of communications and transportation routes, the lack of technical skills, the prevalence of disease—it makes more sense to attack them in accordance with a coordinated general plan than in a dozen national compartments. The disparity in available capital resources between the oil-rich states and the others seems another logical argument for a common program for the development of the region as a whole. Kuwait and Saudi Arabia cannot properly absorb their royalties from oil as fast as they accumulate; the surplus would be better invested in a country like Egypt, Syria or Jordan than spent in ways unrelated to the needs of the community. Some "national" problems, moreover, like that of the explosive population pressure in Egypt, are beyond the power of national efforts to solve. Even with land reform, the most advanced agricultural techniques, industrialization, and the High Aswan Dam, Egypt could not indefinitely support its rapidly expanding population. The obvious solution is to export some of it to less crowded Arab states like Syria or Iraq.

The idea of regional cooperation for economic development in the Middle East is a sound one. If it is to be of any practical use, however, it has to be brought down from the realm of the grandiose regional plan—complete with Director, High Authority, comprehensive long-term programs, and fruitful cooperation among Westerners, Turks, Israelis and Arabs—to what is feasible economically and sensible politically. An economic plan for the Middle East, especially one made in Washington, might not run into all the same troubles encountered by the Western proposals for a Middle East defense organization, but the obstacles would be formidable and many.

The salient fact is that the Middle East is a region of such great variations in economic progress, social structure, and political institutions that general participation in a regional economic program would not be a practicable proposition for some time. The Baghdad Pact nations have undertaken a few joint projects among themselves, but have shown no desire to cooperate with the Arab states. Israel remains economically isolated in its surroundings. The oil-producing states have proposed no share-the-wealth plan. The Saudi Arabian Government may make loans to other Arab states, but it is wary of any scheme that would put its oil or its oil revenues at the disposal of some regional authority. So much needs to be done on the national level in many countries by way of agricultural reform, elementary industries, and technical training that the broader regional requirements seem to them less pressing.

For the United States the most fruitful approach is to encourage and support feasible and promising projects, like river valley development schemes, which involve limited cooperation among different Middle Eastern states, particularly those which link states of the northern tier with those of the Arab world. Among the latter, moreover, the concept of greater economic cooperation is sufficiently real to be deserving of support. Thus far they have concentrated on the negative task of coordinating measures of economic warfare against Israel. Encouragement to pursue something more constructive might be useful in preparing the way for the broader solutions not practical now. Inter-Arab economic projects with sufficient international backing should serve as desirable alternatives, in Arab eyes, to development with Soviet loans on Soviet terms.

Inter-Arab economic cooperation or even union has long been discussed in Arab circles. Syria and Jordan have gone as far as declaring their intention to abolish all economic barriers between them. The difficulty is that political currents often cut across the natural economic ties. For example, Syria's economic development would benefit from close association with Iraq, but for political reasons the Syrian urge toward Arab unity has now taken the form of moves toward union with Egypt, which cannot help Syria economically. The United States will do well to avoid strong initiatives or direct involvement in the jungles of inter-Arab politics, in its desire to promote regional development. In general, it should take a generous and benevolent attitude toward inter-Arab regional projects which have solid local support. If plans such as those involving the use of oil royalties for the general development of the Arab world are to take form, the impetus will have to come from the Arab states themselves. If such an impetus does materialize, and on a basis that respects Western interests, Western governments and oil companies ought to be prepared to contribute material and technical assistance.

Meanwhile, there is still plenty of room for economic development on a national basis. Iran and Iraq have programs which will absorb their capital and energies for some time; they need continuing technical advice and assistance. Turkey and Israel need capital for sound long-term projects, as well as emergency aid. Egypt urgently requires capital, trained personnel and adequate organization to build the High Dam, which should still be of interest to the Western nations unless they prefer to take a chance on the continued deterioration of the situation in Egypt to the point of anarchy.

We should not expect miracles from economic and technical aid to the Middle East. It can help avert nasty situations. It can contribute to stability, or rather to controlled change, by helping to raise living standards or to prevent their decline. It can offer new hope to the people through projects that increase the arable land or wipe out disease. If provided in ways that satisfy the recipients, it can win a certain amount of good will. Still, economic policies and aid for development do not of themselves provide us with the master key to success in the Middle East. They do not guarantee a contented populace plus resistance to communism. They are not a substitute for the solution of political problems. They are, however, a necessary concomitant and lubricant of efforts to solve those problems.

Chapter 16

THE UNITED STATES AND THE
NEW MIDDLE EAST

THE EXPLANATION of failure and the keys to success lie, above all, in the realm of political relationships. We have seen how plans for the organization of defense, for economic development, or for containing the explosive possibilities of local conflicts all depend on the political atmosphere. The West's experience with Abdel Nasser has shown the importance of the new leadership arising in the Middle East. Although he himself and his present regime may be temporary political phenomena, unless the United States knows the nature of the new types of leadership, unless it can devise a political approach which awakens a responsive echo among those who are or will be exercising power, then it has little chance of an effective defense of the area, whether the challenge is military, political or economic.

Because of the inchoate nature of Middle Eastern society, the absence of stable political institutions and the high degree of illiteracy, the role of local leadership takes on special importance. Attempts to influence the course of political development, to succeed, will have to be aimed more at the leaders than at the masses of the people. Leaders, of course, will themselves be concerned with the currents of popular opinion, if they wish to keep or to gain political power. They "make" and guide popular opinion, however, to a much greater extent than do political leaders in the West. Where political power is so dependent on shifting combinations among leaders and on emotional appeals, they understand better than do Western governments the ways and means of holding or gaining it. Especially in the short run, it behooves us to adapt our policies to the facts of Middle Eastern politics rather than to any Western conception of what the situation might or ought to be. In the longer run, as we have seen on the question of economic aid, American policies can and should take account of the new situations in which the people will have a larger role; but here also it will be to the new leadership more than to the amorphous mass that the policies should be directed.

No array of "experts" on the Middle East can be expected to lay out the pattern of the future. History has stored up in this region so many tensions and conflicts, currents and cross-currents, that little except more tension and conflict is predictable. What the U.S. Government has a right to ask of the experts is that they introduce as much clarity as possible into the picture in a way that will have some meaning for the policy-maker. This chapter, drawing on the knowledge of many who know the area well, will mention what seem to be some of the main trends, and the types of policy decisions they seem to call for, without presuming to any special prescience. The problems are complex enough to require almost unlimited study and continuing reassessment.

Old forms and institutions in the Middle East are at various stages of decay or readaptation, while new ones are in process of construction. The ways of the West have proved contagious, although in many instances they have been turned against the West. The new nationalism, in its present strident and uncompromising form, seems to leave the West helpless either to conciliate or to deal firmly with it. Still, the pattern is far from uniform. What is true of Lebanon, of Turkey or of Israel will not hold for Yemen or Oman. A rough judgment may perhaps be made on where the differences are principally those of time, the main trends being the same throughout the region, and where they flow from the separate history and national character of individual peoples. We have to make some estimate of what kinds of societies are developing, what groups and classes are likely to come to the fore, and what general attitudes are taking shape. Will those attitudes open the gates to communism? Will they leave any room for compromise and cooperation with the West, and particularly with the United States?

Turkey

The experience of Turkey may be instructive. A half-century ago the Young Turk revolution turned Turkey's face toward the West, and the subsequent reforms of Kemal Ataturk marked a drastic break with the past. It was not a mere superficial borrowing of Western methods in order the better to combat the West, although that was a part of the motivation behind it, but a studied attempt to give the new Turkey the inner strength as well as the outer trappings of a modern national state.

Economic development and technical progress were part of the transformation, but more important were the fundamental changes in the law codes the Turks lived by, the clothes they wore, the alphabet in which they read and wrote, and the relation of their religion to the state. Ataturk carried through these reforms with a boundless and ruthless energy. While they have gone deeper among the urban population than the peasantry, and although evidence persists of modes of thought neither secular nor modern, Turkey today testifies to the general acceptance of the reforms and to the success of what was in fact a political and social revolution. Turkey is a secular state with a working democratic system of government.

Turkish political leadership, we have some right to expect, should remain purposeful and strong. The democratic institutions which the Turks have developed may not be so well anchored as many apologists, Turkish and American, have claimed. The temptations for a party in power to deal harshly with its opponents, to curb freedom of the press, and to equate strong criticism with disloyalty are still strong. The Democratic government of Adnan

Menderes has yielded to these temptations, as its Republican predecessors did in their day. The election of 1957, which returned the Democrats to power, was not without its charges of fraud and intimidation. Yet basically the trend toward a modern state and society has not changed. The institutions of democracy and the sense of community with the West seem to be firmly embedded in the consciousness of the people.

The United States has every reason to encourage and to help consolidate these trends. This it can do by proffering advice when it is welcome, without any identification with the party in power or the parties in opposition, and above all by material assistance to the government and to the people. Turkey has shown a constancy of policy that has made it the most reliable American ally in the Middle East. Should Turkey waver or be reduced to desperate measures by economic troubles, the entire defense of the Middle East would crumble.

How much is it worth to the United States that Turkey should continue to stand firm, to cooperate in defense plans, and to make available bases on its territory? No one can sanely recommend that it is merely for Turkey to name its price. The United States cannot keep filled a cornucopia with a hole in the bottom. Its foreign aid program is world-wide and must have certain rules that apply to all recipients. For reasons of over-all policy it may decide to put aid for development on a basis which makes no differentiation between allies and neutrals. We may assume, too, that Turkish policies are based on Turkey's national interests. The Turks are with the West because they find this the best way to assure the defense of their country, not because they are paid a price for it in economic aid.

On the other hand, we cannot become the prisoners of our own regulations. We should realize that the Turks tend to look at the whole question of aid as primarily political in character. They therefore take it amiss when the United States turns down their requests with admonitions to put their economic house in order, while offering far more to Egypt or to India. In the past few years Turkey has received an average of close to $100 million in economic grants per year, most of it under the label of "defense support;" but the political benefits have been lessened by the ill effects of stalling off and then turning down Turkey's request for additional support in loans.[1]

Admittedly it is a difficult problem, for many of the Turkish Government's economic policies have been unwise (for example, overcommitment of resources to new and unnecessary industries, overborrowing abroad on short-term credit, and failure to check inflation), and there is no sense in subsidizing folly; good money will follow bad without accomplishing its purpose. Certain reforms are necessary before the Turkish economy will be on a sound basis. Yet these reforms are not politically easy to make, and we should never become so stubborn in our economic arguments or set in the ways of bureaucratic routine that we lose sight of the real objective of mutual security, which must rest on the continued willingness of Turkey to see its security as tied to the West. We are, after all, giving the Turks what amounts to a continuing subsidy, not because their international payments are out of balance or because their agriculture is in need of tractors, but because they are steadfast allies and are standing up to Soviet threats and pressures. Continued haggling and pressure for changes in economic policies may obscure and even obstruct the real purpose of the subsidy.

The Soviets have discovered the political benefits of providing aid "without strings." Here there is a lesson to be heeded. Turkey does not hesitate to declare itself in the world struggle. We need not fear giving offense on that score. Neither the government nor the opposition parties have flirted with neutralism. It is all the more neces-

[1] The Turkish Government requested, in 1955, a loan of $300 million, which was not granted. The United States did, however, adjust its annual aid program to meet Turkey's urgent need for fuel, raw materials and spare parts.

sary, when Turkey is being forced by economic necessity into closer commercial relations with the Soviet bloc and may be pushed by domestic pressures toward totalitarian methods, to help it through its "second revolution," that of economic transformation, and to keep relations on a basis of full faith and confidence. Turkey seems to be in a position further to develop its economy and raise its still pitifully low living standards while maintaining its Western outlook and its inner coherence as a nation. Such situations are rare in the Middle East. Even at some extra cost we have much to gain by encouraging the trend, and possibly everything to lose by not doing so.

Turkey experienced its national revolution a generation ago. It fought for its independence against the Western powers and Greece, and in doing so it sought and received aid from Soviet Russia. In due course it consolidated its national independence and allied itself with the West. Its nationalism is now mature enough to be able to accept Western troops and bases on Turkish soil. If the example has any validity for other nations of the Middle East, then the main question may be whether we are vouchsafed the time required for young, vigorous and presently anti-Western national movements to mature and settle down. Obviously, Iranians and Afghans and Arabs are not Turks, but the possibilities of a generally parallel development are not to be ignored. The experiment at least has the attraction of success, for Westernized Turkey has attained a strength which is the envy of other Moslem nations of the Middle East.

Iran

Kemalist Turkey had an influence on Iran and Afghanistan between the wars, when Reza Shah and Amanullah Shah, respectively, tried to copy some of Ataturk's reforms. Much of their modernization, however, did not go beneath the surface. In backward Afghanistan the power of the religious and tribal leaders was not broken, and they eventually broke the power of the reforming monarch. Reza Shah did a great deal to push Iran into the 20th century but he did not have the national support that Ataturk had in Turkey, and the country remained essentially weak and disunited. The Iranians did not, like the Turks, go through the fires of a combined revolution and war for national independence. The later experience of foreign occupation in World War II, however, was a stimulus to nationalism and also to popular restlessness, evident in the growth of the Tudeh (Communist) Party. Iranian nationalism asserted itself against the Soviet Union in the crisis of 1946, and then even more spectacularly five years later with the seizure of the Anglo-Iranian Oil Company and the revilement of the West symbolized by the figure of Mohammed Mosaddeq. He brought the country to the verge of bankruptcy, but he did it to the accompaniment of the cheers of many, many Iranians. And he set an example that was not lost on the Arabs.

With the fall of Mosaddeq in 1953, the young Shah, son of Reza, and the old ruling groups were able to reassert their power. They chose to repudiate Mosaddeq's policies and to come to terms with the Western powers. They concluded an agreement which, without undoing the act of nationalization, placed the production and marketing of oil of the former Anglo-Iranian concession in the hands of an international consortium. They requested and received additional military, economic and technical assistance from the United States. Iran ignored Soviet threats and blandishments and finally, in November 1955, joined the Baghdad Pact. The reaction from Moscow was a strongly worded note calling this step "contrary to Iran's good-neighbor relations with the Soviet Union and to certain of Iran's treaty obligations." [2] But Iran stood firm.

These events do not mean that Iran has reached the point in its evolution that Turkey has. It has experienced

[2] J. C. Hurewitz, *Diplomacy in the Near and Middle East, A Documentary Record: 1914–1956* (Princeton: Van Nostrand, 1956), v. 2, p. 416. Presumably the reference is to the Soviet-Iranian treaty of 1921 (see above, p. 27).

no such thorough sweeping away of the old order. Its nationalism has not been tempered and disciplined. The violent expression of anti-Western feeling and the religious fanaticism of men who can stir the mobs to violence did not disappear with Mosaddeq. It merely lurks under the surface. While the Tudeh Party has been outlawed, its cause is not without secret supporters. Much, indeed too much, depends on the Shah himself, who rules as well as reigns. The existing political institutions are not rooted in popular acceptance and will attain stability only if they can attract the support of the rising middle class and eventually, the peasantry. Distribution of the crown lands represents an encouraging start, but only a start, toward meeting the needs of the peasants.

In spite of these uncertainties, the policies of the Shah have created for the United States and the West the most favorable situation possible. Because of them, no opportunity should be lost to give his policies a more solid footing by encouraging the trends which give promise of a more stable political system.

These have been the aims of American policy in Iran. Progress has not been spectacular, but the obstacles have been formidable. Military assistance has been instrumental in increasing the prestige of the Shah and his Government, though it were better directed more to internal security than to a hopeless and pointless effort to copy the modern armies of the West. Economic aid has had to be devoted to saving the state from bankruptcy and has therefore contributed little to longer-range goals. Technical cooperation, through the largest-scale program the United States carries on in the Middle East, has sown some seeds which should germinate and flower in due time. All aid programs have run up against the suspicion, inefficiency and corruption that have frustrated many a foreign adviser in Iran in times past. The much-heralded seven-year plans for economic development (the second such plan was begun after the settlement of the oil crisis in 1954) have been slow to show results. The time available for showing results, unfortunately, may be limited.

How far should the United States espouse the cause of political and social reform in Iran? It makes little sense, obviously, to undermine a regime that has courageously joined the Western alliance system and cooperates with the United States. But it is legitimate to ask what is the life expectancy of any regime in a country of strategic importance, and whether it may not be undermined in any case by political and social forces within that country itself. The vital questions for Iran are whether the energies of the new middle class, its numbers constantly being swelled by those receiving higher education at home or abroad, can be absorbed and put to constructive use or will be diverted into opposition and revolution, and whether the peasants and tribes can be gradually introduced into the body politic. On the answers to those questions will depend whether we face a moderate, mature nationalism in the future, or an explosive nationalism opening the gates to political convulsions and possibly to communism or foreign intervention.

As a long-run policy, the United States should do what it properly can, without intervention which would only backfire, to encourage reform in Iran. The aid program, hampered thus far by a measure of waste and lack of direction on our part in addition to obstacles on the local scene, can have some influence toward reform. Real progress in economic development will itself bring changes in the political and social structure. It should encourage young engineers, scientists and administrators to see a future both for themselves and for their country. It will provide the peasants with tangible benefits. Beyond that, there may be occasions when American advice and influence can be directed toward helping the Shah and his Government to choose their policies wisely when the choice is between reform today and revolution tomorrow.[3]

3 T. Cuyler Young, "The Race between Russia and Reform in Iran," *Foreign Affairs*, v. 28 (January 1950), pp. 278-289.

Afghanistan and Pakistan

Afghanistan is in a quite different situation, although its historic role, like Iran's, has been that of a buffer state between Russia and the West. So long as its way of life is largely tribal, the social basis for modern nationalism hardly exists. We may expect its leaders, however—whoever they may be—to resist domination by any outside power and to try to maintain the status of buffer state by seeking a balance between competing outside influences. Regardless of Afghanistan's acceptance of aid, even military aid, from the Soviet bloc, regardless also of possible objections on the part of Pakistan, it is in the American interest to keep open all the channels of communication with Afghanistan, to support projects of economic development in which the Afghan Government is interested, and to treat that Government with respect in the councils of nations. Should a ruling or insurgent group in Afghanistan go so far in its "friendly cooperation" with the Soviet Union as to endanger the country's independence, the United States and other free nations should not be without resources to help patriotic Afghans thwart or reverse such an eventuality.

In Pakistan, the critical decisions for collaboration with the United States were taken by a few strong leaders. Behind them, and behind the front of solidarity with the West, is a nation that has not yet found political stability. Handicapped by its geographical division into two separate territories dissimilar in population, history and outlook, it has been held together by the bonds of religion, by antipathy to India, and by the leadership of men like Jinnah, Liaquat Ali Khan, and Iskander Mirza. How well it will weather the inevitable crises of the future is an open question, but we must assume that its own internal problems and its relations with India will so absorb its energies that it cannot be expected to play a major role in the Middle East. American aid and influence should be devoted, above all, to helping Pakistan find political stability, which concentration on building military strength may jeopardize rather than advance. Moreover, if Pakistan is to have a role in the Middle East it will not be because of its armed strength or its membership in the Baghdad Pact but primarily because, as an Islamic nation of 70 million souls that has preserved some part of its British heritage and found strength in its own institutions, it may exert a healthy influence on other Moslem nations and help to bring Arab and non-Arab states closer together.

Leadership in the Arab World

It is the Arabs who in recent years have presented the United States with its greatest perplexities in the Middle East, and it is therefore to the future of the Arab world that we must devote our most serious attention. Will the Arabs, prey to emotional drives that often seem to defy all reason, ever "settle down" to stable relations among themselves, with their neighbors and with the West? Their experience of Western rule left little in the way of affinity for Western political institutions, except perhaps in Lebanon. The parliamentary forms that still exist in Jordan, Syria and Iraq have little of the content of representative government although they may from time to time reflect the play of contending political forces. When they become inconvenient to those in power, they are manipulated or pushed aside. Egypt's government is a dictatorship with "single-list" elections, while Saudi Arabia and Yemen still have regimes of royal absolutism. That the Arab states may follow the Turkish example is a theory for which supporting evidence is lacking. Turkish political influence is virtually nonexistent, owing to Arab distrust of the Turks as former Ottoman overlords and present partners of the West, and to Turkish contempt for the weakness and indiscipline of the Arabs. Turkey and Iran, let us remember, have existed as independent states for centuries. They have an experience and a sense of continuity in self-government that the newly independent Arab states do not possess.

The future of the Arab world, unless it is swallowed up by Soviet imperialism, depends primarily on the evolution of its own internal forces. The pattern varies from one state to another, but the appearance on the political stage of young army officers and leftist "intellectuals" claiming to represent the national will seems to be a common phenomenon where older institutions, whether monarchical, feudal or parliamentary, prove incapable of meeting the demands of the time. The groups of "free officers" which have come to the top in Egypt and exist also in Syria, Jordan and elsewhere are interested in power for its own sake, of course, but the success they have had or may have in the future is not dependent entirely on the military force at their disposition. In many respects their rise reflects a widespread popular view that the old order meant corruption, injustice and national weakness. It reflects a growing pressure from below for social reform.

The fall of Faruq, for those reasons, was greeted with nearly unanimous approval in Egypt, and the social content of the Egyptian revolution explains much of Nasser's great appeal to the Arab masses. The parliamentary system in Egypt, similarly, has had few mourners, because it was irresponsive to the popular will. The politicians had lost all prestige. In addition to the domestic sources of unrest and revolution, the humiliation of Arab weakness in the conflict with Israel has created a continuing mood of frustration and discontent which any clever demagogue or political manipulator can exploit, particularly if outside assistance is available to him.

These trends are not confined to Egypt and Syria. They are evident in Jordan and Iraq, and even in Saudi Arabia, Kuwait and Bahrein. Unrest in those countries is not just the result of the influence of Abdel Nasser's success or of the work of his agents. It is true enough that his agents have been active, often under cover of diplomatic immunity, and that Egyptian and Palestinian advisers and teachers have had a real impact on the less advanced Arab countries. Cairo's "Voice of the Arabs" provides continuing incitement to revolution. But the basic cause of the instability and unrest is that the old static society is breaking up. It is enough to see what the presence of Western oil companies has meant to the nature and tempo of life in eastern Arabia, or how economic changes are affecting the habits and outlook of the peasants of Iraq, many of whom now flock to the cities to form a new floating proletariat.

America and the Arab Future

These internal political currents and cross-currents in the Arab lands are bound to cause concern to the United States, a concern which has grown with the realization that they have been running more against than in favor of American prestige and interests. For it is undeniable that those elements which generally looked to the West in the past—the kings, the old politicians, the landowners, and the Western-educated business and professional men who tend to be liberal nationalists—are on the defensive against the more dynamic forces that speak in the name of a new era of "liberation," social change, and a nationalism that tends to be totalitarian rather than liberal. Here we have a dilemma which cannot be met by a clear choice on one side or the other, and still less by taking refuge in the doctrine of nonintervention as an excuse for disinterest or for inability to look ahead.

So long as the Arab political future looks as unstable and as murky as it does, the United States should not identify itself too closely with any government or political group. Naturally, it should deal with the governments that exist, but it should be able to make the transitions from one regime to another as they come, in fact to be prepared for them ahead of time. A Hussein may be able to master one internal crisis but not the next; a Nuri es-Said may be able to pass on his special brand of controlled democracy to his successors, but they may not be able to make it work; a Saud may find that a backward desert people cannot be brought into the economic life of the 20th century without raising questions in their minds about the system of medieval absolutism by which their country is governed. The degree to which the Arab peoples accept or reject Western forms of democracy, for which they do not have the traditions and the temperament, need not be a matter of great concern to us. It is more important that they have institutions which help them to absorb the pressures of social and political change and the shocks of popular unrest. The United States, in its approach to them, should endeavor to avoid head-on clashes with traditions, ideas and "complexes" that are deeply rooted in their thinking; to make sure, by conduct and not by preaching, that they are aware of the advantages of good relations with the West and the dangers of flirtation with the Soviet world; and to strengthen the hand of those who are working to give their countries greater stability and staying-power in the face of an uncertain future.

In those countries where the leadership is now anti-Communist, it is largely a matter of encouraging foresighted adaptation and peaceful transition. It may be estimated, for example, that the political system which King Saud inherited from his father can last for another decade; if so, that time may be used more profitably in encouraging gradual reforms and changes which would draw new elements into responsible political life, and in making it easier for the King gradually to move away from the restrictive influence of the mullahs and to build up a bureaucracy and other attributes of a modern state structure, than in awaiting a storm in which the House of Saud and the interests of the West would go down together. The same general considerations apply in Iraq, a more advanced country run by a feudal oligarchy but with a rising middle class which has long demanded greater political freedom. They apply in Jordan, but with the grievous handicap that the time limit is nearer a year than a decade and the new elements are largely Palestinian Arabs deeply hostile to the West.

The Anti-Western Regimes in Egypt and Syria

In countries where the leadership has already gone far in the direction of collaboration with the Soviet Union, like Egypt and Syria, an early change of leadership could hardly be anything but welcome in the West. In some ways it is a measure of the West's failure that such changes have not taken place. But here again the question is more than one of favoring anti-Soviet against pro-Soviet forces. It concerns the nature and permanence of the existing leadership. Are Abdel Nasser and his fellow officers, are the "Social Resurrectionists" and leftist army officers in Syria, unrepresentative cliques which have seized power by force or intrigue, or do they speak with the voice of the people of Egypt and of Syria and even, as they claim, that of the whole Arab nation?

In the case of Egypt, so far as one can judge from evidence that is not conclusive, the regime has not lacked general popular support despite its dictatorial methods. Its leader, with all his limitations of education and outlook, is a man of significance, to most Egyptians a promise of a better future and a symbol of newly attained status in the world. Those who deplore the loss of political freedom are but the few. The West would be foolish to build its hopes on the expectation of a popular demand for more democratic government. Even if the regime should fall victim to the enormous tasks it has inherited or created for itself, the chances are high that it would be succeeded by one of a similar type. The United States will have to get used to dealing with this kind of Arab: energetic, dedicated, self-confident, and adept at the use and abuse of political power.

The case of Syria may be different. Since the Palestine War and the three military *coups d' état* that followed one another with startling rapidity in 1949, Syrian politics have been marked by confusion compounded, in which success has fallen to those best qualified in demagogy, intrigue, and manipulation of the levers of power. In these respects the young men of the Arab Social Resurrectionist or Ba'th Party, allied with elements of the army and with the Communist leader, Khalid Bakdash, have proved themselves more than a match for the leaders of the old political parties. Their path to power was eased by identification of their cause with that of nationalism. Syrians, with some justice, tend to regard their country as the birthplace and center of modern Arab nationalism; [4] their direct experience with the West—under French mandate from 1920 to 1945—left a legacy of hatred; and they seem to outdo their fellow Arabs (other than Palestinians) in the bitterness of their feeling about Israel. Thus it was difficult for moderates and friends of the West to make their influence felt at all, or to avoid charges of antinationalism and even treason. Some chose to keep their jobs without any real power, others to flee the country or to withdraw quietly from the political stage.

There was nothing inevitable, however, in the progress to power of such men as Akram Hourani (leader of the Ba'th Party), Afif Bizri (Chief of Staff, as of August 1957) and Abdul Hamid Serraj (Chief of Military Intelligence). It was rather the absence of effective action on the part of other political forces. Nor is there anything inevitable about the duration of any group's exercise of power. Syrian regimes have not been noted for their longevity. Alternatives to adventurous left-wing leadership exist. The danger is that those who profited from Soviet and Communist support to gain and to hold power may one day discover that they have lost it, together with the independence of their country, to the Soviet Union.

Toward countries where the leadership has been unfriendly, American policy may often have to take rapid

---

[4] George Antonius, *The Arab Awakening* (Beirut: Khayat's College Book Cooperative, 3rd printing, 1955), pp. 79-100.

shifts and turns in relations with the governments. At the same time it is eminently in our interest to devise a set of steady, long-range policies directed to the people. This does not necessarily mean trying to set the people against their governments, but rather reaching their minds and affecting their lives in a number of ways, many of which may be expected to have the consent of the governments. Educational institutions, like the American University of Beirut, can have a far-reaching influence. The need for long-term programs to foster social progress and to combat poverty and disease has already been mentioned.

It may not be easy to measure the success of such programs. Some will not show any success at all. Nevertheless, they have to be undertaken if we are to have any hope of bringing the Western world and the Middle East into relationships that are mutually beneficial or even mutually tolerable. Nor can we, with any degree of safety, leave the field to the Soviets, who have already developed long-range programs of their own. It is not just economic and technical aid that is in question. It is also the use of information programs, establishment of personal contacts, and the influences that exchanges of scientists, technicians, teachers and students can have on popular opinion and on emerging new leadership. Above all, it is a question of attitudes, both individual and national. The peoples of the Middle East must be convinced, and rightly convinced, that America treats them with understanding and respect.

The Meaning of Arab Nationalism

No mere resolve to understand and respect the Arabs, important as that may be, provides the answer to the challenge of Arab nationalism in its present irrational manifestations. The Soviet Union has reaped great gains by encouraging those very manifestations. The American attitude has been equivocal, despite the general tendency to sympathize with "peoples struggling to be free," for we have other interests and obligations which put brakes on our sympathies and counsel circumspection. It is not all attributable to "Zionist pressures." The key to success is not, as some of the more enthusiastic American supporters of the Arab cause have argued, to recognize all Arab national aspirations as just and by supporting them to win the friendship and cooperation of the Arab world. Who defines the aspirations? The United States cannot put the determination of its policies in the hands of an Abdel Nasser any more than in those of a Ben-Gurion. That kind of "friendship" would only encourage the extremists without winning their respect, and at the sacrifice of the ability of the United States to protect essential interests of the free world.

Yet if to appease "Nasserism" is an abdication of policy, to make a frontal assault on it, as the British and French did, could be fatal to our position in the Middle East. The only course with any promise of success is one which frankly accepts the justice of Arab aspirations to self-determination, equality and independence, while setting limits to support of extreme claims which would deny those rights to others. It is the determination of those limits which is so difficult, for Arab grievances range far and wide.

The United States must find some way to win Arab confidence as a means of cutting the ground from under the extremists. Only then will the moderates have a chance to hold their own. First by a more generous recognition of Arab rights in Palestine, and then by practical arrangements on such matters as oil revenues, pipelines, and economic development, the United States may be able to provide moderate and pro-Western leaders some ground on which to stand. They cannot make headway if the West, either by disregard of widely held Arab desires or by weakness in the face of the extremists, persists in making the latter the sole effective champions of Arab nationalism. It is asking much of American diplomacy to draw the fine line between encouragement of "good" nationalists and appeasement of "bad" nationalists, but is there any other

hope of checking and repairing the damage already
wrought by the unholy alliance between the coldly calculated strategy of Moscow and the unbounded ambitions
of anti-Western extremists throughout the Arab world?

Nationalism has, without any doubt, eased the way for
the advance of Soviet influence into the Middle East. But
this has happened not because of any natural affinity between nationalism and communism in the Middle Eastern
mind. It has happened because the targets of nationalism
were positions held by the Western powers. Recent events
have removed some of those targets, and a diplomacy
which offers the Arabs practical benefits while not offend-
ing their sensibilities could remove others. Meanwhile,
Arab leaders may learn some lessons from their intimate
association with the Soviet Union, and the latter may find
that the very success of its drive to become a Middle Eastern power has spoiled the formula which made it possible,
the role of disinterested friend. Conceivably, Soviet imperialism may then become the main target, and nationalism the barrier to Soviet expansion that it now is in Turkey and Iran.

Certainly Islam cannot be counted upon to serve as
such a barrier. The theory that communism and Soviet
influence could never make inroads in the Moslem world
because they are materialistic and atheistic has not been
borne out. Religion does have a significant place in
Middle Eastern society. It colors both popular and official
attitudes. But it does not establish an absolute immunity
to a political virus such as fascism or communism. Communist theory does have certain superficial parallels with
Islamic dogma, and the promise of a better material life is
not inconsistent with it. Above all, the impact of the
modern world on Islam has produced two major trends
which tend to open the door to Communist influence:
first, the inability of traditional doctrines and institutions
to hold the loyalty of the intellectual leaders and the new
generation bent on finding a way out of material backwardness; and second, the revulsion against the West

which, while often reinforcing the sense of dedication to Islam, has often created also a sense of identification with whatever theories and political forces were hostile to the West. Where in Turkey nationalism tends to be secular, in the Arab lands and Iran the anti-Western nationalist movement has had a strong admixture of religious feeling, even fanaticism.[5]

Soviet strategy, in knowing when to emphasize communism and when to stress national rights and hatred of the West, has deftly taken advantage of a receptive frame of mind among many Moslems. While making no basic change within the borders of the U.S.S.R. in its doctrinal hostility to Islam as a religion and its suppression of the national feelings of its own Moslem subjects, the Soviet regime has made certain superficial gestures at home and successfully managed to portray itself in the Middle East as a natural ally of Moslem peoples.[6]

It has been argued that Arab nationalism is so empty of real content and incapable over the long run of satisfying popular desires that it merely paves the way for communism instead of opposing it. Extreme nationalists, those associated with the Moslem Brotherhood, for instance, have dallied with communist ideas and connections as they dallied with fascism in the 1930's, and the young social nationalists and reformers of today are more totalitarian than liberal-democratic in their thinking. The students, a real political force in the Arab countries, have been drawn toward communism and xenophobia by their dissatisfaction with the existing order and their susceptibility to the argument that the West is to blame.[7] That Arab nationalist leaders have offered their peoples more

[5] Manfred Halpern, "The Implications of Communism for Islam," *The Muslim World*, v. 43 (January 1953), pp. 28-41; Walter Z. Laqueur, *Communism and Nationalism in the Middle East* (London: Routledge and Kegan Paul, 1956), pp. 5-7, 246-247, 255-256; Bernard Lewis, "Communism and Islam," *International Affairs*, v. 30 (January 1954), pp. 1-12.
[6] H. Carrère d'Encausse, "La déstalinisation dans l'Islam soviétique," *L'Afrique et l'Asie*, no. 37 (Ier trimestre, 1957), pp. 30-42.
[7] Laqueur, cited, pp. 8-18, 236-259.

sound and fury than constructive statesmanship is true. That some of them have recklessly allied with communism and thus imperiled their own as well as their nation's future is also true. Beside the opportunists, whose name is legion, there have been many of the idealistically inclined who simply accept Soviet policy and protestations at face value. Knowledge of what happened to the Communists' partners in popular fronts all over the world seems not to have penetrated very deeply into the minds of those Arab nationalists eagerly falling in with such tactics today.

Nevertheless, the prospect is not hopeless, for nationalism is more than the mouthings of its self-appointed leaders. It springs from the deepest feelings of the people, who will not knowingly follow the path leading to national subjection. The leaders, too, are basically egocentric, both for their nation and for themselves. The Egyptian regime is obviously trying to get the most it can for itself and for Egypt by taking advantage of the struggle among the great powers. The regime in Syria is attempting to do the same thing, although at greater risk because of its own relative weakness and vulnerability to subversion. The great danger is that Communist penetration may go so far that it will become Communist control before nationalism can successfully assert itself against it. American policy can help to prevent that eventuality by keeping open the lines of communication between the Arabs and the West. When a state such as Egypt or Syria seeks to ease relations with the United States as an anchor to windward in its relationship with the Soviet Union, we should meet it halfway and try to check the drift toward a complete break, not as a sign of trust, which is not warranted, but as a matter of calculated self-interest. We may be irked by an Arab government's partiality or apparent subservience to Soviet policies, but unless it is actually under Soviet domination, run by men who are Soviet agents, it makes sense not to drive it inexorably in that direction by leaving no alternatives.

The Remnants of British Imperialism

Arab nationalism still has two great areas of challenge ahead of it which draw our attention to the map. The first is the series of protected and client states where Arab populations still live under the control of Great Britain. The second concerns relationships and boundaries among the Arab states themselves, the issue of particularism versus the concept of a single Arab nation. How the contending forces will work themselves out, and how the course of events may be influenced from outside, are questions of especial interest to the United States.

The area which the British still control stretches in an arc around the outer edge of the Arabian Peninsula from Aden at the entrance to the Red Sea to Kuwait at the head of the Persian Gulf. The juridical status of the territories varies from a directly ruled colony (Aden) all the way to the nominally sovereign Sultanate of Muscat and Oman. In between are the protected states of Kuwait, Bahrein and Qatar, and the eight "trucial sheikhdoms" of Oman. All of them are tied to Britain by various treaty arrangements and by the presence of British officials or military officers as advisers to the local sheikhs or nominally in their employ. All foreign relations are in British hands.

Except in Kuwait and Bahrein, where oil revenues have had their effect, the life of the inhabitants of these territories is primitive, hardly touched by the modern world; their relationships are personal and tribal, not national. The slogans of nationalism mean little to the people, who are probably better off under their sheikhs and under British protection than they would be if absorbed by their sovereign Arab neighbors. From time to time the world is treated to the spectacle of a "war" on the Yemen-Aden frontier or in Oman. These encounters grow out of local tribal rivalries, magnified by the ambition of an Imam of Yemen to add to his power and his domains, or that of an Imam of Oman to carve out a kingdom for himself, and stimulated further by arms and money provided

by Egypt, Saudi Arabia or the U.S.S.R. as a means of causing trouble for the British. To label such skirmishes as a
national struggle against imperialist domination is to deal
in fiction. The trouble is that just such a fiction becomes
political reality when it has validity in the eyes of millions
of people who know next to nothing of the Aden Protectorate or of Muscat and Oman.

The salient fact is that these people are Arabs. By Western standards they may not be ready for independence, but
they are no less ready than the population of Yemen,
long an independent state. So long as they are ruled or controlled by a Western power, every Arab politician and
every enemy of the West will ceaselessly agitate for it. Such
agitation is already finding an echo within the territories
themselves. Agents from outside dispense arms and promises. Discontented sheikhs are beginning to look to Cairo
or to Riyadh. In time the position of local leaders loyal
to Britain will become untenable; revolts will no longer
be easily stifled by a few sorties of the Royal Air Force.
The Soviet Union, already in the picture through its
courting of Yemen with arms and other favors, will establish its influence more widely and firmly. The United Nations will have before it a new set of disputes in which
Britain and the "colonial powers" will again face the combined onslaught of Arab-Asian and Soviet blocs while the
United States stands uncomfortably in the middle.

This is a prospect which can only complicate long-run
efforts to eliminate sources of conflict and establish common interests between the West and the Middle East. It
is incumbent upon the United States to try to anticipate
a succession of crises over Oman, Bahrein, Aden and the
rest by seeking some understanding with Britain and with
interested Middle Eastern states on the political future of
those territories. For Britons, especially those long associated with the Middle East, there is no joy in retreat
from the last British strongholds in the region. Yet it is
pertinent for them to consider whether the reasons for
taking the strongholds in the first place and for holding

them since are still valid. The original purpose was to protect India and the routes of empire; but India is no longer a British responsibility and most of the British Empire in Asia is gone. A more recent purpose has been to safeguard Britain's vital oil supplies in the area of the Persian Gulf; but surely this is an interest of all Western Europe and of other countries as well, including the United States. Britain's people have reason to ask—as some have—why they alone should bear the burden, financially and politically, of protecting that interest. And other interested countries may question whether a decision by Great Britain to hold these areas indefinitely, using force when necessary, is indeed the best way to assure to all users the continued availability of oil, both from these "protected" sheikhdoms and from the independent countries of the Persian Gulf area.

It may be argued that Britain can handle any local "nationalist" movements, despite the best efforts of Egypt and other Arab states to make these protectorates untenable. On this theory, a strong stand is justified to preserve at all costs, even that of great risk to Western oil operations and political influence in the independent Middle Eastern countries, the oil production of Bahrein, Qatar and especially Kuwait for Britain and the West. The difficulty is that this oil alone, though Kuwait leads all Middle Eastern producers, does not meet Western needs. A "Kuwait-first" policy, moreover, might be the easiest way to lose all the rest of the Arab world; and, if it were in fact lost, the chances of holding an exposed position like Kuwait or Qatar would be slim indeed.

The Western powers would do well to see the problem of these protected states in terms of an eventual accommodation with Arab nationalism which will assure continued access to oil without the burdens of political responsibility and of a running conflict with other Arab states. This does not mean that immediate action is necessary. It definitely does not mean that these areas and their oil resources should be summarily turned over to Egypt or Saudi

Arabia or the Arab League. What does seem necessary is an exploration by the United States and United Kingdom, in consultation with each other and with other states which produce or consume Persian Gulf oil, of possible gradual approaches to a solution that holds more promise of permanence than the present system.

Most of the British client states and sheikhdoms have insufficient qualifications for full independence, and surely the King of Saudi Arabia and the Imam of Yemen have no divine right to annex them just because of contiguity with their own territories, although they do have special geographical interests that merit consideration. Here are problems for which a full examination of the possibilities of federal arrangements and of the international trusteeship system would be in order, an examination in which the Arab states concerned (Iraq, Saudi Arabia or Yemen as the case may be) should take part. Not to attempt some new approach is to risk seeing the relationship between the West and even those Arab states that have been relatively friendly wrecked by a series of Omani revolts and Buraimi disputes.

Arab Nation or Arab Nations

Future relations between the United States and the Arab world may depend in large measure on the unity which the Arabs attain. Shall we be dealing with a single, solidly organized nation or, as now, with a group of sovereign states, each with its own interests and often at odds with its "sister states?" This is the great unresolved point in the ideas and practices of Arab nationalism. The Arabs are Arabs, but they are also Syrians, Saudis, Egyptians, and so forth. It is not always easy to tell which loyalty comes first, for it may depend on the time, the circumstances and the issue.

Pan-Arabism, or the idea of one Arab people, has been the theme of nationalist ideology since the start of the "Arab awakening" in the last century. It had its firm basis in the common literary language and the common culture. Arabs in different localities had undergone differing historical experiences, however, and the ties between them were not always close. The great leaders of nationalism in Egypt, Mustafa Kamil and Zaghlul Pasha, were primarily Egyptian nationalists. The rising leaders of the Bedouin of the Arabian desert had little in common with the Westernized elite of Beirut and Damascus. With the splitting up of the Arab lands into British and French mandates after World War I, political differences were further accentuated, and the movement for self-expression and independence tended to develop in separate compartments. By the time the Arab League was formed, the vested interests in separate sovereignties were stronger than the general sentiment for a confederation or a united Arab state.

The past decade has seen plenty of evidence of "Arab solidarity." There is no question that the consciousness of unity goes very deep with Arabs in all classes of society and in all parts of the Arab world. Political leaders have been well aware of it and have made their appeals accordingly. The new Egyptian constitution (1956) describes Egypt as a part of "the Arab nation." This is not just an invention of Abdel Nasser. Much of his attraction to the Arabs is attributable to his reiterated faith in their destiny as a great and populous nation stretching from the Atlantic to the "Arabian" (Persian) Gulf. The talk of political union between Egypt and Syria is intended to show that these two governments are true to the great ideal of Arab unity.

The Arab world is rent by internal feuds. Ever since Ibn Saud conquered the Hejaz and drove the Hashemite family from the holy cities of Islam, Saudi-Hashemite antagonism has colored the foreign policies of Saudi Arabia and of Iraq and Jordan, both of which have Hashemite monarchs. Only recently has it diminished in intensity, in the light of the improbability of any Hashemite attempt to recover the Hejaz, and of new threats to both royal houses. Relations between Egypt and Iraq, long rivals for leadership of the movement toward Arab unity, have reached a state of acute hostility because of Iraq's choice of a Western alignment and Egypt's association with Russia. Iraq and Syria have been at swords' points over their respective choices of outside allies and over the movement to unite the Fertile Crescent, which has had partisans in both countries. Even Lebanon and Syria, bound together by a real sense of identity among their peoples, have gone separate political ways, with Lebanon's hospitality to Syrian political exiles and Syria's casual attitude toward Lebanon's national sovereignty helping to make mutual irritation endemic. The Nasser regime, meanwhile, has gone into the business of promoting revolution in "sister Arab states" like Lebanon and Jordan as well as Iraq. And King Saud, though allied formally to Egypt, has undertaken to rally conservative and moderate Arab governments against the spreading influence of "Nasserism."

While these divisive influences seem to make a mockery of the continuing expressions of brotherly solidarity on the part of all Arab governments, the idea of unity does have political reality. Most frequently expressed in common attitudes toward Israel, it so permeates the whole political atmosphere that Arab governments feel compelled to vie with each other in loyalty to the cause. Their policies appear often to be marked by a curious duality of motivation. Thus, when the crisis over Syria boiled up in the autumn of 1957, some of the Arab states which obviously were alarmed at Syria's drift toward the Soviet camp, and were expected to be willing to do something about it, suddenly rallied round Syria and proclaimed their intention of rushing to its assistance in case of attack. The result was to lend an air of credibility to Soviet and Syrian charges that the United States was plotting aggression against Syria.

Such demonstrations of Arab solidarity often reflect compelling political facts as well as sentiment for national unity. An Arab government, for example, may be moved by the need to buttress a shaky internal situation by giving proof of its devotion to the larger cause of Arabism. In any case, the public myth of unity must be considered a more or less continuing phenomenon conditioning what American diplomacy can accomplish. Any attempt to mobilize the support of Arab states against another Arab state is almost sure to backfire if the call to Arab unity can be sounded against it.

It would seem wise for the United States to play the same game by taking a general public attitude which is friendly to the idea of Arab unity. This does not mean that we have to make its accomplishment an objective of American policy. That is properly a matter for the Arabs themselves. The purpose should be rather to avoid statements and positions which seem to disparage and to discourage it, and to establish a general reputation of benevolent support. Specific American policies, like those of the individual Arab states themselves, may sometimes tend to be divisive; even then, they will have more chance of success if they are surrounded by an aura of sympathy for aspirations we know to be close to the hearts of so many Arabs.

What the future holds with respect to political unity will depend mainly on the strength of the idea among the Arabs themselves and on the qualities of their own leadership. It is a fairly safe guess that they will not attain it for a long time. The idea of an Arab empire playing the role of a great world power, under the leadership of Abdel Nasser or anyone else, is not one that need unduly concern us, either as something to fear or as something to cheer. It would be short-sighted, on the other hand, to assume that the present configuration of the Arab world is permanent. Many of the inter-Arab frontiers are the results of historical accident or were drawn by outside powers without reference to the desires or needs of the people. Some are bound to succumb to developing pressures.

The urge to unity, where it involves actual political or economic union and not just expressions of solidarity, is likely to make itself felt in particular areas less extensive than the whole broad expanse of territory from Morocco to Muscat. The Arab world is made up of four natural regions: the Fertile Crescent (Lebanon, Syria, Jordan, Iraq), the Arabian peninsula, the Nile valley, and the northern coast of Africa. Each has a different background and history; each has problems of its own that the others do not share. North Africa has a long association with the West which will impel it to seek its own unity and its own future not bound to Cairo and the Arab East. It is logical to expect Yemen and the sheikhdoms of the Persian Gulf to come into close relationships with Saudi Arabia, but not to expect the latter to merge its fortunes with those of Egypt or Iraq. Egypt and the Sudan are bound to be associated together in the natural unity of the Nile valley, despite Sudanese distrust of Cairo, but they are well separated by deserts and by the State of Israel from other centers of the Arab world. This is the main reason why the projected Egyptian-Syrian political union has an air of artificiality about it.

The greatest complexities are those which involve the countries of the Fertile Crescent, their relations among themselves and with the other Arab states. The ideas of "greater Syria" and "Fertile Crescent unity" have long been held by writers, political leaders and many others in those lands.[8] Syria, in Ottoman times, was considered as including what later became Syria, Lebanon, Palestine and Transjordan. The nationalist movements of Syria and Mesopotamia (later Iraq) had close ties. Those who led the Arab revolt during the first World War had no program for the division of the Fertile Crescent into separate states. The mere existence of the separate mandates, however, had its effect on the directions of Arab nationalism, and the tendencies toward unity were not strong enough to overcome the obstacles to it even after Western control was withdrawn. Personal and dynastic factors complicated

[8] Majid Khadduri, "The Scheme of Fertile Crescent Unity: A Study in Inter-Arab Relations," in Richard N. Frye, ed., *The Near East and the Great Powers* (Cambridge: Harvard University Press, 1951), pp. 137-177.

the picture. The idea of greater Syria, when associated with the ambitions of Abdullah of Transjordan, had little appeal for others. And the prospect of Syrian-Iraqi union, besides meeting objections from Egypt and Saudi Arabia, ran into the opposition of all who had vested interests in the continuation of a Syrian republic. Meanwhile Lebanon, under largely Christian leadership and having special bonds with the West, was mainly concerned with maintaining its own unique position.

In present circumstances, when the combined impact of the global struggle and of Abdel Nasser's new brand of Arab leadership have split the states of the Fertile Crescent into rival camps, talk of their unity may seem out of place. From whichever side it comes, it tends to be interpreted as a move in the cold war. Thus for Iraq to advocate union with Syria is interpreted as an attempt to extend the pro-Western bloc and deal a blow at Russia and at Egypt; for Syria to talk of union with Jordan is to raise the specter of the further spread of Soviet influence. This is inevitably the case. Partisans of each side can play with the idea of greater Syria or Fertile Crescent unity in the hope of using it to enlarge their own bloc or to remove a menacing situation. Yet the very dangers of a drastic change in the *status quo,* through a merger of Middle Eastern states or the absorption of one by another, have the effect of a damper on the possibilities of such a change.

Nothing seems less certain, however, than the long-term prospects of any regime or system of government in these countries. That Syria may have a pro-Soviet and Iraq a pro-Western regime does not mean that either has unanimous popular support. Beneath the surface is a consciousness of common interests likely to grow. The United States should see the possibilities as they develop. For some kind of union of Iraq, Syria and Jordan may be the solution of what are today obviously a "Syrian problem" and a "problem of Jordan." It may be a means of ending the Balkanization of this part of the Arab world, giving it scope for economic development, eliminating some of the sources of conflict and the temptations to those who would meddle from outside, and establishing a counterweight to Egyptian ambitions.

In order to keep an open mind and a flexibility of policy in this direction the United States should not commit itself definitely and beyond all possibility of change to the territorial integrity of a state like Jordan. The first demonstration of American policy in the Middle East after adoption of the Eisenhower Doctrine, in the crisis of April 1957 in Jordan, was marked by strong declarations that the United States stood four-square behind the principle of the territorial integrity of Jordan.[9] Ironically, Jordan is the state in the Middle East which has the least chance, and the least justification, for maintaining its integrity over the long run. Created arbitrarily by the British for their own strategic purposes and to establish a throne for their friend Abdullah, its original frontiers were but arbitrary lines drawn or left vague in the desert. Transjordan was never able to stand on its own feet. Its people's loyalty was to the Arab idea or to Abdullah personally, but not to a Transjordanian nation. When Abdullah annexed the west bank of the Jordan, he added an unruly population of Palestine Arabs, outnumbering his own former subjects and generally without loyalty either to the dynasty or to the state. Jordan has since been at the mercy of internal unrest and outside pressures. It depended for its existence on British subsidies until the King was forced to terminate the alliance with Britain and give them up.[10]

Since then, emergency aid from the United States has

[9] White House statement, April 24, 1957 (*New York Times*, April 25, 1957); State Department statement, April 25, 1957 (*Department of State Bulletin*, v. 36, May 13, 1957, p. 768); William M. Rountree, "The Middle Eastern Policy of the United States," same, pp. 755-758.

[10] After the riots of December 1955 and January 1956 and the dismissal of General Glubb in March 1956, the ending of the formal tie with Great Britain was the logical next step. Following the victory of nationalists and leftists in the election of October 1956 the new government announced its intention of terminating the treaty, which, with the annual subsidy of £12 million, came to an end by agreement in March 1957. British forces withdrew from Jordan by July 4, 1957.

helped to keep Jordan afloat. But it is not just a question of money. Jordan is basically unstable, a state which may fall apart even if well subsidized. It could explode from within. It could be absorbed by a neighbor or partitioned among several of them. It is a regrettable fact that Syria, the logical heir to most of Jordan, has moved ever closer to the Soviet orbit. Ideally, the Syrian problem should be dealt with before the problem of Jordan is posed, but when and how it is posed is likely to be beyond the power of the United States to determine.[11] The declarations by the United States on independence and integrity and the current subsidies may be suited to the needs of the moment, but beyond that there should be serious but not public consideration of how Jordan might be partitioned if and when the time comes, so that the process may be peaceful, the results acceptable, and the possibilities of inter-Arab or Arab-Israel strife kept to a minimum.

Perhaps the most effective way to influence, in due course, the trend toward unity in the Fertile Crescent is to work steadily to build up Iraq. Possessed of abundant land, water and oil resources, it is a country basically stronger than Syria and with great economic potentialities. It could exercise a considerable force of attraction. If it is jobs that worry the politicians and army officers who have been the controlling element in Syria, they should be made to feel sure that jobs will also be available to them in any union with Iraq. The United States cannot properly take the lead in this question, which is a matter for the decision of the peoples concerned, but it can do its part by steady policies, both political and economic, which encourage eventual unity of the Fertile Crescent.

Beyond Nationalism

Nationalism has already expended much of its force in Europe. May it not do the same in the Middle East? From

[11] Some of the possibilities and difficulties of partition, in connection with the Arab-Israel conflict, are mentioned below, Chapter 17, pp. 313-315.

all appearances it will remain for some years in the virulent stage. The politically effective slogans are those which speak of national rights and claims and resistance to the foreigner. The frenzy persists, as we have seen, beyond the winning of national independence. The key to political success in many countries continues to be denunciation of the "imperialists" long after they have in fact left. Perhaps Middle Eastern nationalism can only lead to "Nasserism," to communism or to anarchy. That outcome need not be assumed. The United States and other Western nations should at least be alert to the possibilities of a constructive alternative and how they may contribute to it.

The indispensable groundwork involves the removal of remaining grounds of grievance on which frenetic nationalism still feeds. Beyond that, it is partly a matter of showing by example that nationalism by itself, having attained the goal of full independence, has little constructive to offer to the solution of the pressing problems of 20th-century society. More specifically, and without overlooking the fatuity of an economic approach unrelated to the political, the need is for the disinterested promotion of regional and other broad enterprises, as in the field of nuclear energy for peaceful purposes, that may catch the imagination of Middle Eastern peoples and open up to them a prospect of the future in which they can work with each other and with the West and still build a new society that will be their own.

Chapter 17

THE ARAB-ISRAEL CONFLICT

ANY attempt to accomplish anything on a broad scale in the Middle East—whether it be regional defense, or economic development, or merely putting Western relations with the Arab world on a tolerable basis—leads into the conflict between the Arab states and Israel. It colors our relations with every country in the Middle East. It affects the consolidation of the northern tier, for Iraq feels that it must vie with Egypt and Syria in showing its hostility to Israel, and the others are Moslem states which cannot be indifferent to the Arab cause. Even Turkey, though secular in outlook and the only one maintaining diplomatic relations with Israel, cannot go as far in those relations as its strategic and economic interests might dictate; Turkey even withdrew its minister from Tel Aviv after Israel's attack on Egypt. No Western power, as Britain and France learned when the four Middle Eastern members of the Baghdad Pact denounced their action against Egypt in November 1956, can afford to ignore the sensitivity of the whole Moslem world to open Western support of Israel. On the other hand the nations of the West, and especially the United States, have certain obligations to Israel, above all an obligation not to allow it to be attacked and annihilated.

The great danger to American interests is the state of tension and instability in the whole area of the Middle East to which the Arab-Israel conflict so substantially contributes. It is this conflict which has given the Soviet Union its greatest opportunities to exploit Arab grievances and to win Arab favor. The Western powers have found it impossible to gain the confidence and cooperation of the Arab world so long as Arab eyes are fixed on the

295

"loss" of Palestine and on the "menace" of Israel, for both of which they hold the West responsible. We have found that if we want to see a more strong and stable Middle East, we cannot avoid the Arab-Israel problem. The question is: What can we do about it?

The United States has tried in the past to promote a settlement. Early efforts through the U.N. Palestine Conciliation Commission, of which the United States was a member, came to nothing. Later attempts to use the channels of secret diplomacy met the same fate. The indirect approach through a search for agreement on some of the less bitterly contested aspects of the conflict—such as division of the water resources of the Jordan valley—would not work because all aspects were interlocked, and the controlling factor was not rational calculation of economic interest but a fixed political position. As we have seen, neither side was disposed to yield anything. Israel stood firmly on the gains made in 1948. The Arab states would not negotiate with Israel or even recognize its legal existence.[1]

The Sinai campaign of 1956 reduced the meager chances for a settlement even further. Israel's attempt to force Egypt into negotiating peace would have worked only if the outside powers had allowed Israel to complete its victory and dictate terms, or had used the occasion of crisis to insist on a negotiated settlement. They did neither. The Arab governments, after the crisis, were no more willing to talk of negotiation and compromise than they had been before. Egypt still claimed to be in a state of war with Israel. All the elements that had produced the crisis were still there: unsettled boundaries; the Arab refugees; the status of Jerusalem; the disputes over water resources; Israel's claims to freedom of passage through the Suez Canal and the Gulf of Aqaba; and the Arab boycott and blockade. The U.N. machinery for keeping the peace on the borders had proved its inadequacy. The Tripartite

[1] See above, pp. 80-83.

Declaration of 1950 had in effect been torn up by two of its signatories.

The United States is faced with a double problem: first, the immediate need to keep the peace between Israel and its Arab neighbors; second, the need to remove the underlying causes of the trouble or at least to reduce their more poisonous effects. If any lesson has been learned, however, it is that no policy can be built on the expectation of early settlement of the basic issues in conflict. Accordingly, our immediate attention must be given to the stabilization of the existing state of affairs, inherently unstable though it may be, in order to prevent a new outbreak of hostilities, which could hardly do anything but harm to American interests.

Keeping the Peace

The first step is to guarantee peace on the borders. Since the armistice lines are not accepted as the definitive frontiers, it would not be wise to give formal treaty pledges to either side by such a device as a security treaty with Israel or a guarantee of the territorial integrity of Jordan. Legal instruments outlawing violence on either side already exist in the form of the armistice agreements of 1949. The task is to put sufficient authority behind the principle that none of the lines established by these agreements can be changed by force, so that the pattern of raid and counter-raid across them is not allowed to re-establish itself. Israel cannot be permitted to tear up the armistice agreements and say they do not exist. Secretary-General Hammarskjold was quite right in his contention that they constitute the only possible legal basis for *de facto* relations and for keeping the peace, in which the members of the United Nations individually and collectively as well as the parties themselves have an interest.[2] Nor can Egypt

[2] U.N. General Assembly, 11th Session, *Report by the Secretary-General in pursuance of the resolution . . . of 19 January 1957* (*A/RES/453*) (A/3512, January 24, 1957).

be permitted to act on the theory that a state of war continues to exist between Egypt and Israel.

These two legal points, inconsequential as they may seem, deserve further discussion because they are so strongly and seriously put forward by the parties themselves. First, the armistice between Egypt and Israel,[3] although signed by military officers and not by diplomats with plenipotentiary authority, is a valid international agreement binding the governments of both states regardless of the absence of diplomatic relations between them. Israel makes the case that the agreement must be considered as a whole, and because Egypt has violated some of its provisions, Israel therefore cannot be bound by its other provisions; also, that the armistice was intended as a temporary arrangement to be followed by a negotiated peace and cannot be allowed to stand indefinitely, to Israel's disadvantage, because of Egypt's refusal to negotiate a peace settlement. Israel's exasperation is understandable, but its contentions are legally dubious and unacceptable to the world community. Until there is a negotiated settlement—and Egypt cannot be compelled to negotiate—the armistice agreement remains in force. It contains no provision for denunciation by one side. Israel may justly complain of violations by Egypt, but the remedy lies in an attempt to have the agreement enforced, not in its repudiation.

Egypt's contention that a state of war has existed with Israel since 1948, permitting the exercise of certain rights of belligerency such as those of visit and search of ships for contraband and the closure of the Suez Canal to Israeli shipping, is also questionable as a point of law and unacceptable to the world community. While it has been a general rule of international law that a truce or armistice

[3] The other armistice agreements between Israel and Jordan, Syria and Lebanon, respectively, are of a similar character. The Israel-Egyptian armistice is discussed here because it is the one which has generated the legal controversy. For texts of agreements, see U.N. Security Council, *Official Records*, 4th Year, Special Supplements nos. 1 (Jordan and Israel), 2 (Syria and Israel), 3 (Egypt and Israel) and 4 (Lebanon and Israel) (Lake Success, 1949).

does not put an end to a legal state of war, which must await a peace treaty, in any individual instance the application of the rule and the exercise of belligerent rights after an armistice will depend on the special circumstances of the case and the terms of the armistice agreement itself. In this case no state of war was ever declared in the first place, and the armistice is a detailed instrument with political provisions and not merely an agreement to cease hostilities in the field. Competent United Nations officials, including Dr. Ralph Bunche under whose auspices the armistice was negotiated, have stated that in their view its provisions implicitly rule out any exercise of belligerent rights by Egypt under the claim of the existence of a state of war.[4] In 1951 the Security Council, without attempting to pronounce as a court on the legal issues, adopted by a vote of 8 to 0, with three abstentions, a resolution to the effect that "neither party can reasonably assert that it is actively a belligerent" and that Egypt should terminate the restrictions on international shipping maintained on those grounds.[5] Unless the matter is decided otherwise by the International Court of Justice, this is a sound position on which to stand.

If we accept the proposition that the armistice agreements between Israel and its neighbors are valid and must be enforced, the question becomes one of will and means. Since those means which were looked to before the crisis of 1956—the United Nations Security Council, the Truce Supervision Organization and the Tripartite Declaration— did not prevent the progressive breakdown of the armistice system and the outbreak of war, we have either to make better use of them or to look for some alternative.

[4] U.N. Security Council, *Official Records,* 4th Year, 433rd Meeting, August 4, 1949 (Lake Success, 1949), p. 6; see also the statement of General W. E. Riley, U.N. Security Council, 6th Year, *Cablegram dated 12 June 1951 from the Chief of Staff of the Truce Supervision Organization addressed to the Secretary-General transmitting a Report to the Security Council* (S/2194, June 13, 1951).
[5] U.N. Security Council, 6th Year, *Official Records,* 558th Meeting, September 1, 1951 (Flushing Meadow, 1951).

The problem is to combine the necessary pledges and the capacity to back them up in a way which is convincing to Israel and the Arab states and generally acceptable to world opinion. The pledges should be clear and the will to back them up should be firm. In view of what happened in 1956 Great Britain and France, except as members of the United Nations, are best left out of any role as guarantors of the peace in the Near East. The Soviet Union is not interested in stabilizing the Arab-Israel conflict. The major responsibility thus falls on the United States.

A primary role will still rest with the United Nations, which from the start has had special responsibilities in Palestine. The armistice agreements were negotiated with the help of a U.N. mediator. The United Nations helped to restore peace in November 1956. Since the general obligations of the Charter, however, may not be sufficient to assure that the peace will be kept, the question arises whether it can do anything further by way of guarantees, warnings, or preparations for military action. Real difficulties surround any attempt to put the United Nations on record as deciding or recommending the immediate use of force against a state committing any armed aggression across the armistice lines. If passed, such a resolution would provide the U.S.S.R. with a legal basis for military action of its own in the Middle East. If, as is more likely, it were vetoed by the Soviet representative in the Security Council, to the accompaniment of much talk of Western imperialism and Soviet devotion to Arab rights, it is questionable whether the effort would be worth while. Perhaps the soundest course that the United States can follow in the United Nations is to support the continuation and the strengthening of the United Nations Emergency Force, so that eventually it might reach the point where, legally and practically, it could go into action against either side in the Arab-Israel dispute. The U.N. forum will also continue to be important for keeping the world's attention on the danger of a "third round" in the

Near East, and for warning the two disputants that in case of aggression the Charter would be applied as it was in 1956.

What is necessary is that the power of the United States, representing the authority of the United Nations insofar as possible and backed by the will of the United States Government to act swiftly in an emergency, should be placed behind the armistice lines in Palestine. If both sides understand that no "local war" between themselves would be permitted, that any major armed attack across the armistice lines would bring swift retribution from outside and no possible political or other advantage, the chances for peace would be immeasurably improved.

In a sense this would be an extension of the Eisenhower Doctrine by providing for the use of U.S. armed forces in cases of aggression other than by a state "controlled by international communism." However one may choose to interpret it, such an extension in practice to Israel and the Arab states would meet one of the main reservations both have had on the doctrine: its failure to give them any assurance of protection against each other. Official spokesmen have referred several times to the President's statement of April 1956 that the United States would come to the aid of the victim in case of aggression by either side, and have cited the swift diplomatic action taken in November 1956. This is all to the good. But the fact is that it is not considered sufficient by Israel or the Arab states, especially in the light of the specific limitations of the Eisenhower Doctrine. It would be desirable to make a more formal pledge, and to leave as little doubt as possible of our determination to back it up.

The United States, Russia, and Guarantees against Aggression

One of the principles on which the United States must stand is that it will not permit the destruction of Israel by force. The Arab governments frequently say that they do not accept the existence of Israel. Probably they will continue to say so for some time. We need feel no compulsion to require them to make a public renunciation of that position. To many Arabs it is enough to take the long view. Some say they will wait as long as is necessary to dispose of Israel; they point to the fate of the Latin Kingdom of Jerusalem set up in their midst by the Crusaders, which lasted over seventy years but went under in the end. We need not object to their clinging to the idea of eventual victory as a matter of faith. But we should make it clear that, so far as the present and the foreseeable future are concerned, they will not be allowed to wipe Israel off the map.

American policy may well have been misguided in the part it played in the establishment of the State of Israel. The United States ensured for itself a harvest of unending trouble in relations with the Arab world, as many informed Americans foresaw and warned at the time. We cannot, however, go back on those decisions. By encouraging the mass flight to Palestine of the remnants of European Jewry, to whom the Western world offered no alternative safe haven, and by its later support for the U.N. resolution on the partition of Palestine in 1947 (including high-pressure lobbying for votes beside its own) and its split-second recognition of Israel's independence in 1948, the United States established certain moral positions and obligations to both Jews and Arabs which it cannot ignore. Besides, whatever judgment one may make on the record of the past, Israel is a fact of international life. It is a member of the United Nations under the protection of its Charter. The state contains over one and one-half million Jews. It would be impossible for the world to tolerate their being destroyed as an independent nation in Palestine or "driven into the sea."

If the Arabs could be convinced of this fact, they might come to accept it. Israel, by its own military strength, has already shown them that a successful war of annihilation is now beyond their capability. The United States should do what it can to fortify that conclusion by placing American power in the scales to guarantee Israel's existence. Steadfastly maintained, that stand should rule out the prospect of an Arab assault at some later time when Arab armies have been built up beyond Israel's ability to match.

It may be objected also that the Arabs would turn to the Soviet Union, and that the latter would then ensure its capture of the Arab world by promising the destruction of Israel. Again, only a firm American position can reduce the danger from that quarter. Soviet propaganda will doubtless call Israel's continued existence into question, as it has on occasion in the past, but that does not mean that the Soviet leadership will back the Arabs in a war to destroy Israel, if they know it will involve them in hostilities with the United States. The strong probability is that they will not. As for the Arabs, it is well to let them see the limitations of playing the Soviet card. Once they know they cannot count on the Soviet Union to neutralize American power and hold the ring while they crush Israel, they may come to reconcile themselves to its existence.

The other side of the coin is the Arab fear of Israel's further expansion. After Israel's attack on Egypt and obvious reluctance to withdraw from Sinai and Gaza, who can say that this fear is without reality or without justification? The fact is that, ever since Israel's birth as a state, the Arabs' threat to destroy Israel has been less real than their fear of what Israel, with its superior military capabilities, might do to them in a second and now a third "round." Israel's massive border raids between 1953 and 1956, against which the Arab states had no effective defense, were aimed at checking Arab infiltration rather than at territorial expansion. But they glaringly revealed Arab military weakness and stimulated Arab fears. Arab propaganda to the effect that Israel is dedicated to the creation of a Jewish empire "from the Nile to the Euphrates" may be discounted. But an attempt by Israel to round out its borders by taking the Arab remnants of

Palestine is a possibility not to be dismissed, even after the failure to hold any of the conquests of the Sinai campaign. So long as Israel holds open its doors to unlimited immigration and maintains its military advantage, the Arabs are not unreasonable in expecting some explosion from the confines of its present territory into the more extensive lands of its neighbors. They must be able to feel confident that the United States can and will prevent such an explosion, and Israel must know it too.

Some of those neighbors, such as Egypt and Syria, may look to Russia rather than to America for protection. Here again, a bold and firm American policy is the best answer. The United States should make clear that it will not permit the entry of Soviet armed forces into the Middle East, under any guise or any pretext, without itself resorting to force to prevent it. There are conceivable situations in which Moscow would seem to have a good pretext for military intervention (an invitation from an Arab state or a U.N. resolution condemning Israel aggression for example), but this is a point on which the United States must stand firm. If Western forces are to refrain from entering Eastern Europe under penalty of provoking war—this is the actual situation, highlighted by Hungary's fate in 1956, whether admitted or not—Soviet forces must be under similar restraint as far as the Middle East is concerned. Once the Arab leaders know that this is America's position, they should see the limitations of counting on Soviet support. The United States, in turn, must match its firmness on this point by doing everything possible to convince them it is genuine.

Preventing Trouble on the Borders

The deterrence of the initiation of a new war between the Arab states and Israel, through firm pledges to oppose force to any major aggression by either side, is one part of the task of keeping the peace. The other is the prevention of the minor border violations which do so much to raise tension and always carry the threat that they will grow into something bigger. Briefly, the question is how to stop infiltration and fedayeen incursions on the part of the Arabs and how to dissuade Israel from resorting to brutal raids of reprisal. Insofar as it is a matter of vigilance and protection on the borders, the remedies are available if there is the will to use them: an expanded and strengthened U.N. Truce Supervision Organization, maximum physical barriers along the frontiers to prevent illegal crossings, the use of the U.N. Emergency Force, strengthened and enlarged, to patrol and guard a zone covering both sides of all Israel's borders. Successive chiefs of U.N.T.S.O. have correctly assessed the needs on the spot. What is required is the necessary effort and pressure to give them the authority and the facilities they need to do the job. U.N.E.F. has already shown its worth. If it is unreasonable—as it is—to employ it only on one side of one of the troubled borders, then all possible persuasion through the U.N. should be used to extend its functions.

Israel's practice of periodically showing its teeth and demonstrating their sharpness, culminating in the attack on Sinai, was certainly to be deplored. To turn Israel from it the United States and the United Nations should offer a reasonable substitute, in the form of dependable measures against Arab incursions, and should also be prepared to impose certain penalties if Israel continues the practice. Where diplomatic pressures and resolutions of condemnation do not suffice, economic measures should be applied. The United States should be equally willing to apply pressures to one side as to the other and should not hesitate to take the initiative in the United Nations when the occasion demands. It might not be easy to obtain the assent of Asian and African countries to sanctions against an Arab state (any more than to win the support of the U.S. Congress for sanctions against Israel), but they do presumably have an interest in keeping the peace and none in a new outbreak of war in Palestine. If action by the United Nations proves infeasible, the United States still has enough economic power of its own to be able to apply certain pressures against any state which persists in threatening the peace by the practice of organized raids across the border.

The Underlying Issues

All these measures to stabilize the armistice lines and prevent recourse to force are, of course, but palliatives. Even if highly successful, they constitute no guarantee of stability so long as the underlying issues remain, for the real danger in the Arab-Israel conflict lies in the persistence of the deep-seated disputes and problems which emerged with the ending of the British mandate and the war of 1948 in Palestine. These are the problems of permanent boundaries, refugees, Jerusalem, water, and the future status of Israel as a nation which is in but not of the Arab Middle East. However intractable they may be, a long-run American policy has to make some provision for dealing with them, for the lack of progress thus far has had a corrosive influence on the American position in the entire region.

We may as well frankly admit that in the foreseeable future the possibilities of a freely negotiated settlement are nonexistent. The Arab governments will not talk to Israel, and even if they would the two sides are so far apart that no compromise settlement seems possible. Some Arab leaders might be inclined to negotiate, but there is too much political capital to be derived from intransigence and too much danger of political and even physical liquidation for those who talk of settlement. In the present state of Arab opinion one can hardly expect the more reasonable leaders to jeopardize what standing they have and put the game entirely in the hands of the demagogues and the pro-Soviet politicians. Israel, meanwhile, constantly proclaims its desire for a negotiated peace but does not match its willingness to talk with a willingness to compromise.

In the face of that discouraging situation, what can the United States do, to live with the problem while it remains unsolved, to prevent its being exploited by our enemies, and to prepare the ground for the time when the difficulties may be more susceptible of solution? It can, as has already been indicated, discourage resort to violence and take certain firm positions so that all concerned know where America stands. It can take the initiative to set up machinery and procedures for the discussion and eventual solution of outstanding problems, utilizing the United Nations and the influence of non-Western nations whenever possible. And it can make oblique and indirect attacks on the over-all problem by special efforts to deal with individual aspects which are urgent or seem capable of settlement. A "package deal," in which all major issues are wrapped up in one settlement and concessions are more easily made on one item when advantages are gained on others, is often a useful technique of diplomacy. In the Arab-Israel case, however, such an approach, judging by experience and by the state of mind on both sides, seems doomed to failure. Although the issues in dispute are related to one another and not easily separable, the only possibility of progress lies in attacking each aspect of the problem as it becomes ripe for attack, and at least testing to see where are the clogging points, in the hope that in time the log jam may be broken.

Territory

The territorial question is the thorniest of all, and understandably so, for as Isaiah Bowman once said, territorial settlements touch deeply rooted sentiments of individuals and groups and involve "all the complexities of civilization." [6] There is no middle ground between Arabs who lament their lost Palestinian "homeland" and Jews to whom every inch of Palestine is sacred soil of Zion. Never-

[6] Isaiah Bowman, "The Strategy of Territorial Decisions," *Foreign Affairs*, v. 24 (January 1946), p. 180.

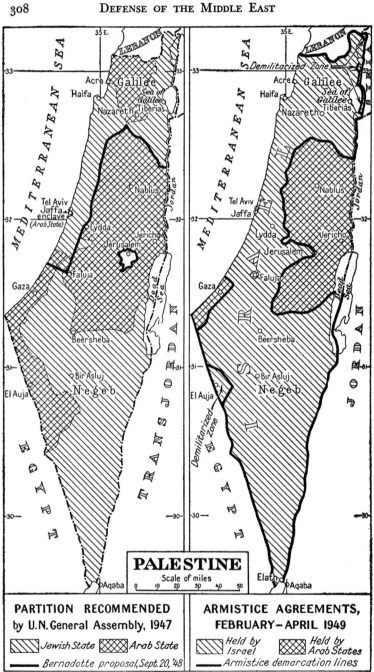

PALESTINE

Scale of miles
0   10   20   30   40   50

PARTITION RECOMMENDED
by U.N. General Assembly, 1947

Jewish State   Arab State

Bernadotte proposal, Sept. 20, '48

ARMISTICE AGREEMENTS,
FEBRUARY–APRIL 1949

Held by   Held by
Israel   Arab States

Armistice demarcation lines

theless, the boundaries have to run somewhere, as long as Arabs and Jews are not going to live together in the same state. At present they run along lines generally acceptable to Israel, except to extreme nationalists, but unacceptable to the Arab states and to those who can speak freely on behalf of the Palestine Arabs. Israel argues that a peace settlement confirming the present lines (with minor modifications) as permanent boundaries would be fair and just. Why, its spokesmen say, should the Arabs with their millions of square miles begrudge tiny Israel its 8,000 square miles? Why, with vast deserts in their possession, should they want more desert territory in the Negev, the only open territory available for Israel to develop for its growing population? Finally, asks Israel, what Arab state has any proper claim to territory in Palestine? None of them had any before 1948; Egypt is in Gaza only as an occupying power; Jordan took the west bank of the Jordan by right of conquest; there was and is no state of Arab Palestine.

The Arab view is that Palestine was an Arab land that did not cease to be an Arab land when Britain admitted hundreds of thousands of Jews under the mandate, or when Israel's armies conquered most of it in 1948. Arab demands are for rectification of the injustice done to the Arabs of Palestine. In its extreme form, generally for home consumption, this is a demand for the extinction of the State of Israel and the establishment of Arab rule over all Palestine. In its more moderate form on the levels of diplomacy, it is a demand for a return to the U.N. partition plan of 1947, which the Arabs themselves rejected at the time. Under that plan three parts of Palestine were to form parts of an Arab state: western Galilee, the west bank area, and a region near the Egyptian border larger than the present Gaza strip (see map, opposite). This plan, say responsible Arab leaders, is the only possible legal basis for any negotiation of permanent frontiers.

The United States, in 1947, gave its support to the partition plan which the U.N. General Assembly approved by a two-thirds majority. Then the fighting and truce arrangements of the following year produced a division of Palestine quite different from that of the U.N. plan; they led also to new partition proposals such as the abortive "Bernadotte Plan," which reversed the original U.N. resolution by assigning the Negev to the Arabs and western Galilee to Israel. U.S. policy floated in uncertainty and contradiction until the presidential election was over, then took the line of "general agreement" with the Bernadotte Plan, with the proviso that any modifications of the lines of 1947 should be roughly equal on both sides; thus, Israel's overstepping of those lines in one area presumably should be matched by negotiated adjustments in the Arabs' favor somewhere else.[7] As it turned out, Israel kept its gains and no corresponding adjustments were made. The armistice lines became the *de facto* frontiers of the State of Israel.

Since 1948 the United States has kept silent on the territorial issue, except to say, as Secretary Dulles did in August 1955, that this country would accept and help to carry out any settlement reached by the parties themselves. Prime Minister Eden went further when he said that a compromise should be found somewhere between the U.N. partition plan and the present armistice lines. Neither suggestion set things in motion toward a negotiated settlement. The Secretary's remarks were largely ignored as offering no incentive to either side to change its position. The Prime Minister's proposal went too far for Israel and not far enough for the Arabs.

For the present, it is hard to see where the solution can be found. Israel is not likely to give up any territory, beyond minor border adjustments, unless compelled to do so by tremendous pressure or by force. The Arab states are not going to be satisfied with anything Israel would be prepared to cede. We may therefore count on the continuation of the *status quo* for some time. But this is, as we

---

[7] U.N. General Assembly, First Committee, 205th Meeting, November 20, 1948, *Official Records*, pt. 1, 3rd Session (Paris, 1949), p. 682.

have seen, a dangerous *status quo,* one which by its pro-
visional character and lack of acceptance makes for instability, tension, and easy exploitation from outside. In
the longer view, toward what solution are we working?
Toward the eventual solidification of the *status quo,* to
which the Arabs may conceivably become resigned as the
years pass, or toward a redrawing of the frontiers in a way
which will give greater satisfaction to Arab aspirations and,
perhaps, greater promise of a durable peace?

In many ways the first course seems the more realistic,
for it is easier to accept a *fait accompli* than to try to undo
it, and it is at least doubtful that anything is to be gained,
in terms of American interests, by great efforts to persuade
or force Israel to cede territory which could hardly satisfy
the Arabs and might only whet their appetite for more.
Nevertheless, the United States has suffered enormously
in the Middle East because of what happened in Palestine; not only the American role in the creation of the
State of Israel but especially the fact that Israel, with no
opposition or restraint from the United States, was able
to retain all the gains it made in the fighting of 1948. We
are, indeed, partly responsible for the fact that the Arabs
of Palestine have been denied the right of self-determination, a right recognized by the U.N. partition plan which
we supported. We have conveniently forgotten about the
statement favoring equivalent gains and losses on both
sides. It is not a comfortable moral position.

It is quite true that the Arab states themselves rejected
the U.N. partition plan and invaded Palestine for the very
purpose of strangling the infant Jewish state in its cradle.
That fact takes away much of the force of the present
Arab plea for a return to the partition plan as the proper
legal basis for any settlement. Nor is morality, even if we
could define it, clearly on one side or the other. The
United States, however, has to look at this as a political
rather than a legal or a moral question. No American who
has anything to do with the Arab world can be unaware
of the depth of Arab feeling on Palestine. It is a real

obstacle to the success of any American policies, for it colors the attitudes of Arabs both literate and illiterate. It goes as deep as political consciousness goes. It strengthens those who are hostile and gravely weakens the hand of those who are friendly. If there is any feasible way in which this country can repair the damage to its position in the Arab world by addressing itself to the territorial problem, without risking more than it could possibly gain, it is worth a serious effort to find.

Only the uninformed can feel confident of knowing how to approach the question. Yet one general proposition seems difficult to avoid, and that is that the United States will remain under intolerable handicaps in its relations with the Arab world unless it puts itself in a position of willingness to recognize that injustice was done to the Arabs of Palestine and that some measure of rectification is in order. The principle is more important than the precise nature of any concrete territorial changes proposed, for to the Arab states the Palestine question is above all a question of principle and of "face." The Arabs were not only defeated in battle in 1948; they were deeply humiliated, and they were humiliated again in 1956. The Arab governments are not really desirous of getting territory in Palestine for themselves. Nor have they in fact shown themselves to be so vitally concerned over the actual fate of the Palestine Arabs as human beings, having made little effort to improve the present pitiful lot of the refugees on their own territory in order not to prejudice their political demands. What the Arab governments want above all is recognition that the present situation is unjust. When and how it may be changed is another matter, but even if the United States is unable to do anything about that, it would do well to take the position, while ruling out change by force, that a negotiated peace settlement (for which Israel is constantly calling) should include a territorial revision in favor of the Arabs as well as Arab acceptance of the existence of Israel. A return to the boundaries of the U.N. partition plan may, indeed, be proposed at some point by the Soviet Union. The United States will not be able to support it. All the more reason, then, to have shown a prior recognition of Arab rights to some revision of existing boundaries.

The United States Government should not, however, commit itself to specific territorial solutions at any early stage. It should encourage full consideration of the question in the United Nations, where it can watch how the possibilities of settlement develop and how they are related to the other matters at issue. Nevertheless, it may be useful to give some attention here to what kind of territorial settlement might recommend itself. In the first place, there would seem to be no good reason to add Palestinian territory to Egypt, Lebanon or Syria. Egypt is separated from the Gaza strip by the Sinai desert. Lebanon has a well-defined frontier with Israel and no desire to change it. Nor should concessions, other than possible adjustments to eliminate the demilitarized zones and some of the anomalies of the present Israel-Syrian border, be made to Syria, whose claim to all of Palestine as part of "southern Syria" is merely a demand for the elimination of Israel.

The case of Jordan, which has already annexed a sizable part of Palestine, is different, for here the present line could well be adjusted in many localities; for example by returning to Arab villages on the Jordan side their former fields and groves now in Israel, and by broadening Israel's corridor to Jerusalem. More fundamentally, the territorial settlement in Palestine is tied up with the fate of Jordan itself, and the two must be considered together. For if Jordan is unable to survive, the area west of the Jordan River will presumably fall to an Arab state which swallows up Jordan or shares in its partition, or it will be seized by Israel, or it will be left hanging in the air. Each of those possibilities seems to pose more problems than it solves, but we should at least give some thought to where American influence is to be thrown if and when the crisis comes.

The Arab Refugees

It is useful to remember that it was not the Arab states but the Arabs of Palestine who lost the territory assigned to them by the U.N. partition plan. Looked at in this light the territorial problem is directly linked to that of the refugees, a fact which may clarify the route of approach to it though without making it any easier to solve. Some 933,000 Arab refugees from territory that is now controlled by Israel are living in Arab lands, mainly in the Gaza strip, Jordan, Syria and Lebanon. There is room for all their number in some of the less heavily populated regions of the Arab world. But for political reasons the problem cannot be solved merely by stating the physical and financial possibilities of resettlement. In the end some of the refugees, probably most of them, will be resettled outside Palestine, but this can only be accomplished within the terms of a negotiated settlement if a certain proportion of them is allowed to live in Palestine. The Arabs insist on the right of repatriation, citing the U.N. resolution of 1948 which says refugees wishing to return and live at peace with their neighbors should be permitted to do so.[8] Obviously there can be no mass return now to their old homes, but there can be acceptance of the return of some of the refugees to territory that is now Israel.

It is here that the question of boundaries enters the picture. Israel cannot be expected to absorb an indigestible mass of hundreds of thousands of hostile Arabs, to add to the nearly 200,000 already within its borders. Israel might properly be asked, however—and this is put forward as a suggestion worth some discussion, not as *the* solution—to give up a portion of territory in western Galilee, to become an autonomous Arab area administered by the United Nations. Western Galilee was assigned to the proposed Arab state under the U.N. partition plan; it con-

[8] Resolution 194(III), December 11, 1948, U.N. General Assembly, *Resolutions*, pt. 1, *Official Records*, 3rd Session (Paris, 1948). On the number of refugees, see above, p. 80, footnote 1.

tains a large part of the Arab population now in Israel, and it has room for some of the refugees.[9] The Gaza strip, although it could not possibly support the number of refugees and other Arabs now living there and might well be somewhat enlarged, could become a similar U.N.-administered Arab area. This change would have the advantage, among others, of eliminating the strip as a base of operations against Israel and a target for Israel's border raids. The two autonomous Arab areas, western Galilee and Gaza, would be outside Israel's jurisdiction but they could maintain economic ties with Israel, as the original partition plan contemplated, as well as with the Arab states.

Taking into consideration the failure of most such experiments in the past, one is understandably hesitant to propose the creation of new "internationalized" areas. But other solutions do not spring to mind, and the United Nations as an organization is already deeply involved in the fate of Palestine. Such a solution, moreover, offers a pattern for the west bank of the River Jordan if the Kingdom of Jordan comes to the point of dissolution or partition. Israel would have good reason to fear the absorption of the west bank into an enlarged Syria or Iraq, yet Israel could not itself take over that territory without adding over one-half million Arabs (original inhabitants plus refugees now there) to its population as a dangerous minority or driving them across the Jordan as a new tidal wave of refugees. The creation of an Arab area administered by the United Nations might be the best way out for all concerned. It would also, with similar areas in Gaza and western Galilee, constitute a return to the general pattern of the original U.N. resolution on partition without making it impossible for Israel to live.

The problem of the Arab refugees is above all a great

---

[9] Such an autonomous Arab area should be smaller than that of the 1947 partition plan, for Israel should be left with a reasonable territorial connection between its central and northern parts. How many Arab refugees the area could absorb is a matter for detailed study of all the technical questions involved; the Jewish immigrants who have moved into the area could be moved out, as part of Israel's contribution to a solution.

human problem, about which the world has a moral obligation to do something. That obligation lies especially on Israel and on the Arab states, but also on other nations, including the United States. It also has a political urgency due to its explosive character. The refugees cannot but be steeped in bitterness and desperation, a prey to agitators and a source of infection throughout the area. For the past two years the Director of U.N.R.W.A. has informed the General Assembly of the urgent need for a political solution.[10]

The Government of Israel, which shrugs its shoulders and says that the Arabs brought the problem on themselves by attacking Israel in 1948, has a responsibility to do more than it has done. It can accept the principle that a reasonable number of Arabs will be permitted to return and that compensation will be paid to others, the number and the compensation to be subject to negotiation or arbitration. Only if Israel takes such a step will it be possible for outside powers or the United Nations to put some pressure on the Arabs to proceed with resettlement of the bulk of the refugees in the Arab world.

The Arab governments, which have put all the blame on Israel and the West, also have a responsibility to the world and to the refugees themselves. They do not discharge that responsibility by asserting the right of every refugee to return to Palestine. Once some reasonable proposals conceding that some may return are on the record, then it may be possible to press the case for resettlement. As a means of persuasion, those states which provide the funds for the refugees through U.N.R.W.A. can gradually shift their use from relief to resettlement, as has been contemplated but not carried out in the past, with the clear warning that relief funds will not be available after 1960, when the agency is due to be terminated. It would

---

[10] *Annual Report of the Director of the United Nations Relief and Works Agency for Palestine Refugees in the Near East . . . 1 July 1955 to 30 June 1956,* U.N. General Assembly, *Official Records,* 11th Session, Supplement no. 14 (New York, 1956) and *Annual Report . . . 1 July 1956 to 30 June 1957,* same, 12th Session, Supplement no. 14 (New York, 1957).

work hardship on the refugees themselves, but it might add their pressure to that of others to get the Arab governments to deal with the question as a practical one to be negotiated and to be solved by agreement. If the Arab governments can be given some satisfaction on the territorial issue which will materialize only if they help in solving the refugee problem, there is some chance that they or their successors will eventually cooperate. On the other hand, they will probably prefer to remain intransigent on both issues as long as they find that intransigence pays off in political success more than does reason or statesmanship.

It may still be possible, even without the concessions each side would have to make for a major agreement, to make some progress around the edges of the problem. Israel may be prevailed upon to pay some compensation to refugees whose property it has taken over. More of the refugees may be absorbed into the economy and society of the countries in which they live. Offers can be made which might induce individual refugees to start life anew somewhere else. One thing can and should be done without delay, and that is to make objective technical studies of the economic and social problems involved in settling refugees in Palestine or elsewhere: what countries can absorb refugees and how many; what are the costs of resettling this or that group or type of refugees; what are the facts on property losses and on adequacy of compensation. A reliable body of information on such questions, not now available, is necessary before such concrete proposals as the creation of Arab autonomous areas in Palestine or the migration of large numbers to Iraq are taken up in serious negotiations.

The Status of Jerusalem

Allied to the territorial problem is that of Jerusalem. The U.N. partition plan of 1947 provided for an internationalized district, a *corpus separatum* belonging neither

to the Arab nor to the Jewish state, to include the city
and its surrounding area. Since then the General Assembly
has twice, with the United States voting in the negative,
recommended that that solution be put into effect.[11] It
has remained a dead letter, for no one knew how to impose
it on the two states that shared possession and were not
prepared to give it up, Israel and Jordan. The unfortunate
city, sacred to three of the world's great religions, remained
bisected by the armistice line and the scene of many a
bloody incident.

The only practical hope is for a modification of the
unsatisfactory *status quo* that will reduce tensions and
safeguard legitimate world interest in the Holy Places.
The Jewish sector of Jerusalem is already established as
the capital of Israel, although not recognized as such by
the United States and many others. There is no strong
reason why this city, overwhelmingly Jewish and containing few of the shrines sacred to Christians or Moslems,
should be taken away from Israel, even if that were a
simple proposition, which it is not. Greater cause exists
for some form of international status for Arab Jerusalem,
where most of the Holy Places are located, but it is hardly
equitable or desirable to enforce it on Jordan alone. Were
the whole west bank area at some time to have some special international status, the solution would of course be
much simpler.

The logical answer at this time seems to lie in an arrangement which would leave the existing sovereignty of
the two states undisturbed, while requiring both to accept
international supervision of the Holy Places only, which
would guarantee their protection and freedom of access
to them by the citizens of all countries. Such a plan was
presented to the United Nations by Sweden in 1950 but
was never adopted, although Israel and Jordan were both

---

[11] Resolution 194(III), cited and Resolution 303(IV), December 9, 1949,
U.N. General Assembly, *Resolutions, Official Records*, 4th Session (Lake
Success, 1949).

willing to accept it.[12] It is far more sensible to seek its general acceptance and thus achieve a practical though imperfect solution than to continue the present unsettled situation and leave on the United Nations' books the unattainable resolutions in favor of a separate international city. The first task is to convince Israel and Jordan, which is not impossible as both would be confirmed in possession of what they have. The next task would be to convince the many Catholic countries (especially in Latin America) which voted for internationalization, and the Vatican, which was the principal influence determining their votes.[13]

The Jordan Valley Plan

The other outstanding major source of conflict is the division of the waters of the Jordan river system. Israel, Syria and Jordan all have need for the water of the Jordan and its tributaries. If each proceeds with its own national plan, drawing on that part of the river system accessible within its own territory, the inevitable result is economic warfare, political conflict, and inefficient use of the available water resources by all three. There is not enough water to supply simultaneously the needs of the state of Jordan, especially if refugees are to be settled on new land, and the requirements of Israel not only in the immediate area of the river but in the central plain and the Negev. No one country could get the most rational use of water without some coordination of its plans with

[12] The United States, with Great Britain and Uruguay, sponsored an amendment to the Swedish resolution which made it acceptable to Jordan. Because of its dim prospects, the amended resolution was never submitted to a vote. See U.N. General Assembly, 5th Session, Ad Hoc Political Committee, *United Kingdom, United States of America, Uruguay: amendment to the Draft Resolution proposed by Sweden* (A/AC.38/L.73/Rev.2, December 13, 1950) and *Summary Records* (A/AC.38/SR.78 and SR.80, December 12 and 13, 1950) (New York, 1950).

[13] Edward B. Glick, "The Vatican, Latin America, and Jerusalem," *International Organization*, v. 11 (Spring 1957), pp. 213-219.

those of its neighbors.[14] The situation fairly cries for an internationally agreed scheme of river control and development based on an equitable sharing of the water. Israel's determination to go ahead with its own plan, and actual start in 1953 on a project to divert Jordan water through a new canal at Banat Ya'qub in the demilitarized zone north of Lake Tiberias, though checked temporarily by a ruling of the head of U.N.T.S.O. upheld by the Security Council, led to intensified efforts on the part of the United Nations and the United States to get acceptance of an international plan.

The plan associated with the name of Eric Johnston, who as President Eisenhower's special representative made numerous trips to the Near East from 1953 to 1955 to obtain agreement to it, was soundly based on engineering surveys conducted under joint American and U.N.R.W.A. auspices. It provided for an agreed division of water and for dams and other works that would contribute to the development of agriculture and industry in all three countries. Accepted by all parties "on the technical level," including the difficult item of allotment of percentages of available water, it ultimately ran afoul of Syria's political objections and dropped out of sight.

The fate of the Johnston Plan shows that the real difficulties are political. The Arab states, apparently, will sacrifice their own economic interests in order to avoid any move that might be taken as a step toward acceptance of Israel. How and when that political objection may be overcome is impossible to say. It depends on the whole climate of relations in the Near East, not merely on new approaches on the subject of water resources. But new approaches should nevertheless be made. If the Johnston Plan is dead, some comparable plan must be devised to replace it. If under neutral or U.N. sponsorship, it might

[14] M. G. Ionides, "The Disputed Waters of the Jordan," *Middle East Journal*, v. 7 (Spring 1953), pp. 153-164; Georgiana G. Stevens, *The Jordan River Valley* (New York: Carnegie Endowment for International Peace, 1956), pp. 244-260.

have more chance of acceptance. The time, unfortunately, is short, for Israel will not wait indefinitely before going ahead with its own ambitious schemes, and once the pattern of national action is set it will not easily be changed.

The Place of Israel in the Arab East

No part of the many-sided problem lends itself to easy solution. No one avenue of attack stands out as the most logical and promising. The idea of fitting all the pieces of the puzzle together in some way that will bring even a tolerable "coexistence" in the near future between the Arab states and Israel is utopian. On the other hand, pragmatic attempts to deal with this or that concrete problem such as the use and development of water resources or relaxation of the Arab blockade and boycott run up against the blank wall of Arab refusal to agree to anything that seems to accept Israel's continuing existence.

Deeply rooted and fanatically held emotional attitudes are not easily modified by outside pressure or exhortation. The United States has urged the Arabs to accept Israel as an established fact and has urged Israel to realize that as a small Middle Eastern state it must find a way to live among other Middle Eastern states and cease to regard itself as a "nucleus . . . of worldwide groupings of peoples of a particular religious faith who must have special rights within and obligations to the Israeli state." [15] But if there is one thing on which Israel and the Arab states do not agree it is that they have a common destiny in the Middle East. Israel, say the Arab leaders, is an alien body established by force in the heart of the Arab world. Israel, say its own most eloquent spokesmen, is a Mediterranean rather than a Middle Eastern country. Despite the increasingly "eastern" complexion of its population, it looks toward the sea and the Western world, not toward the

[15] Address of Assistant Secretary of State Henry A. Byroade, "The Middle East in New Perspective," *Department of State Bulletin*, v. 30 (April 26, 1954), p. 632.

desert. To the Arabs, Israel is the most dangerous manifestation of Western imperialism, for it has come not to
occupy bases or exploit oil resources but with settlers in
unlimited numbers to push Arabs off their own land. To
Israel, the return to the Promised Land cannot be a matter
for compromise or for negotiation; it is of the very essence
of the state of Israel that its doors be open for the "in-
gathering" of all Jews, no matter what the effect on future
relations with the Arab world. The violence of Israel's
reaction to American suggestions that it should limit immigration in the interest of peace is comparable to the
violence of Arab threats to drive the Jews into the sea. If
the men of the Kremlin, for purposes of their own, should
some day decide to "dump" the millions of Jews of the
Soviet Union and Eastern Europe on the world refugee
market, Israel would wish to take them in regardless of
the consequences to its own economy, of Arab objections,
or of contrary advice from Western governments.

The implications of a massive influx of immigrants into
Israel should be clearly understood. If Israel sees this as a
guarantee of its security, the Arabs see it as a guarantee of
their insecurity. Within its present boundaries and before
the Negev is developed to the point where it can support
large numbers (if it ever can be), Israel cannot absorb
another million or more immigrants unless its people are
prepared to accept a Middle Eastern standard of living,
an unlikely possibility. If the United States should stand
aside and do nothing while such a massive immigration
took place, the job of containing the forces building up to
a new explosion would become nearly impossible. If it
should provide the necessarily enormous funds, privately
or publicly, to finance large-scale immigration, the effect
on American relations with the Arab world could be disastrous. Nor would it make sense to encourage heavy Jewish
immigration while trying to induce Israel to accept some
Arab refugees or to give up some of its territory. If the
Kremlin should open the gates and let loose a flood of
refugees, the problem cannot be met solely by trying to per-

suade the Government of Israel to limit its acceptance of Jewish immigrants. Some provision to settle such refugees elsewhere would also be necessary.

To these matters of faith or prejudice which stand in the way of any reconciliation is added the element of fear. Israel naturally fears submergence by the great mass of surrounding Moslem peoples; any concession it made to this hostile environment might fatally compromise the struggle for survival. The Arab governments, on the other hand, fear not only Israel's armies but Israel's potential influence on their own countries. They may call it a manifestation of imperialism, but what Israel in fact represents is a dynamic Western-type society with a working democratic system of government. If it should cease to be quarantined, if commercial and cultural relations were allowed to develop between Israel and the Arab world, these contacts might not be without effect on Arab thinking, on Arab society, and on Arab politics.

Sometimes it is comforting to escape the perplexities of insoluble current problems by taking refuge in the long view. The long view of the Arab-Israel conflict, because of these elements of faith, fear and hatred on both sides, offers no silver lining. Still, one cannot be sure of anything, even of disaster, in the Middle East. Tension may relax simply because it is impossible for people to sustain it indefinitely. Great changes are taking place in Arab society. New political forces, a new generation, may find other issues more important than the barren conflict with Israel. A new generation in Israel may be more aware than the "founding fathers" of the need to adjust to the Middle Eastern environment.

The task of American diplomacy in this affair bristles with difficulties. It is far more demanding than that of Soviet diplomacy, for it is easier to keep wounds open than to heal them, easier to espouse the cause of one side and reap political benefits without responsibility for the consequences than to seek to stabilize a situation basically unsatisfactory to both. If we expect to live on terms of

mutual respect and friendship with both Israel and the
Arab world, as we must if we hope to keep the whole
Middle East free of outside domination, then we have no
alternative to the slow and often unrewarding effort to
help reduce the sources of tension and conflict between
them. The discussion of a number of specific propositions
earlier in this chapter is not intended to suggest that the
solutions are ready to hand if only American officials are
bold enough to propose and support them. There is a long
road between an idea put on paper and a negotiated settlement accepted by governments and by nations. Discouraging as the prospects may be, however, the United States
should bestir itself to attack an issue which has contributed
so much to the deterioration of the American position in
the Middle East.

Having set the framework within which diplomacy can
work by establishing limits beyond which it will not tolerate Soviet intervention, the United States should then
move forward from the proposals made by Secretary Dulles
in 1955 [16] to make the main questions in dispute the subject of an active international effort to reach agreed solutions. Generally, it will not be wise for the United States
to be out in front, though there are some points on which
it may find political advantage in taking a stand. The place
for negotiation, in most instances, is the United Nations.
Where U.N. machinery already exists, it should be per-
fected and used; otherwise it can be created. Commissions
can be set up to keep the problems under study. Every
effort should be made to bring Asian and African countries into the picture in a constructive role, for they have
an interest in peace. India, for example, has no interest in
seeing the Arab-Israel conflict kept at fever heat, even if
Moscow does. Israel and the Arab states are not likely to
be coaxed into concessions by American urging; they will
not be receptive to proposals merely because they bear
the label of the United Nations; but they may be impressed by proposed settlements that have the endorsement

[16] See above, p. 88.

of the greater part of the free world, including important "neutrals" as well as the West.

The ways of diplomacy are slow but they need not be in vain, even if seemingly outrun by events, scorned by the parties to the conflict, and pushed aside in favor of force. The Arab-Israel problem has been with us for more than a decade and will be with us for a long time to come. Constructive American diplomacy may at least reduce its baneful effects within tolerable limits, even if it cannot produce the miracle of a "solution."

Chapter 18

THE UNITY OF THE WEST

THE DEBACLE of 1956 opened a yawning chasm within the Western world, or disclosed one already there, and subsequent developments have not entirely closed it. The initial state of shock having passed, the need for reassessment has been obvious. The major Western powers, jointly and severally, have to consider the changed situation in the Middle East as it affects both their global strategy and their specific interests in the region itself. Additionally, both Western Europe and the United States have the duty to subject their relations with each other to a reassessment in which reason and objectivity are not lost in the "agony" of reappraisal.

It is necessary to state first and foremost that the survival of the West depends on its ability to maintain its essential unity. Perhaps the United States could fight a war against the U.S.S.R. without European allies, although there is small comfort in that thought since such a war would probably destroy the United States as well as its enemies. To carry on in the cold war, in any event, Western Europe and the United States are indispensable to each other. Each needs the other's power, its resources, its moral support, and its prestige and position in the world. It has been a prime purpose of Soviet policy to break down and destroy that Western unity, so that it could eliminate America's power and presence from the Eastern Hemisphere and confront the free nations of Europe, and later the United States, from a position of overwhelming strength.

Western unity is now expressed in NATO, in American cooperation with various European international and supranational organizations, and in certain working relationships between the United States and Western European powers in other parts of the world. We need not try to determine here just what degree of unity on the first two of these points is the necessary amount to ensure the survival of the West in freedom. Probably it will have to be greater than in the past. What concerns us is the third point: How much or how little Western unity is required to meet the challenge in the underdeveloped and former colonial areas like the Middle East where the Communist powers, not without success, are now making their most serious efforts?

In the years since the second World War the United States, the United Kingdom and France have been associated in an informal partnership as the "Big Three" of the Western world. They have had a recognized leading role in NATO (through the so-called Standing Group) and as occupying powers in Germany and Austria. They have acted together, for limited periods and not always in full harmony, in such matters as economic aid to Yugoslavia and the restriction of arms shipments to the Near East. They have sought, though not always attained, "united action" on certain critical problems of the Far East. And they have made it a practice—though not an invariable one—to consult on matters all over the world carrying any danger of a war which, involving one, would probably in the end involve all. In theory the three powers have had a special relationship among themselves which they did not share with others, because only they had both the rank of great powers and responsibility for global interests.

It was never a precisely defined or automatic relationship, because of the wide gaps between the relative power of the parties to it and the frequent differences in their interests and points of view on particular issues. In general France has wished to apply the principle of tripartite consultation and common policy as broadly as possible, in order to ensure for itself the standing of a great power, a voice in Western strategy, and support for its own interests. The French have been extraordinarily sensitive to signs of a special relationship between the United States and Great Britain from which France is excluded. Successive British governments, on the other hand, have sought to preserve the unique bilateral relationship with the United States forged in the recent World War and based on certain imponderables as well as a general similarity of interests all round the globe. They have also looked on the formula of tripartite understanding and the procedures of NATO as useful in putting a checkrein on American policies, especially in the Far East, deemed too adventurous or provocative.

The United States has had no consistent attitude. It has assumed a general unity of purpose with Britan and France in confronting the Soviet threat. As the one power able to hold the world-wide balance with the Sino-Soviet bloc, however, it has not wished to have its hands tied by British and French caution. This has been evident especially in the Far East where American security and American emotions are more directly involved and where, in American eyes, the British often have seemed more concerned with not provoking the Communists than with stopping them, and the French merely with trying to preserve the remnants of a dying empire. In these generalizations the views of all three powers are perhaps too starkly put, but they correctly show the different strains on the concept of Western unity when it confronts concrete situations outside the NATO area. They show the tendency of each partner to look to the concept as a means of furthering the pursuit of his own interests, and the absence of any specific agreement on its meaning in practice.

Strains on Western Unity in the Middle East

In the Middle East, during the first postwar decade, the separate interests of the three powers were only partially subordinated to a common Western strategy or to accepted procedures for coordinating individual strategies. The

heritage of the past was a heavy burden: it tended to set
the French and British against each other and the new
Middle Eastern nations against both of them. The United
States, wary of being tarred with the brush of imperialism,
sought middle positions on many questions at issue between its European allies and Middle Eastern nationalism,
a tactic not always appreciated by the former. As between
Britain and the United States, general identity of policy
on defense of the region was marred by competition and
rivalry in the oil industry which inevitably had some effect
on intergovernmental relations.

The Tripartite Declaration of 1950 represented an
agreed Western policy on how best to maintain security
on the troubled borders of Israel, and the Middle East
Command proposal of the following year associated all
three powers in the attempt to build a security system
against Soviet aggression. As Middle Eastern problems
grew more critical, however, some of the weaknesses and
contradictions behind the façade of unity were revealed.
One was the anomalous position of France, historically a
great power in the area but now retreating almost everywhere and incapable of playing a major role. After its
departure from Syria and Lebanon in 1946, France had no
pied-à-terre at all in the Middle East, only cultural connections and a commercial and financial interest in the
Suez Canal. It had been included in the policy declarations of 1950 and 1951 more by courtesy than by reason
of its power or influence in the Middle East. When the
United States, Britain and Turkey moved ahead with the
northern tier alliance in 1954, they ignored France, provoking vigorous protests from Paris on the grounds that
French interests were being slighted, particularly its special concern for the independence of Syria allegedly
threatened by the new bloc.[1] Objectively, such protests

[1] Metellus, "Politique de la France au Proche-Orient," *Politique Étrangère*,
20ᵉ année (December 1955), pp. 677-688; Edouard Sablier, "La tension en
Proche-Orient et la politique des grandes puissances," same, 21ᵉ année
(January-February 1956), pp. 21-26.

would seem to be based on little more than nostalgia—the last thing the Syrians wanted was the solicitude and protection of France. The fact remains that they represented a view strongly and widely held in France.

France was directly involved in the Arab world, of course, through its presence in North Africa but did not thereby earn recognition of its claim to a major role in the Middle East. On the contrary, the course of events in North Africa, especially after the outbreak of the Algerian rebellion in 1954, only made the situation more difficult. France, looking to its Western partners to help save its position in North Africa, was inevitably disappointed and embittered by the lukewarm support it got from the United States. As the United States saw it, however, even the moderate position it tried to take on North Africa was earning the ill will of the whole Arab world. American attitudes came more and more to be influenced by the fact that association with France was a handicap to good relations with Arabs. Meanwhile, French attitudes toward the Middle East were increasingly colored by the situation in Algeria, where the rebels were receiving help from Egypt. After the nationalization of the Suez Canal Company France virtually wrote off the Arabs and turned to the idea of the use of force against Egypt in the company of its newly found friend, Israel. Solidarity with the United States had not helped France in her agony, Frenchmen reasoned; they would not allow quixotic loyalty to it to restrain them from the desperate action that seemed the only way out.

The breakdown of unity between Britain and the United States was less noticeable but even more serious. Despite differences of approach the two powers seemed to be agreed on the importance of defense of the Middle East against the Soviets. Both supported the Baghdad Pact. Minor troubles reflecting differences in attitude toward Iran, Egypt or Saudi Arabia were not permitted to shake the general agreement on the main lines of policy. That policy, judging by the British acceptance of the withdrawal from the Suez base in 1954 and later from those in Iraq, seemed to envisage a gradual Western retreat from positions that local nationalism would no longer accept. No agreement existed on how far and how fast the process was to go. As in the past, the degree of pressure which nationalism could generate would probably be the determining factor. But the idea of a gradual transition to a new system based on consent seemed to be at least tacitly accepted by both Great Britain and the United States.

When this consent was not forthcoming, it was no easy thing for the British to accept the accelerated loss of positions which by 1956 seemed to be the goal of the rabid nationalism of Abdel Nasser and his followers. Under this onslaught British Conservatives thought more and more in terms of "holding their own" in the Middle East against those who were attacking at every vulnerable point. The Eden Government, under criticism from its own party as well as from the opposition for inaction and mistakes on a number of issues, was increasingly touchy about new blows to British prestige. With Abdel Nasser putting his stamp on Arab nationalism, British officials became increasingly skeptical of the theory, still held by the United States, that it could and must be won over as an ally against Russia.[2] And so, behind the fictions of a common front which marked the conferences and consultations over the Suez Canal after July 1956, unity of policy did not exist. London took the fateful decisions on the use of force, not only in association with France but in action tied to the parallel use of force by Israel, the one sure means of uniting the whole Arab world behind Nasser, precisely what the United States was doing its best to prevent. So strong were the ties of tradition that the Americans did not expect the British to act alone without even prior consultation, and the British expected the Americans, after the first shock of surprise, to give tacit support to their venture. Both were mistaken, and both were resentful of the other's failure to play the game.

[2] See above, pp. 78-79, 101-102.

The Aftermath of the Crisis

The Anglo-French attack on Egypt and the instantaneous American reaction certainly cleared the air of many illusions. But there was no certainty as to what would take their place. It was immediately apparent that the standing of Britain and France in the Middle East would never be what it had been before, and that the United States would have to assume a more active role of leadership if the advantages were not to be left entirely in Soviet hands. The questions to be answered were whether Western Europe was in fact "finished" in the Middle East, what Western interests remained there for the United States to protect, and how, if at all, its continuing ties with Europe should be allowed to affect the new role of champion of the nations of Asia and Africa the United States appeared to have assumed.

In the first flush of excitement over the "moral" stand taken by the United States in the United Nations and amid the plaudits of the Arabs and other "new nations," some American voices were raised in favor of a clean break with "colonialism" and with pussyfooting attempts to mediate between the European powers and the peoples of Asia and Africa. Vice President Nixon spoke of a "declaration of independence," implying that our earlier policies had been virtually determined in London and Paris instead of in Washington.[3] The spectacle of overwhelming majorities in the General Assembly following American leadership to uphold the law of the Charter encouraged the idea of a new emphasis in American diplomacy on the United Nations and the newly independent nations. If this tendency did not go so far as to write off the Western alliance itself, it did assume the end of Western unity in almost all the rest of the world outside Europe. It implied that the United States would have to "go it alone" in the Middle East.

[3] Summary of speech made in Hershey, Pennsylvania, in *New York Times,* November 3, 1956.

Anger in official circles at what Britain and France had
done helped to stimulate this kind of thinking. But
American policy developed in response to the concrete
problems of liquidating the aggression in the Middle
East, not to outraged feelings and new theories. And, as it
developed, some of the gloss wore off the shining hopes
for cooperation from the Arabs. Abdel Nasser was interested chiefly in making sure of a great political victory.
He expressed public appreciation of America's stand
against aggression, but showed no signs of changing his
basic policies of the past year. The American rejection of
the High Aswan Dam was no distant memory. The source
of arms was still Russia. Many Arabs persisted in thinking
that the Soviet Union had done more to help them in their
moment of peril than the United States had, an idea encouraged by much of the Arab press. The American votes
in the United Nations had not wiped out the stain of
earlier American support of Israel, and the leaders of Arab
opinion had long discounted heavily American talk of law
and moral principles.

Another sobering influence was the realization of the
depth and bitterness of anti-American feeling in Britain.
In France it was less noticeable; though the French had
taken the lead in the Suez venture and supported it more
strongly, they seemed to take their defeat more philo-
sophically. To the British, despite the fact that many of
them had opposed the Government, the outcome brought
a sense of national humiliation for which the United
States was held largely responsible. The theory of some
Americans that Britain would continue to be a staunch
ally in Europe while fading entirely out of the Middle
Eastern picture was seen to be based on a misjudgment of
its people. Faced with the real risk of permanent weakening of the Anglo-American relationship, the Administration took steps to restore some of the balance that had
been lost. The Vice President took the occasion of a major
speech to stress the ties with our Western allies and to
concede that mistakes on both sides had contributed to

the debacle.[4] By December, before British and French troops were out of Egypt, the United States was putting its full efforts into helping Europe meet its oil shortage.

Both governments, indeed, had come to the conclusion that some repair work must be done. The resignation of Sir Anthony Eden helped to clear the atmosphere, although many Englishmen would have liked to see it clarified further by the retirement of Mr. Dulles. Then, at Bermuda in March 1957, the Middle East once again was the subject of frank and friendly discussion between the highest officials of the two nations. Again in October, when Prime Minister Macmillan visited Washington, solidarity was evident in the firm joint declaration of support for Turkey under the North Atlantic Treaty.

The Essential Common Interests

The problem for the future, of course, involves more than willingness to speak again together on friendly terms. It will not be enough to put relations back on the old terms, because the old terms did not work when put to the test. What is needed is a more precise understanding than existed before on what are the essential common interests of the West in the Middle East and on how they should be protected.

It is a fact, which tends to be overlooked by enthusiasts for winning new Middle Eastern friends at the cost of losing old European allies, that the defense of Europe and the defense of the Middle East are not separable. NATO, through Turkey, extends into the very heart of the Middle East, which is its most vulnerable flank. From the standpoint of global strategy, the American concern with holding the Middle East is in large part a function of the need to hold Europe. This is stated as a strategic fact, without implying that the Middle Eastern peoples have less right to freedom than do the peoples of Europe

[4] Address to the Automobile Manufacturers Association, *New York Times,* December 7, 1956.

or America. Further, to stress once more the importance
of Middle Eastern oil, European nations have to have
access to it to keep their economies alive. They cannot be
expected to disassociate themselves from the Middle East as
long as this is so. And it is vital to the United States that
those interests of theirs should be protected.

The United States and Western Europe thus have de-
finable common interests in the Middle East which may
be summarized as follows: (1) prevention of Soviet gains,
either by military or nonmilitary means, that would
menace Western Europe's security; (2) access to Middle
Eastern oil and its assured transport to Europe. In the
first instance the United States should reach a basis of
understanding with Great Britain, for they are the two
Western powers which still have a "position" in the area
in the form of political responsibilities and the ability to
bring power to bear. The British, still holding certain
territories and membership in the Baghdad Pact, are not
to be counted out yet. Proceeding from agreement on the
nature of the essential common interests, the two powers
should attempt to work out the best ways of dealing with
such questions as the future of Cyprus, the British protectorates in the Persian Gulf region, and treaty relationships with the Middle Eastern states.[5] Both powers should
be in frequent consultation with France, the German
Federal Republic, Italy and other Western states, preferably through regular NATO channels, so that all may
have their say on how to safeguard interests which are
generally Western and not exclusively American and
British.

The question of Algeria, while not strictly of the Middle
East from a geographic viewpoint, presents grave difficulties
affecting the future position of France and indeed of the
entire West in relations with the Arab world. Obviously the
equation has many factors which may contravene or out-

[5] The substance of these questions has already been discussed. They are
mentioned again here only to re-emphasize the need for Anglo-American
understanding on how to deal with them.

weigh those of policy toward the Arabs. The Algerian problem has many facets, and their analysis is beyond the scope
of this book. But one conclusion, wholly relevant to the fate
of the West in the Middle East, seems clear: the outcome
will be some form of autonomy or independence for Algeria.
Unless France and its Western partners seek a solution
which recognizes that this is what lies at the end of the road,
and which makes possible a partnership between Europe
and Arab North Africa, then the most likely result is the
lasting alienation of Tunisia and Morocco, now favorably
inclined toward the West, and the compounding of the
West's troubles in the Middle East. France cannot play any
constructive part in the Middle East while the war in Algeria continues, and the West as a whole is seriously handicapped.

Questions of security, requiring a certain amount of
consultation between the United States and its NATO
allies, and common planning for the contingency of war,
do not by any means require a common approach to
Middle Eastern governments. Experience has shown that
the West cannot organize the defense of the Middle East
by itself without local cooperation, nor can it win such
cooperation for a joint effort. Whatever Western military
strength can be mustered for the defense of the area will
have to be provided by the United States and Britain, and
indeed, because of physical and political limitations on the
British role, almost entirely by the United States. American military strategy, accordingly, and political strategy
also, must be aimed at protecting the security of Western
Europe as well as other interests of the United States,
whether the threat takes military or other forms. The
Eisenhower Doctrine, or "American Doctrine" as the official statements are pleased to call it, had to be unilaterally
American because that was the need of the time both at
home and abroad. But in practice it must be an instrument to serve the vital interests of Europe also. Joint
action may not often be indicated, but consultation—with

NATO regularly and with Britain more or less continuously—becomes a virtual obligation of the United States.

The West and Middle Eastern Oil

Questions relating to oil have a special importance to all of Western Europe, but the burden of decision rests mainly in the hands of governments of the United States and Great Britain and of the private oil companies. Most of the latter represent American or British capital, although the French have a minority share in the Iraq Petroleum Company, one of the largest producers in several countries of the Middle East. Some of the problems of meeting the threat of nationalism and of working out arrangements with the Middle Eastern nations have already been considered.[6] What concerns us here is the need for Anglo-American agreement, and indeed general Western agreement, on how to ensure the continued flow of oil.

The first point to be sure of is that rivalries between companies, whose role by the very nature of their operations tends to be political as well as economic, do not damage governmental relations. In the postwar period the share of American companies in total Middle East oil production has been going up while that of British companies has been going down. In 1946 the American share was 35 per cent and the British share 50 per cent (57 per cent including British-Dutch interests). In 1955 the figures were reversed, 58 per cent American and 35 per cent British.[7] Saudi Arabian production, exclusively American, has come from nothing twenty years ago to a production of over one million barrels per day. In Kuwait, the leading producing country in the Middle East, the operating company is 50 per cent American-owned. In Iran the crisis over nationalization was settled to Britain's satisfaction in 1954, but one of its results was that an international con-

---

[6] See above, pp. 231-244.
[7] Arabian American Oil Company, *Middle East Oil Development*, 4th edition (Washington, 1956), p. 27.

sortium (40 per cent American) went into operation where the exclusively British-owned Anglo-Iranian had operated before.

The American gains have been due to the fortunes of business and of politics, but the mere fact that they took place created suspicions that it was an aim of American policy in the Middle East to displace British companies in favor of American companies. This has been a favorite theme of Soviet propaganda intended to stir up trouble within the Western world. When Anglo-American relations hit their low point in November 1956, it took its place among the numerous complaints about America heard in Great Britain. It is a point on which the British should have the most categorical assurances. The U.S. Government cannot guarantee the future of British oil companies, but it can pledge that it will do nothing to lessen their chances of staying in business and of finding opportunities to increase their share of Middle Eastern production.

The United States has no interest in driving British enterprise out of the Middle Eastern oil business. American and British firms are now partners in ownership of some of the largest operating companies and are closely associated in marketing arrangements.[8] American capital is established in several British-controlled areas. Neither party would gain if these relations were disrupted either by business rivalries or by the theory that British oil interests represent "imperialism" while the American do not. Similarly, the established companies should not resent the appearance in the field of other Western companies, such as the Italian firm recently granted a concession in

[8] Iraq Petroleum Company, operating in Iraq, Qatar and other areas is 23.75 per cent British Petroleum, 23.75 per cent Royal Dutch Shell, 23.75 per cent French, 23.75 per cent Standard Oil of New Jersey; Kuwait Petroleum Company is 50 per cent British Petroleum and 50 per cent Gulf Oil Company; Bapco, operating in British-protected Bahrein, is 100 per cent American; Aramco in Saudi Arabia is 100 per cent American; the International Consortium in Iran is 54 per cent British, 40 per cent American.

Iran, as long as the new entrants do not disrupt the pattern of relationships with local governments. Attention cannot safely be diverted from the main problem that confronts American, British and all other Western companies, that of ensuring the continuance of production through good working relations with the local governments and a capacity to absorb the shocks from local nationalism.

The companies may be able to act more effectively on their own than in open association with their governments. So much the better if they can. Nevertheless, in the last analysis the oil question is one of national and international strategy with which the Western governments must concern themselves. They may find it necessary to enable the companies to keep producing even under conditions which might induce the latter, if they considered only their own private interests, to throw in the sponge. And in return for having undertaken this type of business, which has been profitable, the companies will have to take guidance on political relations from their governments. The British companies are already on rather tight leading-strings (some are partly owned by the British Government), and Aramco and other American companies have close informal contacts with the U.S. Government.

The companies are bound to feel constricted between the pressure for concessions to the local situation and the acceptance of guidance from their own governments. As long as they operate in the Middle East, however, they are acting, willy-nilly, on behalf of the whole of Western Europe, whose economic life depends on continuing production and transport of Middle Eastern oil. This is a matter so important to the nations of Western Europe which depend on that oil that their governments should be apprised of developments and consulted on strategy. Their economy should not be put in jeopardy by any purely American decisions, governmental or private, nor should they be confronted with such a situation as that of 1956 when all had their supplies of oil cut off as the result of a strategy which two of their number had concocted strictly on their own.

The Suez Canal

The question of the pipelines to the Mediterranean is similarly of concern to all the Western nations, as is the Suez Canal, on which they are dependent for general maritime commerce as well as for the transport of oil. The great controversy provoked by the nationalization of the Canal Company in 1956 was almost lost to view after the Anglo-French invasion raised larger and more urgent questions, and then sputtered out owing to the West's impotence. Events have shown that Egypt cannot be induced by persuasion or compelled by force to accept internationalization of the operation of the canal. The Western powers have therefore been constrained to get the best bargain they could by American negotiations with Egypt. What they have obtained, Egypt's "Declaration" of April 24, 1957, registered with the United Nations,[9] falls far short of the guarantees they were seeking against arbitrary control of the canal by Egypt, or by one man in Egypt, and even of the "Indian Plan," the proposal of the minority at the first London conference in 1956, which Egypt might have accepted then.[10]

The Western nations should look at the Suez Canal strictly in terms of what their vital economic interests re-

[9] U.N. General Assembly, *Letter dated 24 April 1957 from the Minister for Foreign Affairs of Egypt, addressed to the Secretary-General* (A/3576, S/3818, April 24, 1957), *Letter dated 24 April 1957 from the Secretary-General, addressed to the Minister for Foreign Affairs of Egypt* (A/3577, S/3819, April 25, 1957). In connection with the declaration, Egypt formally accepted the compulsory jurisdiction of the International Court of Justice (*Letter dated 18 July 1957 from the Minister for Foreign Affairs of Egypt, addressed to the Secretary-General, relating to paragraph 9 (b) of the declaration,* A/3576/Add. 1, S/3818/Add. 1, July 23, 1957).

[10] The Indian Plan provided for an international advisory board, which would consult with Egypt on the operation of the Suez Canal and would report periodically to the United Nations. (See Department of State, *The Suez Canal Problem, July 26-September 22, 1956,* Washington: G.P.O., 1956, pp. 174-178, 243-249, 288-289.)

quire and what political conditions will permit. Economic interests require only that the canal be freely open to the traffic of all nations.[11] It remained open after the nationalization until the crisis broke at the end of October; it has been open again since its clearance by the United Nations. The interests of the Western nations as a whole are not served if some of them act in anger over blows to their prestige or insist on guarantees they cannot obtain. As long as the Suez Canal runs through Egypt's territory and no foreign troops are in occupation of it, its operation cannot be "insulated from the politics" of Egypt, and paper guarantees are useful only to the extent they can be enforced.

The Western nations do not have to be satisfied with Egypt's "Declaration," which has little, if any, binding legal force. They can and should try to obtain an international agreement that provides greater assurance that navigation will in fact remain free and open, but without urgency and without making it a "showdown" issue between West and East. Eastern nations, after all, have an interest of their own in a firmer assurance of free navigation through the canal. Turkey, Iran, Pakistan and Ethiopia supported the majority plan for internationalization at the first London conference. India, Ceylon, and Indonesia supported the proposal for an international advisory board. The question might well be left to mature while it is studied in the United Nations, so that the weight of those common interests can make itself felt.

As long as Egypt recognizes the validity of the principle of free navigation and of the Constantinople Convention of 1888 which established it, and does not in fact

[11] The United States has properly taken the position that freedom of navigation should extend to Israel. If the legal aspects of the dispute can be adjudicated by the International Court of Justice, the United States should support efforts through the United Nations to have the Court's decision respected. But it is not incumbent on the United States or any group of Western nations to assume alone the task of forcing Egypt to open the canal to the ships and commerce of Israel. On the legal issues, see L. M. Bloomfield, *Egypt, Israel and the Gulf of Aqaba in International Law* (Toronto: Carswell, 1957).

violate it, the situation is one which the Western nations can tolerate. Unless they are willing to accept a comparable degree of internationalization for the Panama Canal, the Bosporus and Dardanelles, and other such waterways as they demand for the Suez Canal, they are not likely to make good their demand.

The Western Approach to the Middle East

The issues vital to the West in the Middle East are few, involving security and oil. Naturally, they have wide ramifications and are affected by many other issues. Attempts to coordinate policy, however, on a host of matters which are subsidiary or unrelated to the vital ones will only create unnecessary practical difficulties among the Western nations themselves and serious political difficulties in their relations with the Middle East. Each Western nation may have interests of its own, which it can properly pursue in its own way. The trouble has come in the past when individual Western nations have in their own way gone about pursuing "national" interests which in fact concerned the whole Western community. A special responsibility lies on the United States to avoid such practices if the West's vital common interests are to be better safeguarded in the coming period of American leadershp than they were in the past. It also has a special responsibility, after having prevented Britain and France from protecting their vital interests in the way they chose, to make every effort to find an alternative way to protect them. Again, a question of agreed definitions of vital interests is involved.

The emphasis which the foregoing analysis gives to Western solidarity might seem to carry the implication of an intent to impose the will and views of the West on the nations of the Middle East. In the current state of opinion in most of those nations any such implication strengthens the voices of those who see an "imperialist front" in any tendency of the Western nations to stand together. The

Western nations will find, even on the vital issues, that it may be desirable to avoid presenting a common front even when they are generally agreed. Projects for a NATO or European program for the economic development of the Middle East represent a total misreading of sentiment in most of the region. With such a label they are bound to be rejected as a new manifestation of imperialism. At the present time England and France may do better by remaining in the background. The United States, on some issues, may find it wise to do the same. Close attention to matters of form may have a bearing on success in matters of substance. If the West can begin to overcome the Middle Eastern complex about imperialism, the Middle Eastern nations may in time come to see, as some already have, that the vital interests of the West do not in fact conflict with their own; that Western concern for the defense of the region is the best assurance of their own independence; and that maintenance of the flow of oil to the West is the best guarantee of their own economic progress.

It may be a long time before we reach that happy state, but the history of relations between the West and the Middle East would seem to justify both taking the long view and retaining a degree of hope and of confidence. As we look ahead into the moderately distant future, it is well also to look back at the long distant past. Europe has historic ties with the Middle East, especially the lands of the Eastern Mediterranean, in the common roots of great religions, in the interpenetration of cultures and in centuries of trade. The struggles between Christianity and Islam, the West's industrial revolution, the expansion of its political power into the Middle East, and finally its export of technology and of ideas (including nationalism) to the Middle East combined to disrupt those historic connections but not to break them entirely. Once the fact and the idea of overlordship disappear, once nationalism loses some of its anti-Western bite, the ties may be reknit and refashioned. The Middle East needs an outside partner, and Europe is its natural partner.

It is up to the United States to help revive the association of the Middle East with Europe, not to give it the *coup de grâce*. Playing a lone hand and holding the British and French at arm's length after the debacle of 1956 was wise as a means of drawing on whatever political capital was stored up in the Arab world as a result of American support of Egypt in the United Nations. The Eisenhower Doctrine was a unilateral declaration, and it was only natural that Washington undertook by itself the diplomatic efforts to keep Saudi Arabia and Jordan out of the Syrian-Egyptian bloc. Over the long run, however, the United States cannot itself carry the whole burden and should not try. Unilateralism is not a permanent basis for policy; it could be a formula for losing the West without saving the Middle East. Lasting Western disunity, after all, will merely assure the success of Soviet efforts to fragmentize the free world.

Chapter 19

GUIDELINES FOR POLICY

WHATEVER conclusions on policy emerge from this examination of the problems confronting the United States in the Middle East should be judged against their complex and murky background, and with a recognition of the limitations on the capacity of the United States alone to direct or to determine their solution. In the past few years it has become commonplace in this country, whichever party holds the presidency, to call for a clear and well-defined Middle Eastern policy and an end to muddling, although the critics of today are generally the muddlers of yesterday and *vice versa*. It is not surprising that no such policy has been produced. It will take more than the application of common sense, or of a slogan or formula—whether it be anti-colonialism, or guarantees for Israel, or justice for the Arabs, or economic development for all—to give the Middle Eastern story a happy ending, if that is possible at all. We shall make better progress if, mindful of long-range aims, we set limited immediate objectives and do not leave an unbridgeable gap between what is and our idea of what ought to be.

The United States, to protect its security and worldwide interests, has had to take up many burdens that could no longer be carried by others and to "move into" many parts of the world, in the sense of developing policies to prevent their being engulfed by the Communist flood. The realization of the need to play this role in the Middle East came haltingly and late. It came amid uncertainty on the part of the American people as to the extent of their own interests, in the absence of a workable understanding with our Western allies, and at a time when the nations of the area itself presented a picture of un-

345

resolved conflict, immature or irresponsible leadership, and vulnerability to Soviet penetration. Important elements in the Middle East were already looking to the Soviet Union as their great and good friend.

In a region with no united will for defense against the Soviet danger, a region of many conflicting aims and interests, the United States Government has had great difficulty in finding firm footing in the role of partner or of leader in organizing free-world strength. It has had to act against the background of an ever changing situation, including strong political pressures at home and manifold criticism abroad. Inevitably, because this country was obviously the citadel of power and dispenser of largesse for a large part of the world, the tendency of others was to look to America for support of particular interests—and to be critical of the absence or inadequacy of such support.

While having longer-term solutions in mind, the U.S. Government has generally found itself able to do little more than meet the crises as they arose, guided by the general purpose of obtaining the cooperation of all concerned—European powers and Middle Eastern nations, northern tier and southern tier, Arabs and Israel. Washington's diplomatic efforts have followed two roads simultaneously: the road of mediation and compromise, to settle the annoying conflicts which stood in the way of general cooperation (for example: the controversies over the Suez base and the nationalization of Anglo-Iranian Oil, the Arab-Israel disputes, inter-Arab rivalries, and the dispute on the Suez Canal); and the road of moving ahead with the building of a barrier (hence the initiative for the northern tier alignments, the courting of Egypt, and the Eisenhower Doctrine). Both roads were strewn with obstacles. The mediation was not always effective, many of the disputes being beyond America's capacity to solve, while the exercise in barrier-building, though not fruitless, often exacerbated the conflicts and suffered from the obvious defects of measures which were necessarily unilateral or partial in character.

The United States has now taken the great step of declaring itself. But the challenge, as we have seen, is not to be met by declarations of intent or the pronunciation of doctrines. It is a political challenge calling for a combination of political responses, for a flexible diplomacy making proper use of military dispositions, economic measures, propaganda and covert activities in the service of well-understood aims. Looking to the future, we cannot attempt to predict all the types of situations that may arise in the Middle East. We should have, however, certain guidelines by which we may legitimately hope to devise and to carry out those policies best suited to the objective of keeping the Middle East anchored in the free world. The following guidelines are offered by way of summary and conclusion. Some are already reflected in official United States policy. Others suggest certain changes in direction or in emphasis.

Suggested Guidelines

First, while the major threat is not military, it has continuing military components which can be met only by certain minimum military dispositions on the part of the United States consonant with its global military posture. Such dispositions, including the maintenance of American armed forces where they can make their influence felt in holding the military balance in the Middle East, are a necessary backdrop to the success of a political strategy to meet what is primarily a political threat. Beyond that minimum, which seems attainable politically, attempts to pursue the mirage of absolute military security or full regional cooperation through defense pacts, base arrangements and the raising of large forces promise only to produce political disadvantages which would outweigh the intended military advantages.

Second, the Eisenhower Doctrine was a significant and a

necessary declaration, both as a deterrent to Soviet aggression and a statement of national concern. It is, however, largely irrelevant to many of the real challenges to American policy. Its limitation to "overt aggression" by states "controlled by international communism," and to cases where aid is requested, makes it inapplicable to most of the critical situations likely to arise in the Middle East, including aggression by Israel against the Arab states or *vice versa*. And because it is the major American statement on record, proposed and adopted with much fanfare, the tendency of the public, and apparently of some officials also, is to think that if the terms of the doctrine do not cover a given situation, then no decisive action is called for.

Third, the heart of the problem is to develop the means to prevent, or to reverse, the "subversion" of any country in the Middle East; that is, any situation in which such a country, without military aggression, is seized from within or falls or drifts under the dominating influence of the Soviet Union and its agents. This is much more than a matter of police measures or skill in "countersubversion." It requires more than the adoption, as "policy," of the proposition that the United States "will not permit" the Soviet Union to extend its control over countries of the Middle East. We are not always able to pick the precise point at which control is about to pass, or has passed, into Soviet hands,[1] or to act decisively when that moment comes; and if decisive action means military action, in many cases it will be politically impossible. Some policies have to be strictly of a short-term character, in order to forestall moves by the other side or to eliminate Soviet "beachheads." Diplomacy must be combined with other means of bringing influence to bear at the critical points.

[1] Secretary Dulles, when questioned on this point at a press conference with reference to Syria, stated his view as of that time that in a borderline case the President probably would not make a finding that a state was controlled by international communism until such time as it actually committed armed aggression (*New York Times*, September 11, 1957). This is an example of the uncertainty likely to confuse other nations as well as ourselves with respect to applicability of the Eisenhower Doctrine in specific critical situations.

It may mean taking risks and "playing rough" on occasions where it is feasible and can be effective. Quick reflexes and a basket of tricks, however, do not meet the long-term problem, that of strengthening within the region all the trends toward internal security and orderly progress, so that the Soviets find no ready-made opportunities and the desperate emergencies do not arise.

Fourth, as a solid foundation for the future the United States should maintain and enhance the strength, and the solidarity with the West, of the nations of the northern tier. In recent years the Arab states have made more noise and caused more trouble, but in the total balance they are probably of less importance than Turkey and Iran. Moscow's concentration on the Arabs is in part a reflection of its failure to make inroads on those two countries on the borders of the U.S.S.R. True, Soviet influence has leaped over them, but the fact that they have stood firm has made the difference between a difficult situation and a disaster. Everything possible should be done to give strength and confidence to Turkey and Iran, to confirm them in the choice they have made, and to increase the influence which they, as Moslem nations well acquainted with Soviet aims and practices, can exert throughout the Middle East. In general the same considerations apply to Pakistan, but we should not exaggerate the role Pakistan can play, militarily or politically, in the Middle East, and should keep in mind the limitations imposed by the requirements of our relations with India and the other uncommitted nations of Asia. It is Turkey, more than any other nation, which is needed for Middle East defense, both military and political. And it is Turkey which stands firmest against all threats and blandishments from the north. Whatever the efforts that may be necessary elsewhere in the Middle East, they should not divert us from recognition of this political fact, or from the measures required to assure its permanence.

Fifth, beyond the immediate claims of the troubled situation in the Arab lands, the United States must work steadily and at greater perspective to link the Arab future with the West. The least effective way to do so is to press for participation in military pacts or political alignments. The approach should be a search for long-term common interests which will give the Arabs the sense that they have a stake in partnership with the West, and that the partnership actually strengthens their independence. In making the approach we should recognize the fact of change in Arab society and avoid permanent identification with lost causes and dying institutions. The crucial decisions may involve the when and the how of the transition which will see power shift from an absolute king or a feudal oligarchy to other elements. Of various lines of action that suggest themselves, among the most promising are those which will strengthen and expand economic enterprises linking the West and the Middle East on a basis which makes all possible concession to local nationalism and desires for progress and to the idea of Arab unity, while setting irreducible limits of Western interest. Of all the Arab states, Iraq has the greatest potential despite present political uncertainties. It links the Arab world with the northern tier. At the moment Baghdad cannot displace Cairo as a center of attraction, but it should be given every opportunity to show all Arabs the real rewards of the wise use of natural wealth combined with a practical cooperation with the West, especially as the hollowness of leadership of the demagogic type becomes ever more apparent.

Sixth, further attempts to build a system of pacts and alliances in the Middle East would be self-defeating. The Baghdad Pact, the concrete expression of that policy, is of limited importance. The United States should not abandon it, but neither should we lose flexibility of policy by joining it or attempting to expand it. Similarly, to make acceptance of the Eisenhower Doctrine or any other form of alignment a test of friendship or of eligibility for assistance will be unwise. Some Middle Eastern nations will voluntarily choose alignment with the West. Their choice need not be discouraged. American political strategy should be broad enough, however, to accept a variety of attitudes on the part of Middle Eastern states. Neutralism is a force with which we shall have to live. Nothing is gained and much is lost by acts that push genuine neutrals into the Soviet camp, or, unless the evidence is incontrovertible, by the assumption they are already there. It is enough that they should have the will to defend their independence.

Seventh, we shall have to put much seemingly unnecessary effort into convincing people, who should know as much from what they can see, that Western imperialism is a spent and dying force. We shall have to proclaim, more times than seems sane, our adherence to the principles of national sovereignty and noninterference in the internal affairs of others, and to flatter those who regard these principles as the answer to the world's problems. Nevertheless, we owe it to the world and to ourselves to look some distance ahead, and to try to get the leaders of Asia and the Middle East to do the same. For they must come to the knowledge eventually, by sad experience if not by persuasion, that so far as these principles and slogans are concerned the Soviet Union has no more concern for them in India or Egypt than in the "sovereign peoples' republics" of Bulgaria and Outer Mongolia; that the day is past when man's aspirations can be satisfied within the frame of nationalism and national sovereignty; and that the choice will be between an internationalism which leaves scope for national freedom and human dignity and one which destroys them.

Eighth, the Arab-Israel dispute cries out for further and more steadfast efforts to bring it nearer to settlement. The State Department, like any foreign office, can always find reasons why the time is not ripe to take a bold step. Almost anything that is proposed threatens to complicate other problems and to disturb relations with one side without earning any thanks from the other. The fact remains that, in the absence of any step toward agreement, the conflict hangs like a poisonous cloud over the entire Middle

East. The United States, at the very least, should see that the various issues in dispute are put into proper U.N. channels for discussion and possible settlement. Time has not solved the problem of the Arab refugees. Something has to be done about it. For too long the United States has been paying out money to carry along the problem in its present unsolved state, to the great political benefit of all those elements which exploit it to the disadvantage of our standing throughout the whole region. Even in the likely event that no solutions are reached, the United States can only gain by itself taking a position that it can defend as in accord with its own past political and moral commitments and as a reasonable satisfaction of Arab claims to justice. The American commitment to Israel is to its continued independent existence, not to its existing boundaries or policies.

Ninth, certain economic measures are necessary to support political strategy, both immediate and long-range. In taking them, we should keep our eye especially on the pattern of local political leadership. We should recognize the obvious need to use economic means for political and military purposes, although generally they should not be so advertised. Beyond these specifically directed measures involving both trade and aid, the United States should contribute generously to long-term economic development in the Middle East, both national and regional. Such aid should be accorded to allies and neutrals alike on the basis of economic need, without "strings" in the form of formal commitments objectionable to the recipients as infringing their independence or demanding their alignment in the cold war. A part of it should be extended through the U.N. or by some other multilateral arrangement. In any event a steady, long-term economic program is needed to keep the situation from growing worse. It will not ensure its growing better unless there is parallel progress on the political front.

Tenth, the Western world must find a new unity to replace the supposed unity shattered by the crisis over Suez. No principle of "standing by one's friends" or general concept of Western solidarity is sufficient to meet the test of specific critical situations certain to arise in the Middle East. The first requirement, of course, has been to repair to the degree possible the damage done to our relations with Britain and with France by what happened in 1956. This is partly a matter of attitudes, which time and a measure of good will on both sides may help to cure. Beyond that, the Western powers should reach some understanding of what their minimum essential common interests are in the Middle East and on how they may best be protected. With respect to France, the first requirement is a resolution of the question of Algeria, so that it will cease to burden the West's relations with the Arab world. Even in that fortunate event, it is difficult at best to see a major political role for France in the Middle East in the future, but the cultural and economic connections which France and other European nations have had with the Middle East are valuable connections which should be fostered and not lost. The United States and Britain, which will carry the main responsibility for the West, must make the effort to rise above fixed past attitudes on "colonialism" and "anti-colonialism," and to agree on the practical measures needed to preserve the common Western interest in the security of the Middle East and the accessibility of its oil.

Finally, the United States has to consider its direct relationship to the Soviet Union in the Middle East. Partly it is a balancing of military power. Partly it is a direct competition in the many facets of the cold war. Beyond those two aspects lies a third possibility, that of negotiation with the Soviet Government. The mere invocation of the processes of diplomacy, as the world has had occasion to learn again and again, especially since the last great war, does not open the way to those general and enduring settlements with the Soviet Union which have been the goal of the Western nations. For where Soviet policy aims at the subversion or domination of an area within the reach of Soviet power, the only limits it accepts are the physical and political obstacles that stand in the way. The Soviet leaders do not seek compromise with outside powers or non-Soviet neighbors in the interests of international amity and world peace, but only agreements that give recognition to the Soviet Union's "special position" in the area in question, or that constitute a meaningless accord on principle under cover of which they proceed to make the position even more "special." The Soviet Union may in time be brought to accept a rough balance of power and position which the West can also accept. But there is no basis for believing it can be negotiated into accepting it in the near future. Western success in negotiation can only be a product of success in checking the trends which have opened the Middle East to Soviet influence.

The issue of whether or not to negotiate, whether or not to "recognize" the U.S.S.R. as a Middle Eastern power, is essentially a false one. The U.S.S.R. obviously is a Middle Eastern power. And any government can negotiate with another by sending it diplomatic notes. The United States should always be ready to explore the possibilities of agreement on Middle Eastern as on other issues. But willingness to negotiate does not answer the challenge. The Soviet Union has not been pushing into the Middle East just for the sake of making an agreement guaranteeing Western interests there. The real issue is whether the United States can agree that the Soviet Union should establish a position in the Middle East similar to its own, with bases, military aid programs, and all the rest of it; or whether it can agree with Moscow to "neutralize" the area.

The first proposition might sound reasonable to an objective observer from Mars or from India. If the United States has alliances and bases in an area which is on the Soviet Union's doorstep, is it logical to deny to the Soviet Union an equal right to allies and bases in the same area, which happens to be half-way across the world from America? It is, from the standpoint of the security of the free world, both logical and necessary, for the proposed equality would alter the world political and military balance against the West. In that sense we stand for inequality with the Soviet Union in the Middle East, as we do in Western Europe. Soviet arms are already going to Egypt, Syria and Yemen. Moscow's relations with those three countries may be approaching, or may have reached, the point of tacit alliance. Bases being constructed on their territory could become, at a given point, Soviet bases. All this the United States has accepted, in the sense that it has not used force to prevent it. But that is no reason to give its formal blessing to situations which are so dangerous to Western security, and which it should bend every effort to reverse.

Proposals to neutralize the Middle East raise similar difficulties. The establishment of Soviet influence in Syria raises the possibility of seeking its elimination by trading Western influence in other states and neutralizing them all. Again, this may seem to some a reasonable and equitable course. But it is not one compatible with the objective of keeping the Middle East in the free world. A part of the area is and probably will remain neutral, in the sense that some states will choose not to align themselves with either side. That is a tolerable situation. However, any great-power agreement to "neutralize" the Middle East (presumably covering fixed arms levels and the forswearing of bases and military alliances) would mean the dismantlement of the Western military position, based chiefly on Turkey. If Turkey, as a NATO country, were excluded, the proposal might appear to be worth at least some consideration. As there are few Western bases outside Turkey, tacit or formal neutralization of Iran, a number of Arab states and Israel might not make such a great difference in military terms. It might be possible to set up a system of international control to detect violations and ensure compliance.[2] It is the political effects that would

[2] Senator Hubert H. Humphrey has proposed the creation of demilitarized zones (not defined) and an internationally supervised inspection system. See *Control and Reduction of Armaments: Disarmament and Security in the Middle East*, U.S. Senate Subcommittee on Disarmament of the Committee on Foreign Relations, Staff Study no. 6, 85th Cong., 1st sess. (Washington: G.P.O., 1957), p. iv.

hold the great danger. For the Soviet Union and its followers in the area would have a free field to establish
political dominance in one country after another. An
agreement on neutralization, from that viewpoint, would
be a bad bargain to begin with, even if it were honored
by the Soviet Union. As for the peoples of the Middle
East, they would take it as the capitulation of the West,
as proof that the future lay with "the camp of socialism."

The Soviet leaders are using their offers of negotiation,
like their talk of coexistence, as a weapon of propaganda
and a means of throwing on the United States the blame
for continuing the cold war. Behind that front they are
free to wage it themselves by whatever means they find
suitable to the problem at hand. Obviously we cannot afford to ignore the effect which apparent Soviet reasonable-
ness has on the peoples of the Middle East and elsewhere.
To some extent we have to use the same tactics and to
make clear that it is Soviet aims and actions that we oppose, not the reasonable principles which Moscow pre-
tends to support. Moreover, there will be certain specific
problems for which we can seek negotiated solutions
through the United Nations (such as the Arab refugees)
or through direct arrangements with the U.S.S.R. (such
as the limitation of arms deliveries to certain Middle Eastern states), taking care in every case not to make irretriev-
able concrete concessions in exchange for Soviet promises.

Continuation of the cold war has its dangers. Competition between great powers for influence in a congeries of
weak states can put the peace of the world at the mercy of
a coup which replaces one group of local politicians with
another. It is a dangerous game, but we have to play it;
and, in playing, there is no need to make the task more
difficult than it already is by subjecting our own policies
and decisions to a Soviet veto, whether in the United Nations or in four-power conferences, in pursuit of the chi-
mera of a negotiated settlement. That day will come, if
it comes at all, only when the Soviet Union is willing to
negotiate about the Middle East on the basis of a funda-

mental change in policy, and probably only in the context of progress toward acceptable agreement on such issues as unification of Germany, the future of Eastern Europe, and the limitation of armaments.

The Middle East, for all our concentration on it as an area of crisis, is only part of a larger picture. While the Soviets have made gains there which cause us concern, they also are and will be engaged on many other fronts, including the home front. It is no reason for panic if the problems of the Middle East look insoluble. Some can only be solved in a broader framework and in changed world conditions. Soviet tactics in the Middle East are part of a larger strategy to win the whole "in-between world" of Asia, Africa and even Latin America over to cooperation with the Soviet bloc under the pretext of building a vast "zone of peace." [3] The task of the West is to expose and defeat that strategy, both in the Middle East and elsewhere, by policies that respond to the basic aspirations of peoples.

To return to the theme of the opening chapter, the United States can successfully defend the Middle East against Soviet imperialism only if it can find a basis of common interest and common understanding with the peoples of the Middle East. Success has been but partial. The great difficulties arise out of fundamentally different ways of looking at the same thing or of interpreting the same words. This goes deeper than mere misunderstanding. There are differences in evaluation of the Soviet threat and of Israel, differences even over the purposes and the means of economic development. Not that there is any uniformity of attitudes in the Middle East itself. Turkey, Iran and Israel are closer to the West in their views. They do not fit the pattern of Arab views and complexes. Still, the stirrings of every one of the Middle Eastern nations reflect an urge that goads them all: the urge to build a

[3] The phrase used by Khrushchev in his Report of the Central Committee to the 20th Congress of the Soviet Communist Party (*New Times,* no. 8, February 16, 1956, Documentary Supplement, p. 13).

new society, to take their place in the modern world, without becoming the instruments of others or losing their national and cultural identity in the process.

The United States and the Western world can accept and support that basic aspiration. Common interests, despite the myopia of both sides, do exist. They must be identified, strengthened by enlightened policies, and defended against those who would attack or undermine them. Common understanding is less easy to define, but the essential ingredient is a necessary minimum of mutual respect between peoples. One cannot expect any great number of American citizens to be experts on Islam or on all the forces and ideas which move the men and women of the Middle East to think and act as they do. Those who are responsible for determining policy, however, and those who are charged with carrying it out should have that understanding, a sympathetic understanding. The American public, for its part, must be sufficiently informed, unprejudiced and mature to give responsible officials the necessary freedom to translate it into effective policies. The public cannot be so informed without a major effort on the part of the officials themselves to find sound policies and to explain them.

Defense of the Middle East will be a long and arduous task. Despite what some of their leaders say, it is beyond the capacities of the Middle Eastern nations themselves. It will depend also on what is done by the West, by the so-called uncommitted nations, and perhaps by the captive peoples of the Soviet empire itself. It will require American leadership, simply because the United States as the strongest and richest nation of the free world cannot avoid that role, even if it purports to consider only its own national interests.

The strategy for success is not clear-cut or easy to carry out. It should not aim at the impossible. The Middle East will not be strong or stable for as far as we can see into the future. Western attempts to make it so have met setbacks in the past, and will meet more The road has many

turnings beyond which we cannot see. Let it be conceded
that in the past the United States has shown no remarkable
capacity for success in such a task, which calls for a re-
silient diplomacy plus national perseverance in a game
which at times may not seem worth the candle. But we cannot concede that the continuing successful defense of the
Middle East is beyond our capacities in the future, for our
survival as a nation may depend upon it.

SELECTED BIBLIOGRAPHY

The following list of titles may be useful to the reader as an indication of background material used in the preparation of this book and as a guide to further pursuit of one or another aspect of Middle Eastern affairs. It is confined generally to the Western languages. For reasons of space it is limited also to published books, although much of the material on a current topic such as the subject of this book must necessarily come from periodicals and newspapers. Among the periodicals especially devoted to the Middle Eastern field the following should be mentioned: *The Middle East Journal* (Washington); *Middle Eastern Affairs* (New York) ; *The Muslim World* (Hartford); *The Royal Central Asian Journal* (London); *Revue du Monde Musulman* (Paris); *Revue des études islamiques* (Paris); *Cahiers de l'Orient Contemporain* (Paris); *L'Orient* (Paris); *Oriente Moderno* (Rome); *Die Welt des Islams* (Berlin; Leyden); *Sovetskoye Vostokovedeniye* (Moscow). Entire issues of *The Political Quarterly* (London, April-June 1957), *Social Science* (Washington, October 1957), and *Current History* (Philadelphia, November 1957) were devoted to the Middle East.

GENERAL

Boveri, Margaret. *Minaret and Pipe-Line: Yesterday and Today in the Near East.* New York: Oxford University Press, 1939. 438 p.
One of the best general works on the prewar situation.
Brockelmann, Carl. *History of the Islamic Peoples.* New York: Putnam, 1947. 582 p.
Translation of a classic from the German, with an added section covering events since 1939. Invaluable for the historical background.
Europa Publications. *The Middle East 1957.* 5th ed. London: Author, 1957. 444 p.

Invaluable handbook and directory of important individuals and institutions.

Fernau, F. W. *Moslems on the March.* New York: Knopf, 1954. 312 p.
English edition of a survey first published in German in 1953.

Fisher, W. B. *The Middle East: A Physical, Social and Regional Geography.* New York: Dutton, 1950. 514 p.

Frye, Richard N., ed. *The Near East and the Great Powers.* Cambridge: Harvard University Press, 1951. 214 p.
A symposium including informative papers by Charles Malik, Ralph Bunche, Majid Khadduri and others.

Giannini, Amedeo. *L'Ultima Fase della Questione Orientale 1913–1932.* Rome: Istituto per l'Oriente, 1933. 416 p.
A first-class documented history.

Hoskins, Halford L. *The Middle East: Problem Area in World Politics.* New York: Macmillan, 1954. 311 p.
General survey by a long-time student of the area. Less informative than Lenczowski (see below).

Hurewitz, J. C. *Diplomacy in the Near and Middle East.* Princeton: Van Nostrand, 1956. 2 v.
A very useful compilation of documents, with explanatory notes giving their historical setting. The first volume covers the period 1535–1914; the second goes through 1955.

Kimche, Jon. *Seven Fallen Pillars: The Middle East 1945–1952.* New York: Praeger, 1953. 439 p.
A talented journalist's story, well worth reading despite its pro-Zionist bias. Expanded version of the English edition published in 1950.

Kirk, George. *The Middle East in the War.* London: Oxford University Press, 1952. 511 p.

——. *The Middle East 1945–1950.* London: Oxford University Press, 1954. 338 p.
These two volumes, issued under the auspices of the Royal Institute of International Affairs, are part of the *Survey of International Affairs.* In many ways they are invaluable, being based on painstaking research in many contemporary sources, but they are uneven and the author's point of view often shines through his factual narrative.

——. *A Short History of the Middle East from the Rise of Islam to Modern Times.* London: Methuen, 1948. 301 p.

Laqueur, Walter Z. *Communism and Nationalism in the Middle East.* New York: Praeger, 1956. 362 p.
Excellent account of Communist parties in the individual states, with a useful and original analysis of interrelationship between communism and nationalism.

Lenczowski, George. *The Middle East in World Affairs.* 2nd ed. Ithaca: Cornell University Press, 1956. 576 p.
A most useful combination of recent history and current problems, organized by country but with some attention also to area-wide problems.

Middle East Institute. *Evolution in the Middle East: Reform, Revolt and Change.* Sydney Nettleton Fisher, ed. Washington: Author, 1953. 97 p.

————. *Nationalism in the Middle East.* Washington: Author, 1952. 68 p.
This and the preceding volume are collections of addresses presented at the annual conferences on Middle East Affairs, sponsored by the Middle East Institute. The contributors are leading scholars in the field.

Morris, James. *Islam Inflamed.* New York: Pantheon, 1957. 326 p.
Perceptive and well-written impressions of the Middle East by a British journalist, as of the time of crisis, November 1956.

Roosevelt, Kermit. *Arabs, Oil and History.* New York: Harper, 1949. 271 p.
A stimulating book, stressing the need for greater awareness of the Arab side of Middle Eastern questions and clearer thinking on the part of Americans.

Royal Institute of International Affairs. *The Middle East: A Political and Economic Survey.* 2nd ed., revised. London: Oxford University Press, 1954. 590 p.
A valuable background and reference work.

POLICIES OF THE GREAT POWERS

Great Britain

Bullard, Sir Reader. *Britain and the Middle East.* London: Hutchinson, 1951. 195 p.
Excellent account by the former British Ambassador to Iran.

Kedourie, Elie. *England and the Middle East*. London: Bowes & Bowes, 1956. 236 p.
The best available study of the critical period during and after World War I.

Royal Institute of International Affairs. *Great Britain and Egypt, 1914–1951*. Information Papers no. 19a. London: Oxford University Press, 1952. 216 p.
A thorough study focused on the treaty negotiations. Documentary appendix.

Seton-Williams, M. V. *Britain and the Arab States: A Survey of Anglo-Arab Relations, 1920–1948*. London: Luzac, 1948. 330 p.
A competent historical study, with a useful documentary appendix.

Storrs, Sir Ronald. *The Memoirs of Sir Ronald Storrs*. New York: Putnam, 1937. 563 p.
Recollections of a ranking British pro-consul and diplomat versed in the lore of the Near East. The period covered is 1904–1932. (Published in England as *Orientations*, London, Nicholson and Watson, 1937.)

U.S.S.R.

Lacoste, Raymond. *La Russie Soviétique et la Question d'Orient*. Paris: Les Editions Internationales, 1946. 238 p.
Deals especially with Soviet policy toward Turkey and Iran.

Smirnov, N. A. *Ocherki Istorii Izucheniya Islama v SSSR*. Moscow: Akademiya Nauk SSSR, Institut Istorii, 1954. 275 p.
A history of Islamic studies in the U.S.S.R. Not primarily a history of Soviet policy in the Middle East, but it throws considerable light on it. An analysis of the book, with a critical introduction by Ann K. S. Lambton, was put out as *Islam and Russia* (London, Central Asian Research Centre in association with St. Antony's College Soviet Affairs Study Group, 1956, 87 p. mimeographed.)

Spector, Ivar. *The Soviet Union and the Muslim World, 1917–1956*. Seattle: University of Washington Press, 1956. 158 p. (preliminary mimeographed edition).
Based largely on Russian sources hitherto unused by Western scholars.

United States

Agwani, Mohammed Shafi. *The United States and the Arab World, 1945–1952.* Aligarh: Institute of Islamic Studies, Muslim University, 1955. 184 p.
Interesting because written by an Easterner. The author makes full use of American sources.

Brookings Institution. *The Security of the Middle East: A Problem Paper.* Washington: Author, 1950. 66 p. (lithographed).
A study by the staff of the Brookings Institution laying out alternative policies for the United States. Out of date but still useful.

Hoskins, Halford L. *Middle East Oil in United States Foreign Policy.* Public Affairs Bulletin no. 89. Washington: Library of Congress, Legislative Reference Service, 1950. 118 p.
States the essentials of the problem in brief compass.

Howard, Harry N. *The Development of United States Policy in the Near East, 1945–1951.* Department of State Publication 4446. Washington: G.P.O., 1952. 13 p.
———. *The Development of United States Policy in the Near East, South Asia, and Africa, 1951–52.* Department of State Publication 4851. Washington: G.P.O., 1953. 19 p.
———. *The Development of United States Policy in the Near East, South Asia, and Africa during 1953.* Department of State Publication 5432. Washington: G.P.O., 1954. 21 p.
———. *U.S. Policy in the Near East, South Asia, and Africa—1954.* Department of State Publication 5801. Washington: G.P.O., 1955. 70 p.
———. *U.S. Policy in the Near East, South Asia, and Africa—1955.* Department of State Publication 6330. Washington: G.P.O., 1956. 63 p.
This series of pamphlets constitutes a detailed exposition of the development of official policy over the entire area as it developed year by year.

Hurewitz, J. C. *Middle East Dilemmas: The Background of United States Policy.* New York: Harper, for the Council on Foreign Relations, 1953. 273 p.
A balanced but critical analysis of policy problems facing the United States since the second World War.

Lilienthal, Alfred M. *There Goes the Middle East.* New York: Devin-Adair, 1957. 300 p.
A plea for a more pro-Arab policy on the part of the United States, by an anti-Zionist American Jewish author.

Reitzel, William. *The Mediterranean: Its Role in America's Foreign Policy.* New York: Harcourt, Brace, 1948. 195 p.
A geopolitical study, somewhat dated, placing the Middle East in the broad strategic picture of the Mediterranean.

Speiser, Ephraim A. *The United States and the Near East.* Revised ed. Cambridge: Harvard University Press, 1950. 283 p.
A pioneer study of U.S. policy, especially concerned with the Anglo-American relationship.

Thomas, Lewis V., and Frye, Richard N. *The United States and Turkey and Iran.* Cambridge: Harvard University Press, 1951. 291 p.
Competent studies of U.S. policy toward the two countries, each done by a separate author.

Utley, Freda. *Will the Middle East Go West?* Chicago: Henry Regnery, 1957. 198 p.
A critique of American policy in the Middle East. The main theme is the parallel with China.

TURKEY

Heyd, Uriel. *Foundations of Turkish Nationalism.* London: Luzac, 1950. 174 p.
Concentrates on the life and writings of Ziya Gökalp, ideologist of Turkish nationalism.

Hostler, Charles W. *Turkism and the Soviets.* New York: Praeger, 1957. 244 p.
Mixture of ethnology and history, not very enlightening on policy questions but of interest because of the use of Russian and Turkish in addition to Western sources.

Howard, Harry N. *The Partition of Turkey, 1913–1923.* Norman: University of Oklahoma Press, 1931. 486 p.
Thoroughly documented study of the critical period 1913–1923.

International Bank for Reconstruction and Development.

The Economy of Turkey. Washington: Author, 1951. 276 p.
Report of a mission to Turkey.

Jäschke, Gotthard. *Der Islam in der Neuen Türkei.* Leyden: Brill, 1951. 174 p.
An important study stressing secularism. The reader can supplement it with an article by Howard A. Reed, "Revival of Islam in Secular Turkey," *Middle East Journal,* v. 8 (Summer 1954), pp. 267-282.

Lewis, Geoffrey L. *Turkey.* New York: Praeger, 1955. 224 p.
A concise and informative history, mainly devoted to the last thirty years, by a Lecturer in Islamic Studies at Oxford.

Thornburg, Max, and others. *Turkey: An Economic Appraisal.* New York: Twentieth Century Fund, 1949. 324 p.
A thorough study intended to lay the "intellectual groundwork" for U.S. economic policy toward Turkey including aid programs. In some ways outdated, as some of the pressing problems of today had not yet appeared.

Toynbee, Arnold J. *The Western Question in Greece and Turkey.* London: Constable, 1922. 420 p.
A classic. May be supplemented by Toynbee's contributions on the Near East to the early volumes of the *Survey of International Affairs* published by the Royal Institute of International Affairs.

Vere-Hodge, Edward Reginald. *Turkish Foreign Policy, 1918–1948.* Ambilly-Annemasse: Imprimerie Franco-Suisse, 1950. 191 p.
Brief but useful summary.

Yalman, Ahmet Emin. *Turkey in My Time.* Norman: University of Oklahoma Press, 1956. 294 p.
Autobiography of a well-known Turkish journalist and public figure long associated with the nationalist movement.

IRAN

Elwell-Sutton, Lawrence Paul. *Persian Oil: A Study in Power Politics.* London: Lawrence & Wishart, 1955. 343 p.
The dispute seen from the Iranian side.

Geyer, Dietrich. *Die Sowjetunion und Iran.* Köln: Böhlau-Verlag, 1955. 99 p.
Survey of Soviet policy from 1917 to 1954.

Haas, William S. *Iran.* New York: Columbia University Press, 1946. 273 p.

Excellent survey by a German educator who served as adviser to the Iranian Government in 1935–1940. It covers political, economic and cultural affairs.

Hamzavi, A. H. *Persia and the Powers.* London: Hutchinson, 1946. 125 p.

Documents and commentary on the period 1941–1946 by the then Iranian press attaché in London.

Ivanov, M. S. *Ocherk Istorii Irana.* Moscow: Izdatel'stvo Politicheskoi Literatury, 1952. 467 p.

A history of Iran including a significant and carefully edited Soviet version of events between 1945 and 1951.

Lenczowski, George. *Russia and the West in Iran, 1918–1948.* Ithaca: Cornell University Press, 1949. 383 p.

Competent monograph. The author, now a recognized American scholar, had first-hand experience in Iran as a Polish official.

Millspaugh, Arthur C. *Americans in Persia.* Washington: Brookings Institution, 1946. 293 p.

The personal story of an American financial adviser's second mission to Iran.

Sykes, Sir Percy M. *A History of Persia.* 3rd ed. London: Macmillan, 1930. 2 v.

The best history in English.

Warne, William E. *Mission for Peace: Point 4 in Iran.* Indianapolis: Bobbs-Merrill, 1956. 320 p.

The author was Director of the U.S. Technical Assistance mission in Iran for four years.

Wilber, Donald Newton. *Iran: Past and Present.* 3rd ed. Princeton: Princeton University Press, 1955. 288 p.

A summary history followed by concise treatment of resources, economy, government and people in the early postwar period.

AFGHANISTAN AND PAKISTAN

Ahmad, Mushtaq. *The United Nations and Pakistan.* Karachi: Pakistan Institute of International Affairs, 1955. 162 p.

A frank presentation of the Pakistan viewpoint on current issues before the United Nations.

Arnold, F. B., ed. *Pakistan: Economic and Commercial Conditions, May 1954.* London: H.M.S.O., 1955. 291 p.

A comprehensive descriptive survey, with an excellent bibliography.

Caspani, E. and Cagnacci, E. *Afghanistan, Crocevia dell'Asia.* Milan: Vallardi, 1951. 275 p.

Well-informed survey by two Italian diplomatic officials.

Fraser-Tytler, Sir William Kerr. *Afghanistan: A Study of Political Developments in Central Asia.* New York: Oxford University Press, 1950. 330 p.

History plus discussion of contemporary problems by a former British Minister in Kabul.

Sykes, Sir Percy M. *The History of Afghanistan.* New York: Macmillan, 1949. 2 v.

The only good history in English.

Wilber, Donald N., ed. *Afghanistan.* New Haven: Human Relations Area Files, 1956. 501 p.

A comprehensive handbook.

THE ARAB WORLD

Antonius, George. *The Arab Awakening: The Story of the Arab National Movement.* Philadelphia: Lippincott, 1939. 471 p.

The classic history of the rise of Arab nationalism.

Atiyah, Edward. *The Arabs.* Harmondsworth, Middlesex: Penguin Books, 1955. 242 p.

Ellis, Harry B. *Heritage of the Desert.* New York: Ronald Press, 1956. 311 p.

An informative report by a correspondent of the *Christian Science Monitor.*

Faris, N. A. and Husayn, M. T. *The Crescent in Crisis: An Interpretive Study of the Modern Arab World.* Lawrence: University of Kansas Press, 1955. 191 p.

Views of two well-known Arab scholars who have made a special study of Arab nationalism.

Hitti, Philip K. *History of the Arabs.* 6th ed. New York: St. Martin's Press, 1956. 822 p.

New edition of a well-known general history.

Izzeddin, Nejla. *The Arab World: Past, Present, and Future.* Chicago: Regnery, 1953. 412 p.

The author is a Druse from Lebanon, educated in the U.S. The treatment is comprehensive and frankly sympathetic.

Khalid, Khalid Muhamad. *From Here We Start*. Washington: American Council of Learned Societies, 1953. 171 p.
Translation of an Arabic work much discussed in the Arab world. It stresses the social answers to the problem of Arab backwardness.

Nuseibeh, Hazem Zaki. *The Ideas of Arab Nationalism*. Ithaca: Cornell University Press, 1956. 227 p.
A largely theoretical study by a Jordanian official.

Thomas, Bertram. *The Arabs*. New York: Doubleday, 1937. 364 p.
Valuable study by one who knew Arab life and history very well as a traveler and a British official in various Arab lands.

Tütsch, Hans E. *Die Arabischen Völker am Kreuzweg*. Zürich: Verlag der *Neuen Zürcher Zeitung*, 1956. 237 p.
Brief, pungent survey by a Swiss journalist.

IRAQ

International Bank for Reconstruction and Development. *The Economic Development of Iraq*. Baltimore: Johns Hopkins Press, 1952. 463 p.
The report of a special mission sent by the World Bank at the Iraq Government's request.

Ireland, Philip W. *Iraq: A Study in Political Development*. New York: Macmillan, 1938. 510 p.
Careful study based largely on British sources and the Iraqi press.

Khadduri, Majid. *Independent Iraq: A Study in Iraqi Politics since 1932*. New York: Oxford University Press, for the Royal Institute of International Affairs, 1952. 291 p.
A thorough and scholarly work, admirably supplementing that of Ireland.

Longrigg, Stephen Hemsley. *Iraq, 1900–1950*. New York: Oxford University Press, for the Royal Institute of International Affairs, 1953. 436 p.
A valuable compact history of modern Iraq by one with long experience in its problems.

Marinucci de Reguardati, Costanzo. *Iraq*. Rome: Centro per le Relazioni Italo-Arabe, 1955–1956. 2 v.
A comprehensive work with useful appendices and tables.

Salter, James Arthur (Lord). *The Development of Iraq: A Plan of Action*. Baghdad: Iraq Development Board, 1955. 252 p.
Authoritative treatment by a noted British economist and public servant who helped to launch the Iraq Development Board.

Stewart, Desmond and Haylock, John. *New Babylon: A Portrait of Iraq*. London: Collins, 1956. 256 p.
A recent and readable account.

LEBANON AND SYRIA

Abouchdid, E. E. *Thirty Years of Lebanon and Syria (1917–1947)*. Beirut: Arab Publishing Co., 1948. 614 p.
A disorganized but sometimes informative review of the mandate period.

Farra, Adnan. *L'Industrialisation en Syrie*. Geneva: Grivet, 1950. 262 p.
A general economic analysis showing the possibilities and limits of industrialization.

Haddad, George M. *Fifty Years of Modern Syria and Lebanon*. New York: Hafner, 1950. 264 p.
A combined history and handbook.

Helbaoui, Youssef. *La Syrie*. Paris: Librairie Générale de Droit et de Jurisprudence, 1956. 305 p.
A survey of the Syrian economy and its prospects.

Hourani, A. H. *Syria and Lebanon*. New York: Oxford University Press, for the Royal Institute of International Affairs, 1946. 402 p.
An excellent historical review of the modern history of the Levant states up to 1945.

International Bank for Reconstruction and Development. *The Economic Development of Syria*. Baltimore: Johns Hopkins Press, 1955. 486 p.
Report of a World Bank mission on all aspects of the current Syrian economy with detailed recommendations for future development.

Rondot, Pierre. *Les Institutions Politiques du Liban*. Paris: Institut d'Etudes de l'Orient Contemporain, 1947. 148 p.
A good monograph, unfortunately out of date.

Ziadeh, Nicola A. *Syria and Lebanon*. New York: Praeger, 1957. 312 p.
A good supplement to Hourani's book, with information on the political developments of the past decade. The author is a historian at the American University of Beirut.

JORDAN

Abdullah. *Memoirs of King Abdullah of Transjordan*. v. 1, Philip P. Graves, ed. New York: Philosophical Library, 1950. 278 p.; v. 2, Washington: American Council of Learned Societies, 1954. 121 p.
The late King's recollections contain some interesting points on the Arab liberation movement of World War I and the Palestine war of 1948.

Glubb, John Bagot. *The Story of the Arab Legion*. London: Hodder and Stoughton, 1948. 371 p.
Glubb Pasha's story of the force he created and commanded.

International Bank for Reconstruction and Development. *The Economic Development of Jordan*. Baltimore: Johns Hopkins Press, 1957. 488 p.
Report of a World Bank mission, replete with useful data and recommendations to the Jordan Government.

Kirkbride, Alec Seath. *A Crackle of Thorns: Experiences in the Middle East*. London: John Murray, 1956. 201 p.
Impressions received in a career spanning the years from 1916 to 1955. Interesting information on the establishment of Transjordan but generally disappointing.

Lias, Godfrey. *Glubb's Legion*. London: Evans, 1956. 230 p.
The whole story from beginning to end, supplementing Glubb's own book.

Phillips, Paul G. *The Hashemite Kingdom of Jordan: Prolegomena to a Technical Assistance Program*. Chicago: University of Chicago Press, 1954. 191 p.
A brief but useful economic study, bringing together data not easily available elsewhere.

EGYPT, SUDAN AND LIBYA

Abbas, Mekki. *The Sudan Question: The Dispute over the Anglo-Egyptian Condominium, 1884–1951.* New York: Praeger, 1952. 201 p.
An informed study by a Sudanese official in the British Administration.

el-Barawi, Rached. *The Military Coup in Egypt: An Analytical Study.* Cairo: Renaissance Bookshop, 1952. 269 p.
Story of the nationalist movement since World War I by a supporter of the new regime.

Colombe, Marcel. *L'Evolution de l'Egypte, 1924–1950.* Paris: Maisonneuve, 1951. 361 p.
Primarily a political history.

Duncan, J. S. R. *The Sudan.* Edinburgh: Blackwood, 1952. 283 p.
A civil servant writes on the history and conditions of the Anglo-Egyptian Sudan.

Issawi, Charles. *Egypt: An Economic and Social Analysis.* New York: Oxford University Press, for the Royal Institute of International Affairs, 1947. 219 p.
Valuable both for data and interpretations.

Lacouture, Jean and Simone. *L'Egypte en Mouvement.* Paris: Editions du Seuil, 1956. 480 p.
A detailed account by two French journalists assessing events since the revolution of 1952, including the subject of Communist penetration.

Lloyd, George Ambrose, 1st Baron. *Egypt since Cromer.* New York: Macmillan, 1933–1934. 2 v.
Worthy sequel to Lord Cromer's *Modern Egypt.*

Lugol, Jean. *Egypt and World War II.* Cairo: Société Orientale de Publicité, 1945. 402 p.
Translated from the French. The author is editor of *La Bourse Egyptienne* of Cairo.

MacMichael, Sir Harold A. *The Sudan.* New York: Praeger, 1955. 255 p.
This American edition of the book published in England in 1954 by the former Governor-General discusses many aspects of the Sudan, including political developments up to 1953.

Naguib, Mohammed. *Egypt's Destiny: A Personal Statement.*
New York: Doubleday, 1955. 256 p.
Personal story of the nominal leader of the revolutionary
movement. The discussion of his relations with Abdel
Nasser is of interest.

Nasser, Gamal Abdel. *Egypt's Liberation: The Philosophy of
the Revolution.* Washington: Public Affairs Press, 1955.
119 p.
Observations on the nature and tasks of the revolution
and Egypt's place in the Arab and Moslem world.

Villard, Henry Serrano. *Libya: The New Arab Kingdom of
North Africa.* Ithaca: Cornell University Press, 1956. 169 p.
The first U.S. Ambassador's rather optimistic report on
the prospects of the fledgling state.

THE ARABIAN PENINSULA

Dickson, H. R. P. *Kuwait and Her Neighbours.* London:
Allen & Unwin, 1956. 627 p.
Discursive but informative memoirs by a British official
long resident in the area.

Faroughy, Abbas. *The Bahrein Islands (750–1951).* New York:
Verry, 1951. 128 p.
A short historical and descriptive narrative.

———. *Introducing Yemen.* New York: Orientalia, 1947. 123 p.

Morris, James. *Sultan in Oman.* New York: Pantheon, 1957.
146 p.
A fascinating account of the Sultan of Muscat and Oman's
sweep through the interior of Oman in 1955, by a British
journalist who accompanied him.

Nallino, Carlo Alfonso. *L'Arabia Sa'udiana.* Rome: Istituto
per l'Oriente, 1939. 303 p.
A comprehensive work by a noted scholar touching on
politics, economics and culture.

Philby, H. St. John B. *A Pilgrim in Arabia.* London: Hale,
1946. 198 p.
An illuminating record of 20 years' travel and experience
in the Arabian Peninsula.

———. *Sa'udi Arabia.* New York: Praeger, 1955. 393 p.
A history by a noted authority, traveler and long-time
friend of the Arabs of the Peninsula.

Sanger, Richard H. *The Arabian Peninsula*. Ithaca: Cornell University Press, 1954. 295 p.
An informal survey by a leading scholar and officer of the Department of State, covering both Saudi Arabia and the sheikhdoms and protectorates.

Twitchell, K. S. *Saudi Arabia*. Princeton: Princeton University Press, 1947. 192 p.
Descriptive work by an American engineer.

Van Der Meulen, D. *The Wells of Ibn Sa'ud*. New York: Praeger, 1957. 270 p.
Illuminating recollections of a Dutch diplomat who spent over ten years in Saudi Arabia. Sympathetic but critical.

ISRAEL

Davis, Moshe, ed. *Israel: Its Role in Civilization*. New York: Harper, 1956. 338 p.
Symposium with 21 contributors including Allan Nevins, Carl J. Friedrich and Abba Eban.

Eban, Abba. *Voice of Israel*. New York: Horizon Press, 1957. 304 p.
A selection of speeches.

Horowitz, David. *State in the Making* (translated from the Hebrew by Julian Meltzer). New York: Knopf, 1953. 349 p.
Valuable for the period 1945–1948.

Hebrew University of Jerusalem. *Israel and the United Nations*. New York: Manhattan Publishing Co., 1956. 322 p.
Report of a study group set up by the Hebrew University of Jerusalem. One of a series put out by the Carnegie Endowment for International Peace.

Lehrman, Hal. *Israel: The Beginning and Tomorrow*. New York: Sloane, 1952. 358 p.
The report of an able journalist, sympathetic to Israel but balanced in its judgments.

Lilienthal, Alfred M. *What Price Israel?* Chicago: Regnery, 1953. 274 p.
A passionately argued condemnation of Zionism, of Israel, and of American policy. He pleads for a clear separation between Judaism and Zionism.

Weizmann, Chaim. *Trial and Error: The Autobiography of Chaim Weizmann.* New York: Harper, 1949. 498 p.
Indispensable source for the history of Zionism.

Barbour, Nevill. *Palestine: Star or Crescent?* New York: Odyssey Press, 1947. 310 p.
Good reporting based on first-hand experience. First published in England as *Nisi Dominus: A Survey of the Palestine Controversy* (London: Harrap, 1946. 248 p.).

Bernadotte, Count Folke. *To Jerusalem.* London: Hodder & Stoughton, 1951. 280 p.
The U.N. Mediator's journal of his truce efforts of 1948, published posthumously with a final chapter by his chief of staff.

Ellis, Harry B. *Israel and the Middle East.* New York: Ronald Press, 1957. 260 p.
Largely the story of the Palestine conflict, by an objective American reporter.

Esco Foundation for Palestine. *Palestine: A Study of Jewish, Arab and British Policies.* New Haven: Yale University Press, 1947. 2 v.
Although frankly pro-Zionist, this cooperative publication contains much useful material.

García-Granados, Jorge. *The Birth of Israel: The Drama as I Saw It.* New York: Knopf, 1948. 291 p.
Observations of the Guatemalan Representative on the U.N. Special Committee on Palestine. Very pro-Israel.

Goitein, S. D. F. *Jews and Arabs: Their Contacts through the Ages.* New York: Schocken, 1955. 257 p.
Traces the political, economic and religious contacts between these two peoples from their beginnings up to their present conflict. Scholarly and moderate.

Hurewitz, J. C. *The Struggle for Palestine.* New York: Norton, 1950. 404 p.
A documented and objective study, carrying the story through the partition and war of 1948.

Hutchinson, Elmo H. *Violent Truce.* New York: Devin-Adair, 1956. 199 p.
Personal experiences of a U.S. Observer in the U.N. Truce Supervision Organization. Very critical of Israel.

Hyamson, A. M. *Palestine under the Mandate, 1920–1948.* London: Methuen, 1950. 210 p.
Conscientious account by a British official in the mandatory administration.

Jeffries, Joseph M. N. *Palestine: The Reality.* New York: Longmans, 1939. 728 p.
Comprehensive statement from the Arab viewpoint.

Joseph, Bernard. *British Rule in Palestine.* Washington: Public Affairs Press, 1948. 279 p.
Critical Zionist interpretation.

Polk, William R., Stamler, David M., and Asfour, Edmund. *Backdrop to Tragedy: The Struggle for Palestine.* Boston: Beacon Press, 1957. 399 p.
Interesting experiment in combined scholarship by an American, a British Zionist, and a Palestine Arab.

Royal Institute of International Affairs. *Great Britain and Palestine, 1915–1941.* Information Department Papers, no. 20a. London: Oxford University Press, 1946. 177 p.
A useful factual review.

Schechtman, Joseph B. *The Arab Refugee Problem.* New York: Philosophical Library, 1952. 137 p.
An analysis by an authority on refugees and population movements. His views favor the official Israeli position.

THE SUEZ CANAL AND THE CRISIS OF 1956

Bromberger, Merry and Serge. *Les Secrets de l'Expédition d'Egypte.* Paris: Editions des 4 Fils Aymon, 1957. 269 p.
Interesting revelations presumably based on sources within the French Government.

Calvocoressi, Peter and Wint, Guy. *Middle East Crisis.* Baltimore: Penguin, 1957. 141 p.
An admirable little book giving the background of the crisis of 1956, some judgments on the policies of the powers, and recommendations for the future.

Henriques, Robert. *A Hundred Hours to Suez.* New York: Viking Press, 1957. 206 p.
An account of the military campaign in Sinai, from the Israeli side.

Johnson, Paul. *The Suez War.* New York: Greenberg, 1957. 145 p.

The editor of the *New Statesman* gives his account of the crisis, highly critical of the Eden Government.

Schonfield, Hugh J. *The Suez Canal in World Affairs.* New York: Philosophical Library, 1953. 174 p.
A convenient survey giving the main outlines of the problem up to the date of publication.

U.S. Department of State, *The Suez Canal Problem, July 26-September 22, 1956: A Documentary Publication.* Washington: G.P.O., 1956. 370 p.

Watt, D. C., ed. *Documents on the Suez Crisis, 26 July to 6 November 1956.* London: Royal Institute of International Affairs, 1957. 88 p.
A convenient collection of documents with a thoughtful introduction. The same author's *Britain and the Suez Canal: The Background* (London: Royal Institute of International Affairs, August 1956, mimeographed) is a good supplement to it.

Wilson, Sir Arnold. *The Suez Canal.* London: Oxford University Press, 1933. 224 p.
An indispensable book on the history of the canal.

ECONOMIC AND SOCIAL

Bonné, Alfred. *State and Economics in the Middle East: A Society in Transition.* London: Routledge & Kegan Paul, 1948. 427 p.
A competent analysis by a well-known professor of economics at Hebrew University in Jerusalem.

Caroe, Sir Olaf. *Wells of Power: The Oilfields of South-West Asia.* New York: Macmillan, 1951. 240 p.

Cooke, Hedley V. *Challenge and Response in the Middle East.* New York: Harper, 1952. 366 p.
Problems of economic development, covering the period since 1919.

Fisher, Sydney N., ed. *Social Forces in the Middle East.* Ithaca: Cornell University Press, 1955. 282 p.
Symposium of papers presented at a conference sponsored by the Social Science Research Council.

Longrigg, Stephen Hemsley. *Oil in the Middle East: Its Discovery and Development.* New York: Oxford University Press, for the Royal Institute of International Affairs, 1954. 305 p.

A sound history based on research and personal experience. The author was long associated with the Iraq Petroleum Company.

Mikesell, Raymond F. and Chenery, Hollis B. *Arabian Oil.* Chapel Hill: University of North Carolina Press, 1949. 201 p.

The economic and technical side of American oil operations in the Middle East.

Shwadran, Benjamin. *The Middle East, Oil and the Great Powers.* New York: Praeger, 1955. 500 p.

A well-documented study of the oil industry, country by country, but marked by the strong opinions of the author.

U.N. Department of Economic and Social Affairs. *Economic Development of the Middle East, 1945–1954.* New York: United Nations, 1955. 236 p. (mimeographed).

Supplement to the *World Economic Report, 1953–54.*

———. ———. *Economic Developments in the Middle East, 1954–1955.* New York: United Nations, 1956. 151 p. (mimeographed).

Supplement to *World Economic Survey, 1955.*

———. ———. *Economic Developments in the Middle East, 1955–1956.* New York: United Nations, 1957. 135 p. (mimeographed).

Supplement to *World Economic Survey, 1956.*

Warriner, Doreen. *Land Reform and Development in the Middle East: A Study of Egypt, Syria, and Iraq.* New York: Oxford University Press, for the Royal Institute of International Affairs, 1957. 197 p.

An excellent and objective study which supplements the author's *Land and Poverty in the Middle East* (New York: Royal Institute of International Affairs, 1948. 148 p.).

CULTURAL

Frye, Richard N., ed. *Islam and the West.* The Hague: Mouton, 1957. 215 p.

Discussion of the prospects for an Islamic renaissance by a Harvard Summer School conference.

Gibb, Hamilton A. R. *Modern Trends in Islam.* Chicago: University of Chicago Press, 1947. 141 p.

Keen analysis by a noted scholar in the Oriental field.

Kohn, Hans. *Western Civilization in the Near East*. New York: Columbia University Press, 1936. 329 p.
A penetrating study by an authority on nationalism well acquainted with the area.

Morrison, S. A. *Middle East Tensions: Political, Social and Religious*. New York: Harper, 1954. 198 p.
The author is a British missionary with long experience in the Middle East.

Smith, Wilfred Cantwell. *Islam in Modern History*. Princeton: Princeton University Press, 1957. 317 p.
A deeply perceptive book concentrating on the doctrinal and cultural rather than the political aspects.

Young, T. Cuyler, ed. *Near Eastern Culture and Society*. Princeton: Princeton University Press, 1951. 250 p.
A symposium resulting from a conference held in 1947. The contributors include noted scholars from both the West and the Middle East.

INDEX